CW01667855

NINE STEPS TO HEALTH, STRENGTH, AND HAPPINESS

This is the first book by Dr. Andrew Smith. Andrew is a leading expert in recovery from developmental trauma. He has lectured internationally on the subject, and has written widely. When not working in his busy private psychotherapy practice, he is the editor of the Journal of Modern Psychotherapy, and a Lecturer at Regents' University, London.

NINE STEPS TO HEALTH, STRENGTH, AND HAPPINESS

Dr. Andrew Smith

Rooster Winterfae Publishing
London

Acknowledgements

I firstly want to thank each and every client I have had the privilege of working with. It is always an honour to have someone share their emotional process in the consulting room. It is the hope of alleviating suffering that keeps me doing this work, and I have always strived to do my very best. And let's face it, life can be so hard. However, in learning about your story, I learn about my own, and together, we grow. I hope this book genuinely helps and supports you with your ongoing development. Thank you.

I would like to thank my patient partner, who gave me space to write this book. We often think that relationships need to be co-dependent and cloying, doing everything together, and losing our sense of self in the process. However, you gave me the time and distance to allow me to complete this project, whilst always offering support and patience when requested. My love for you remains strong and steady.

I acknowledge the input of my humble father. You have always taken an interest in what I'm doing, and I know you live in awe of what I have achieved, which is a joy to me. It is because of your support that I am where I am. You introduced me to a love of writing and reading by telling fairytales to me as a child, and you supported me through university, and your pride in my achievements leads me to aim for more. And even though my mother passed to the Summerlands many years ago, I sense her around me. Because of the stories and songs she taught me, I developed a love for what I do.

I am also thankful to all of the editors, agents, publishers, printers, and people who have connected via social media. Sometimes there is nothing more growthful than a well-placed comment from a loving place.

I also thank my five fur babies – you would be surprised at how useful it is to have a chihuahua or cat steer us away from the screen when feeling jaded or tired. They have provided me with many a deflection from the work at hand.

I am especially thankful to all at Rooster Winterfae Publishing, for believing in me as a writer.

Finally, I thank my therapist, colleagues, and friends for their interest, support, and patience during difficult times. I especially thank those esteemed colleagues who generously offered a review of the book; I remain grateful. Although I am totally out of my comfort zone, it is the presence of you also that continues to spur me on.

And even though we often struggle with negative feedback, we cannot grow without being offered a growing edge. The trolls help me grow the most.

Andrew x

First published in the United Kingdom by
Rooster Winterfae Press, 2022

ISBN: 978-1-3999-2403-0

British Library:

Printed in the United Kingdom and online.

 The author of this book does not dispense medical advice or prescribe the use of any technique as a form of treatment for physical or medical problems without the adivce of a physician, either directly or indirectly. The intent of the author is only to offer information of a general nature to help you in your quest for emotional and spiritual wellbeing. In the event you use any of the information in this book for yourself, which is your constitutional right, the author and the publisher assume no responsibility for your actions. No previous client of Andrew Smith is referred to directly or indirectly in this work – the citations are archetypes. Any similarities are due to chance.

A catalogue record for this book is available from the British Library.

ISBN 978-1-3999-2403-0

9 781399 924030 >

CONTENTS:

1. Introduction

Purpose of the book

This book is specifically geared towards anyone who has experienced emotional health challenges as a result of their history or current life experiences. This is anyone who is is alive today! None of us escape the pressure of work, love, or life, and most of us have experienced loss. The pressure of social media adds an additional layer of trauma that entraps us all, and our brains are responding accordingly.

You do not need to be open to exploring spiritual practices yourself, but I ask that you are open to thinking about them at least. My view is that traditional therapies and treatments will only take you part of the way towards recovery. In order to fully recover and manage stress, we need a raft of practices, and a regime change rather than a 'light touch'. By embracing metaphysical spiritual practices from around the world, you will maximise your chances of complete transformation, as opposed to survival. This book can serve as a practical tool for supporting your recovery or healing using spirituality.

It may be surprising, but even professionals such as myself have experienced difficulties with our emotional health; I would guess that most therapists are wounded healers in some way, shape or form. Most of us have a reason that draws us towards helping others. But it wasn't just therapy that helped me, it was a range of things that successfully helped me emerge from my personal darkness, like a bog monster from the depths of a slimy swamp.

I have taken the time to formulate all of these techniques into an accessible therapeutic process that you can read, digest, and practice. Should you choose to. The techniques are curated specifically to support you not only recovering from your history, but buffeting yourself from the toxic effects of daily life. Neuroscientists tell us that the brain is evolving in alarming ways, such as deteriorating attention spans, dysregulation, and disconnection. These practices have the purpose of supporting you in supporting yourself.

In terms of privacy, the benefit of working with this book is that you do not have to share any of this with anyone if you do not wish to. This book will lead you to your own solution; your space. And while you might pay thousands for an individual course of therapy, which is an important thing to consider, there is a sufficient amount of information here to help change your life. I cannot promise an instant transformation, but these methods have been effective for myself and many others, and hope you can use them in a way that works for you. Only you have the power to work this out for yourself.

This book could support your transformation and lasting change, but only with the work and effort you choose to make. I also substantiate what I say with evidence; I don't encourage people to do things that may be unhelpful. I support change from methods that have been proven to be helpful. Therefore, learning from science is encouraged throughout the book, alongside numerous exercises to help you discover what will now work for you. This book isn't just about chalk and talk, but about developing your own self-reflexive process in pragmatic ways.

The exercises are also a start on your metaphysical journey of growth. My therapeutic approach requires real action to achieve change. In order to accomplish this in my practice, I frequently use this book as a bolster to my therapy both for groups and individuals. I support people around the world with their journey towards recovery, so if you would like to connect with me and begin the direct element of your recovery, please do get in touch.

I reach out to you, unquestioningly, with no judgement, just a connection, and I hope you can experiment with some of the suggestions in this book. And the suggestions are only that; suggestions, or at least ideas that worked for me and my clients, which I believe can also support you. Let me know how things go. The benefits from spiritual practice are immense, as I hope you discover.

The Spiritual Approach to Healing

I want to explain a little bit about why spirituality is important for healing. The relationship between people and religion/ spirituality is complex. Although the following research is from the U.S., it suggests that the same applies to anyone around the world. The research states that Americans tend to fall into four categories:

* 29% are both spiritual and religious;
* 18% are spiritual but not religious;
* 22% are not spiritual but religious; and
*31% are neither spiritual nor religious.

Overall, 65% of Americans are neither spiritual nor religious, and younger Americans are more likely to be spiritual but not religious. Spiritual folk (but not religious) are also likely to be liberal, and higher levels of spirituality are strongly related with higher life satisfaction across a range of measures, and more apt to engage in pro-social behaviours (Raney et al., 2017). It seems that increasing spirituality and decreasing religion is a way to increase society's pro-social behaviours and liberalism. We clearly need to start this sooner rather than later!

People turn to spirituality for many reasons. In one way, it is as though the dissatisfaction with the world (especially world leaders) has led to people looking to the past for effective ways of healing. However, it is not just because of a dissatisfaction with politics. People also adopt spiritual approaches for a range of other important reasons: some as a thinly veiled resistance to growing fears around societal changes; others as a way of reconnecting with the environment, and others as a way of becoming part of a movement that does not have controlling religious beliefs. The reasons for becoming involved in spiritual practices are multifarious. What is, perhaps, more important, is for you to think about what brings you to spiritual healing. Terence McKenna once said, "Nature is not mute, it is man who is deaf." Spirituality offers the opportunity to switch on our hearing. I hope you take this as an opportunity to switch on yours.

My personal belief is that adopting a spiritual practice serves various needs. Firstly, it enables us to embrace being different (to the 'norm'). It also helps us to develop practices such as celebrations and ceremonies, which help us feel differently about ourselves. The practice of spirituality helps us change and accept the things that might seem overly tricky to us as individuals. Being part of an accepting group of people who come together through spirituality also means that, for those of us considered different, we can find kith and kin. Being part of a clan is a primordial need for human beings, and this approach therefore creates a vital way of being part of a vibrant community of individuals.

Most importantly, adopting a spiritual practices helps coordinate the four key parts of our brain. Spirituality is known to help people process difficulties, reduce stress, and subsequently reduce the impact on our neurological functioning. I believe that adopting a spiritual practice is essential in such trying times.

The research also suggests that the impact of adopting some kind of spiritual or religious practice impacts not only ourselves positively, but can develop our capacity to form relationships with others in our communities. There is, therefore, a need to include spirituality in any healing process, albeit individual or group. As I will demonstrate in future chapters, humans have been spiritual for thousands of years, and whilst a questioning of religion is always appropriate, this should not mean we leave all spiritual practices behind. We are wired to be spiritual beings. Indeed, spirituality even co-exists comfortably with science. I will show you how this can work for you in the chapters to come.

For all round health, we know that healing isn't just about a 1-2-1 in a consulting room. Our recovery requires an holistic approach: we also need movement to fix the physical issues; we need amazing food to fuel the body; we need art and music to nourish the soul; we need a mentor to talk to and process difficulties; we need something to believe in; we need a clan to be involved with; we need stories. All of these components have featured in some way both in our pagan and religious histories as a constant. The 'God' of Science now tells us of their benefit, and so I have incorporated as much as possible within the approach here.

Much of my approach is pre-Christian, focused upon a group of cultures we now identify as pagans. Pagans have existed since time immemorial. In pre-Christian times, pagans are what we all were across the planet. In a scary and unpredictable world, our spiritual beliefs helped our fears appear less dangerous. By having spiritual beliefs in which paganism holds, we were able to create certainty for those phenomena that we could not understand. For example, we created a goddess for the sun because we could not understand how the sun rose each morning and descended each evening. We also could not understand who brought the winter each year, so created a story that would make sense of that, helping us understand the world. We factored in rituals to manage the uncertainty – for instance, if we offered a sacrifice, we would ensure a better crop. These stories led into myths and legends, and our whole language became imbued with spirituality. We would also create ceremonies to worship and rejoice in the wonders of the natural world.

As we evolved overtime and developed our scientific thinking, we became more ambivalent and questioning of spiritual approaches. We began to leave church in our droves, and became more questioning of our communities. Society now sneers at spirituality. However, Church in particular had offered us an opportunity to meet people in our community every week, and now churches are disappearing, this has left us with a void; no longer can we meet and support others close to us in real life. I say 'real life', because obviously we can join lots of virtual groups, but this will never replace reality.

As pagans, we were also essentially tribal. I know 'tribal' is a controversial term now. However, we needed communities to thrive, and our brains developed to heighten our empathic ability towards other people, to communicate and work more effectively with others to ensure survival. This was a genetic and vital human adjustment to the world. Even our brains adapted. There are areas in our brain that effectively deal with fight, flight, or freeze, and we are equipped to respond to hunger, fatigue, and stress in various ways. There are also areas in our brain that deal with anger. In addition, evolution has developed our brain into three parts - the triune brain.

The triune brain consists of the reptilian complex, the paleomammalian complex (limbic system), and the neomammalian complex (neocortex). These structures were sequentially added to the forebrain in the course of evolution. In layman's terms, there are three layers of the brain, with the most basic parts deep in the centre, and the more recent parts on the outside. The neocortex increased in size in response to pressures for greater cooperation and competition in early ancestors. With the size increase, there was greater voluntary inhibitory control of social behaviours, resulting in increased social harmony. Our brains evolved as our needs evolved. However, this did not happen in twenty years, or even a hundred years, but thousands. In fact, our brains continue to evolve, and we are already seeing unhelpful evolutionary changes in response to social media.

I share this because there is an expectation in civilisation that we suddenly adapt to the current living conditions, and somehow shut off from those feelings and behaviours that served us extremely well in the past. We tell our kids to be quiet when they have a natural instinct to talk and communicate; we bracket off sexual desire to fit in socially, even though our species requires sexual intercourse to survive; we wait to eat when we are in a meeting, despite being ravenous, and then over-eat later.

In fact, our brains have slowly evolved over thousands of years to deal with these factors - threat, short lives, hunter-gatherer existence – so the expectation of suddenly ignoring these powerful internal processes have led us to where we are now. We are similarly forced to 'be kind' online when we might not feel kind. There is something particularly worrying in online behaviours, whereby we are exposed to more extreme material than ever before, and the subsequent impact on our emotional health is massive. We are a disaster waiting to happen, children's attention spans are already much shorter, and the corporations are so immersed in their greed. Neuroscientists confirm this belief. On top of those worries, our nation also struggles with morbid obesity, a lack of real connection with others, soaring suicide rates amongst men in particular, a massive increase in self harm, and mounting division in the world. These changes in our living and spiritual experiences have an impact on every aspect of our lives. I would argue negatively.

So, my spiritual approach to health and happiness takes all of this into consideration. I offer a therapeutic opportunity for recovery, which robustly uses what we already know to inform our healing process. We need this to return to that which we left behind – our relationship with spirituality. However, it would be impossible to re-establish that which went before, so we need to acknowledge the benefits and create our own spirituality – a neo-spirituality. When we talk about healing and growth, we need to incorporate our knowledge of healing and recovery from history and science and combine it with our understanding of spirituality. The combination of the three forces is potent. Through my own study, I realised that there is no one panacea that will make everything good enough. We need to incorporate many practices; many ways of improving our health and happiness.

In a way, the history of our spiritual practices is more important than a randomised control trial. Whilst scientific evidence from such a trial is helpful, I tend to err on the side of caution with new material. As an example, fifty years ago we used science to inform our views on smoking, and we 'discovered' that people didn't die of Alzheimer's if they smoked. So, we deduced that if we smoke, we won't get Alzheimer's, which could be true, but only because we would die of lung cancer before the Alzheimer's had a chance to take hold. As I've already said, I tend to trust that which we have done for thousands of years, and which has stood the test of time.

Workbook

Please write down your answers to the following questions. Take some time on your own before answering to ponder these questions in your workbook:

- **What is your current knowledge of spirituality?**
- **What feelings are triggered when you think about the word 'spiritual'?**
- **What do you feel you need to learn about?**
- **How do you feel about learning about history?**
- **Which part of the world do you live in?**
- **Where are your descendants from?**
- **How do you feel about ancestry?**

Structure of the book

The book is divided into nine sections, each section holding one of the keys to recovery. You are welcome to use as many as you need to help you. You do not have to read the chapters chronologically, and you are welcome to read and practice them out of sync. Each is a self-contained approach to suggest ways of structuring your life and spiritual practice for optimum benefit. The book will detail how you can use spiritual practices to really develop a life that will help you flourish, move away from troubles in your past, and carve out the life in which you have always hoped.

My approach is traditionalist at best, based on the texts and ideas I adore and reflect on, yet contain truths that we have always wondered about as humans; truths that re-emerge in most religions under different guises. I have consolidated my own practice with current scientific evidence. Whilst I do not think that science gives us all the answers, and some things may never be answered properly, it is helpful to assimilate information that other people have spent time exploring and understanding.

My approach is also integrative – you can be a Christian as well as spiritual, or a spiritual Druid, or any other combination. Or nothing at all. You can even choose to be a non-spiritual person if you like, but choose to use some of the ideas. How you define yourself is your business, not mine. My business is my earnest commitment to you and myself, which is consolidated with my determination to support your growth and overall development. As a psychotherapist, I can tell you that aligning too closely to one position or modality generally leads to problems, so try to remain open to diverse approaches and a healthy level of experimentation.

My spiritual approach is not strict or rigid, but flexible and holistic. You can also assimilate into your practice anything else you wish, and should do so if you feel so inclined. For example, if you like to attend Church each Sunday, please complement your practice with that. You may also like a particular form of yoga that I do not cover in this book, so again, please continue adding whatever you value in your own spiritual approach. The key principle under-pinning this book is to work out what fits for you, to open yourself to new practices and stop practicing those things which do not fit for you. We will return to this idea variously throughout the book.

At the beginning of each chapter, I include an archetype. Archetypes are images or ideas that represent a typical example of a certain kind of person or thing. Carl Jung believed that archetypes were a primitive mental image that we inherited from our earliest ancestors. They are supposed to be present in the collective subconscious. I offer a brief description of each one, but the purpose of this is for you to meditate on the archetypes in relation to the topic of the chapter, and discover what they mean for you. For example, in the chapter on sacred love, I offer the archetype of the Lover. Whilst my descriptions may describe the archetypes as we know and understand them, it is within your own meditation practice to situate the archetypes and discover where your reflections take you. The universe is your oyster.

You can use and apply the techniques and strategies in this book to truly revitalise yourself and your life, or just to try something different. I have used these techniques successfully for over twenty years, but they are for anyone, regardless of your age, gender identity, or culture. You can begin to learn how to feel again, how to relate to others, the earth, and magic, and how to use different techniques to reduce stress. The tried and tested ways of years gone by are, arguably, the best, not least because they have lasted the longest. And as the techniques and processes speak for themselves, hopefully you will learn to find your own, and speak your own truth.

Each chapter covers aspects of how to apply the 9 steps within your life – the use of ritual to replenish your energies, how to eat spiritually for health and vitality, and how to incorporate art and music into your life in order to tap in to your inherent creativity. These are, obviously, just suggestions, so if anything feels out of balance to you, or if you do not accept anything you read, then please, do not try to apply it. "It is the beginning of wisdom when you recognise that the best you can do is choose which rules you want to live by, and its persistent and aggravated imbecility to pretend you can live without any." It is of enormous benefit to be able to make that choice for yourself. And especially if you are in distress and need support, do not forgo seeking out that support. The book will still be here.

Each chapter incorporates a workbook section in which you are encouraged to consolidate the reading with practice. A range of techniques and exercises will be offered as well. It is best to write things down in a book that is specially set aside for this process. The notebook can be anything on hand, and should not cost an arm and a leg, just choose one that is right for you and has plenty of pages, which you will fill. It may also be a good idea to decorate the notebook specifically for you – find magazines and posters, then cut and stick images that resonate with you. Or paint – even a few well-placed splotches of colour can transform anything. You may even want to bind some pages together yourself. I would encourage you to write from the heart, and keep it private – I have a secret drawer in my desk where mine is kept. Also, try to be as creative as you like – use colour, different art materials, and try to tap into your subconscious as much as possible.

Each chapter also contains relevant research in the field – for example, there are sections where I discuss what we know about rituals from history, but also from current research in that area. It is important that you develop your awareness from a solid evidence base, rather than just theory. I also incorporate case study material from my therapeutic practice throughout the book; an important element because we often grow from hearing other people's experiences. Everything is anonymised and confidential to protect my clients and the people I have connected with in the past.

There is no reference to any client, past or present, in this book. This is to ensure anonymity and protection of those I have worked with. Whilst I would love to celebrate the work we have completed together, there is no consent for this. And, I do not believe that talking about those we have worked with is safe anyway.

Another focus of the book is trying to help you understand where some popular practices have originated from. This context is indispensable as it helps us to make informed decisions about what to practice. Never do something blindly. Jean Paul Richter once said, "Courage consists not in blindly overlooking danger, but in seeing it, and conquering it." This book, I hope, will help you to not only identify the dangers in your life and practice, but support you in conquering them.

My Own Journey

I would like to share a story with you; in fact, one of the oldest stories in the U.K. That story is entitled 'Taliesin'. This tale of pre-Christian times survived despite the Roman-Christian destruction of much of the U.K.'s ancient spiritual practices. Somehow, as the Roman's tried to burn and discard our spiritual heritage, this story was preserved. The story of Taliesin (written by Taliesin) serves as a window into past times, informing us of significant beliefs and values that we had at that time.

The narrative itself presents a rich tapestry of symbolism, metaphor, and fantasy, telling us of Ceridwen's wrath at Taliesin, after accidentally developing Awen (spiritual insight), and embedded with themes of transformation, determination, survival, and growth. And, of course, magick. Indeed, many contemporary spiritual practitioners use the tale to illustrate parallels between then and now, and to bridge the gap between both time periods. Taliesin is also told as a way of reconnecting to our past, aiming to preserve our ancient belief systems (in the U.K. at least). It is certainly worth a read, and indeed, I tell the story myself in story-telling sessions, specifically for these reasons.

I share this story to you to illustrate how our histories inform the present, and to show that they are intimately connected; we do not just appear now. In fact, our survival and growth depends upon learning the lessons from our past. I also share this story to demonstrate that having spiritual belief systems is nothing new. In truth, they are as old as humanity itself.

My own spiritual story began in childhood. We were, as a family, immersed in a range of spiritual practices – we had aunts who read tarot cards and attended spiritualism circles, and extended family members who were strict Christians. In a way, being spiritual was nothing abnormal. However, my spiritual awakening started some years ago, but somewhat later than the story of Taliesin!

While working as a psychotherapist, enjoying the profession immensely (still do), I found great benefit from helping others. I had also been in therapy myself as part of my training, so was comfortable talking about feelings. There are various psychotherapies that are centred upon spirituality, so was both familiar and comfortable with notions of spirituality as an intrinsic part of being human. I also worked as a yoga teacher and experienced meditation practitioner, so was healthy, relatively chilled, and reflective. I enjoyed life and had lots to be thankful for.

I particularly enjoyed my work. I loved the connection with people and appreciated making a difference to people's lives. This was important to me - I was not a therapist for the sake of it, my own therapy had taught me to value the work of being both around and close to people. In fact, I do not think many people can complete four years of psychotherapy training and not value this aspect. If they do not, I would suggest that it is possibly not the best career choice for them! And yes, I had some vulnerabilities, and my own therapy had helped me to scope out my own history. I, like many wounded healers, had my fair share of traumatic scars from childhood experiences, some bigger than others, but I was doing well.

I also enjoyed life as a 'professional'. People from my history often struggle to survive, let alone thrive, but I had surmounted difficulties and used them for my benefit. In some ways, I was probably self-assured; confident about my capabilities, and reassured in the visible signs of my success. Things were trundling along magnificently; I had a healthy clientele and had a meaningful worthwhile reputation with professional colleagues; I earned good money, maintained a stable relationship with my partner, had no financial woes, and looked forward to conducting some further research in my field. I had nothing to worry about. And then, one day out of nowhere, I received a voicemail from my dad, the kind of call you do not want to receive, made worse by us being in the U.S. at the time. Unable to hide his distress, he let me know that my brother, Michael, had ended his life. And my world discombobulated.

Initially, I felt like I had left my body and dissociated from life; the world felt as though it had become a cartoon. The image from Trainspotting when Ewan McGregor is laid out, gouching, springs to mind. Once I put the phone down, everything moved in slow motion, and it felt like my insides had dropped from my body. I was stunned, mortified, and panicked. I needed to sit down and take some air. In Taliesin, this could have been where Gwion accidentally spilt the potion on himself, invoking the wrath of Ceridwen.

I sat in the living room and reflected on my life with Michael, my oldest brother. I could see him sitting there in the room, staring back. I had not spoken to him for some time, both of us being caught up in conflict and disharmony. He was vulnerable, and it had been hard to find a joint resolution. The conflict was distressing for us both. He felt alone; exactly how I felt in that moment, completely alone. Stunned more because he had always been so likeable and charismatic, and I could not process how someone with such a wonderful life could become so desperate. I could not make the connection, even though I had known him all my life. This may connect with those of you who have experienced suicide. Someone close to me ending their life, a lifelong dread of mine, became reality, and I found myself on a precipice. My ultimate spiritual test had arrived, and like so many before me, I had the choice to accept or decline the test. Would I choose to either sink or fly?

Even the beautiful, the affluent, and the fortunate can feel emotionally destitute, and Michael's passing reminded me of that. I recalled how Michael would characteristically minimise his discomfort, explicitly assuring me he was fine, often joking that he was 'not suicidal'. For men in particular, we are taught to protect and support others, not ourselves. We often grow up with a silent voice telling us we can talk about the things we are interested in (often things as opposed to people), but not about our vulnerability. Any of us who are British will understand the importance of humour to deflect unwanted attention. No-one can crack a joke like me, and I can deflect like the best of them; Michael was similarly adept. I wondered if we were too similar, and I asked myself if I had missed something. I knew the research told us that if someone was minded to end their life, they would, and they would not disclose it, even in therapy, but this knowledge was no consolation.

I cancelled my diary for the week and rang my supervisor for support. I am fortunate to have had these resources; trained people who can immediately offer help. My supervisor put things back into perspective, and I came out of flight/fight mode, into flatness; my supervisor had had similar experiences. I remember being surprised but reflective. His/her support ameliorated the impact on me, and I was able to return to work. However, something deep inside had been triggered. I felt broken.

I realised how inadequate my psychotherapy training was on

its own. Whilst therapy is helpful, and there is lots to gain from it, we often treat it as an autonomous, self-sustained and sustaining practice. Many practitioners are encouraged to think about themselves as that independent sovereign: the master of their own practice; the all-omnipotent personality ready to absorb the woes of the client. However, whilst therapy was helpful in some ways, it was not everything to everyone and never could be. It certainly was not helpful to me, in itself, in that moment. It was also not successful for Michael, even though he had tried several times; if we view success as supporting someone to stay alive against their personal choice.

Describing this period of my life is difficult. I was in life but not part of it; I was living but not fully alive, if that makes sense? The sense of failure stung deeply. And I missed my brother, which was difficult to reconcile inside, leading me to be around people without being with them. I had dissociated from my feelings, and I considered leaving my career. I thought about other options, anything to help me get out of the quagmire. In hindsight, my saving grace was that I wanted to leave the quagmire.

For a long time, I wondered where I had failed Michael, what had I missed, and what I had not done. Ever the perfectionist, I wracked my mind for missed opportunities, signals, signs. Had I missed something? I tried to take responsibility for Michael's actions. In fact, I can still imagine him perched on the edge of the sofa at home, diminutive, attractive, intelligent, great personality, everything to live for. Not dissimilar to myself. But I felt as though I had lost him; like I had lost myself. Like you may also feel lost. Inevitably, how Taliesin may have felt making such a catastrophic mistake against Ceridwen.

And so, I tried to identify what would help me feel differently. I read more widely - sometimes we have to explore the threat and understand it, not shy away. I found that, out of every client who thinks about suicide and is in therapy, 70% of them will not tell their therapist, let alone their family. This is because their therapist would need to refer them to established mental health services, and relationships within families are often too enmeshed. This was correct for Michael. Also, a client considering suicide isn't a secret a therapist can keep, and the law requires us to 'grass' people up when they share their most painful parts – this remains such an impossible binary to hold. And I do not imagine any of my family members could sit on this.

Subsequently, most people fail to share their suicidal thoughts. Would you share yours? This is the first hurdle for therapists working with suicide - as long as we need to betray someone's trust in the therapeutic alliance, we will never encourage them to share their suicidal thinking. You may also not tell anyone about those natural existential urges we all experience at times, which is normal. And I firmly believe that the impact of historical religious expectations and dogma remains, still lingering in our subconscious. We are taught that it is not acceptable to end your life.

I went back into psychotherapy, not because I imagined finding a cure for my feelings, but because I wanted to understand what I might have missed if I had been his therapist; I needed to comprehend the clues, not just for Michael, but for myself, so I could pass this on to others. I also wanted to spend time in therapy to process the trauma of Michael's suicide, so I could move on from it.

Therapy was unsuccessful. I liked my therapist, but weekly sessions for only fifty minutes were not enough. The sessions touched the surface, but not the rocks below, which made me realise that we often put all our eggs in one basket, usually the therapist, when we need a range of baskets. In my therapy, I found that I was generally more experienced than other therapists. They did not seem to feel confident supporting me. No client should feel the need to protect their therapist. My need to be held by someone strong and steady did not appear to be available. My therapist constantly deferred to me, expecting me to know the answer and subconsciously applying further yet unwanted pressure. These sessions made me feel more lost and unhealable, so I eventually left. As a result, a horrifying realisation overwhelmed me - I had nowhere left to turn. Where do psychotherapists go when therapy isn't working?

I worked as a psychotherapist to help others and to also find solutions to my own process. My historic difficulties returned with vengeance. Feeling low and dissociative began to feel normal for me. My practices helped alleviate the discomfort, but my wish to bow out of life remained. Even though I remained available for clients psychologically, and although I had developed relationships, including intimate relationships, the pulse that ran through my veins permeated everything. I hid my feelings well, like you probably do too. I continuously struggled with feelings of wanting to end my life; I felt enraged and had nowhere acceptable to take it. I read about suicide and understood how people performed the actual act. And somehow, I stayed here and remained clear that I had no active plan to die, but continued to carry the feeling that I did not want to be alive. For those who have lost someone in this way, this is probably a familiar process.

Months and months of feeling flat, numb, and deeply depressed extended into years. I gradually shut out everyone to the bare minimum and stopped contacting the rest of my family. I got to a point of only connecting with people, strangers usually, on social media. I found that old wounds and vulnerabilities opened, and PTSD symptoms from childhood returned. Life became dark. I would go weeks without talking to anyone outside of work. I lost my voice. And no one would have known.

As I write this book, I think about the common approach to suicide and acute mental distress from professionals and society in general. Thousands of well-intentioned people post things on social media like, 'Just talk to someone', or 'Ring the Samaritans'. You have all read and heard the messages, which all claim that the solution is talking. Perhaps controversially, in all the time I struggled with suicidal ideation, not once could I have talked to anyone about it openly. When we are so burdened by hurt, we buckle, albeit internally. Whilst I accept that talking about it might have helped, not once would I have trusted anyone to respond in a way that would have fit for me. I am also not convinced that talking is automatically helpful – sometimes we do not need to open up. And for me, there was nothing new that psychotherapy could offer me. In fact, I can only talk about this in retrospect.

Tragically, services are also just not able to effectively deal with suicide. Whilst some support may be helpful to some, the people at real risk, like me, would never touch those services, mainly because they are difficult to trust. They are staffed with unfamiliar professionals who act in the service of the organisation, not the individual. Consequently, many suicidal people lack trust in them and do not see them as an option. Whilst there may be some benefit to some services, and I would always recommend relevant ones, the solution often comes from elsewhere.

I remember one day picking up a book titled, *A Child Called It*, a famous memoir about childhood abuse. Whilst reading the book, I was reminded me of the suffering of others; how many other people have transcended so much difficulty, far worse than mine. This reminder had the effect of grounding me; as I had a naturally empathic response to the author, it took me out of my own process. I looked around for other stories, which all reminded me of my clients, some who often experienced severe harm and abuse. As a result, I had an 'a-ha' moment, like Taliesin did when realising how he should escape from Ceridwen. I fathomed my way forwards.

My way forwards was two-fold; I needed to find my voice and a way to work myself out of the emotional fog that clouded my life. Overall, I needed to heal. I had developed bad habits, but I needed to get back on the wagon and truly enjoy the wonderful opportunity for life I had been given. My trauma had impacted my capacity to enjoy the 'here and now', and I realised that I needed to clear the decks, symbolically and literally. In a way, this was quite straightforward; I had to use those tools I knew worked, but incorporating known psychotherapy tools with those things that were less well known, but still as important – my spiritual beliefs and practices. In my view, my spiritual beliefs and practices were more effective than a 'standardised', NICE-recommended treatment. I instinctively knew that the fundamental key to my own recovery was spirituality.

So, I returned to my books. I got my hands on everything I could and read as widely as possible; buddhism, meditation, shamanism, spiritualism, paganism, and every other 'ism' you could imagine. Learning about these topics was not new for me. My maternal family were travellers, so I had lots of traveller friends growing up, meaning that I had become familiar with a variety of traditional, spiritual practices through my own heritage. In my childhood, it was normal to have your cards read when worried about something, and to meet with spiritualists for more ethereal guidance. But I modified my yoga practice and developed my meditation practice much further. I enrolled on mindfulness courses, Buddhist courses, and began druidic training. I sought answers and became determined to find them. I also incorporated my doctoral research into my life. There was no way I would lose anyone else, and more importantly, no way I would lose myself.

I also knew that I was impacting my body and brain negatively by living around such a high level of environmental stress. I didn't want to end up with other health issues in the future, so this made the quest to develop my practices more essential.

Over time, I developed a range of practices that supported me in the most effective way possible. I extracted the gems I knew worked and practiced them daily. The key to any change process is practice – we have to get on the treadmill of life, begin to walk, and keep walking. Life is movement, and although many spiritual belief systems encourage us to stop, being stationary is not where we grow or heal from that which has befallen us.

After years of application, study, and spiritual guidance, here I am. I have developed an approach that works for me, and I believe the steps can work for you too. I have successfully incorporated these techniques within my practice for over twenty years now, and have also helped many people with their recoveries over the past two decades. Not only have I devised this approach for use with others, but have also used it effectively for myself. I continue to test it empirically. It is time for you to begin your own journey.

And so, after some real struggle, I began to recover. I started to enjoy the outdoors again and connect with my spiritual practice. My mood lifted, and I lost weight. I re-developed my daily calisthenics and meditation practice. Not only did I begin to recover, but I could also protect myself from further harm, move forwards, and thrive.

Getting to that stage is the absolute challenge for myself as a psychotherapist/healer, and it is the problem that keeps me awake at night. I am passionate about doing everything possible to help people change, grow, and heal from whatever has happened to them. I can see myself working on this for the rest of my life, and I will always work incredibly hard to help people make lasting changes in their life. This book may be a potted version of my therapy practices and lectures, but it is based upon a dense history of reading, practice, and experience.

And so, we also leave the story of Taliesin behind here. I worked out a solution to prosper, as did Taliesin. The next steps are designed to help you work out your own story.

Workbook

Throughout this book, I will encourage you to pick up some paper and a pen and reflect on the issues presented. I ask that you spend time on these exercises rather than just skimming past. There is power in both the practice of reflection, but also the specific topics you will explore during workbook practice. Right now, I wonder if you could spend five minutes exploring your own relationship with emotional difficulties:

- * What distresses have you experienced in your life?
- * What experiences have you survived?

Whilst there is no need to write anything down just yet, you might want to reflect on these points in writing as an opportunity to scope out your emotional landscape.

2. *Connecting with our Spiritual Past*

The Ruler

I will firstly introduce you to the concept of the Ruler. The Ruler is a powerful archetype. I have used the idea of the Ruler in relation to this chapter on the history of spirituality, and have been specific in my approach, because we associate the Ruler archetype with power over others. The power exists whether in terms of law or emotion. Obviously, rulers in history have impacted our ability positively or negatively to practice spiritually, but history itself continues to rule over us. I think, therefore, that this archetype is inexorably and irrevocably linked with any thoughts or discussions about spirituality in history. In popular culture, we have literature and films that are replete with rulers. Immediately, I think of Don Corleone in the Godfather, or characters such as King Lear. I use the idea of King Lear because rulers are not always powerful or strong, but can be at the Twilight time of their lives.

The Ruler archetype is a character with legal or emotional power over others, giving them inherent strengths, such as omnipotence and status. Weaknesses refer to things like aloofness and being out of touch with the world at times. I include this archetype in our thinking about history, so we can remember the primordial issues about our past, such as the challenges in reliably understanding the events that have occurred before, but also ways in which we may prioritise certain parts of our history over others. It is important to always maintain balance and equilibrium.

Workbook

Let's spend a few minutes reflecting on the notion of the Ruler. In your workbook, write down as many things that you associate with rulers in history. If there is a spiritual link with a ruler, focus on that. Try to avoid criticising your points or observations, just let your mind run with the archetype.

I shared a bit of my personal backstory in the introduction and detailed my own struggle with mental and spiritual health. I offered a bit of my history to help you understand what brings me to this field of work, and how my work resonates with my life and experiences. I also shared my past to show you that I am very much a human being, and that we are a product of our histories.

I also believe that we are not just impacted by our own recent histories, but by the wave of history before that. And this isn't just a belief - this is corroborated by hard evidence. We are part of the continuous flow of life, inextricably linked and impacted by what has happened before. And it is now time to begin our own process of recovery and spiritual fulfilment.

My history was tough to share, especially for someone with a professional identity; many people presume that professionals should be 'sorted'; not messy. In a way, there is some truth in this – people just do not pay us to support us, they pay us for us to support them, and psychotherapists need to be 'ok' to work effectively. Subsequently, I needed to think carefully about the implications of such disclosure. But it is an important message to share; that even therapists have backstories. We are all human. In fact, I think it is more important that people know we are all human. But you do not have to have had a massive abusive history to benefit from these techniques – none of our parents met every single need of ours in childhood. Part of this work is about identifying your hurts, what impacted you, and then, more importantly, what we can do about it. However, make no bones about it, we are all wounded healers.

Moving forwards, I wanted to write you a chapter that explored the backstory of spirituality. By going back in time, we learn what worked for our ancestors; we can find out what they did and why, and how this helped them in whatever context. And even more widely, we can explore our own histories, backstories, and at the very least, revisit them. We can then learn what underpins how we think and feel now, even if we do not consider ourselves spiritual. We can extract whatever may be useful in the 'here and now'.

In fact, holding respect for our ancestors is a spiritual practice in itself; remembering what has occurred before is not only respectful, but a way of holding the 'there and then' in the 'here and now', or holding our history in the present. We exist in a continuous zone of time and space, and whilst we cannot know our futures just yet, we can know our pasts, which can help us recalibrate and revisit to exist differently. In doing so, we heighten our consciousness through experiencing the now. We also build continuation and connection rather than separation and difference. After all, we are where we are precisely because of our ancestors, and they deserve some respect.

Finally, our history offers ways of understanding the rationale for having a spiritual practice in the first place. Spirituality practice – across continents – helped manage difficult experiences, such as death, although this is not the only reason. Through my research, I discovered that there are multiple ways of thinking about spirituality, and the function varies through cultures, with similarities. I want to share this with you as a way of providing a basis on which we can then begin our journey together.

Workbook

Have a think about your history, and consider one of your experiences that have had a positive impact on you. It could be anything, such as passing a difficult exam or having an amazing birthday. Now reflect on the impact that event had on you.

- **How did it shape your subsequent life?**
- **Did you feel confident about other exams?**
- **Did you expect to always have great birthdays?**

Write your thoughts down in your workbook.

History of Spirituality and the Rise of Christianity

In visiting history, I want to start by exploring and defining the term 'pagan' a bit more. Although this isn't a book about becoming pagan, there is use in understanding the concept as it refers to so much in our past. Also, because the term 'pagan' refers to non-religious spiritual practices, it can lack specificity. Therefore, if we understand the term and its context, we can develop our own practice. I also understand that this still may be a triggering for those with a Christian practice, so try to manage that process.

The actual term 'pagan' is Latinate in origin, derived from the word 'Paganus', revived during the renaissance. 'Paganus' can mean '[a] region delimited by markers', which also suggests a freedom of beliefs and practices, i.e. unlimited. As we try to understand the meaning of pagan, the notion of having markers or boundaries is interesting as the concept of pagan is also associated with the idea of being unlimited or without spiritual boundaries. Ludwig Feüerbach, in his book, The

Essence of Christianity defined paganism as, "...the unity of religion and politics, of spirit and nature, of god and man", suggesting that there is a value within paganism of embracing polarities within belief systems. In a way, this is what this book is aiming for, and I hope you can sift through the information and absorb contradictory qualities and values to support your spiritual development. Feuerbach also qualified the observation that man in the pagan view is always defined by ethnicity, i.e., Greek, Roman, Egyptian, etc. Each pagan tradition is therefore a national tradition, which is an important concept to consider as paganism is about unity, unifying those disparate forces in life, and creating order out of chaos.

In effect, our world is full of separation, despite the sameness. Thus, in order to move towards more cohesion and solidarity, I define paganism as a general way of referring to everything non-religious but incorporating everything spiritual and scientific, which is especially important when history has had such a conflicted relationship with non-religious entities.

Indeed, the term 'pagan' was first used by early Christians for people in the Roman Empire who practiced polytheism; there were alternate terms for the same groups within Christian texts. Predominantly, these were 'Hellene', 'gentile', and 'heathen' (Peter Brown, 1999, Late Antiquity). It was Christianity that led to paganism being thought of as a distasteful practice, as originally the term for pagan was used in a derogatory sense (Davies, 2011). It seems that being called 'pagan' was akin to being called a 'yokel' or 'bumpkin' in current parlance; this belief appears to have stuck. However, paganism is really a word that refers to having a non-religious spiritual practice.

It should be mentioned, though, that the ancient Britons who inhabited this island at the time of 'Christ' were a mixture of tribes, prior to the Romans interbreeding with them. We were a mélange of folk from Gaul and Italy with a 'sprinkling of barbaric mercenaries from the north of Europe as well as elements from the East.' (Branston, 1957: 15). These people used to be referred to as Aryans but are now more commonly referred to as Indo-Europeans. The preponderance of shamanic-like activities may also bear witness to our connections with those from the North of Europe.

Pope Gregory the 'Great' attempted to mass convert the pagans to Christianity at one point, possibly influenced by scripture references such as that found in Deuteronomy 18;9-12:

"When you come into the land that the Lord your God is giving you, you shall not learn to follow the abominable practices of those nations. There shall not be found among you anyone who burns his son or his daughter as an offering, anyone who practices divination or tells fortunes or interprets omens, or a sorcerer or a charmer or a medium or a necromancer or one who inquires of the dead, for whoever does these things is an abomination to the Lord. And because of these abominations the Lord your God is driving them out before you."

He attempted to build churches on the sites of old temples, not realising that the pagans were one step ahead, and they incorporated pagan symbols, such as Green Man, within the architecture. Calling out pagans as devil-worshippers became the new norm, which is ridiculous given the name doesn't appear until the New Testament, and that the name is a mis-translation as 'Ha-satan' and 'diabolos', simply meaning 'opponent' or 'adversary'. The Devil is a Christian invention, and there is no mention of him before the New Testament. This may well have contributed to the Christian persecution of paganism under Theodosius I.

Theodosius I began his reign in 381 after a period of time as the co-emperor in the eastern part of the Roman Empire. He reiterated a ban on pagan sacrifice and Haruspicy (divination through an animal's entrails). Evidently, the Indo-Europeans found benefit in this practice! Theodosius was also responsible for breaking up some pagan associations via the destruction of pagan temples. Not content with this, he also enforced a ban on the remaining pagan holidays and refused to restore the Altar of Victory in the Senate House, as requested by pagan senators. However, temples and festivals were still celebrated until the law of 386, which declared that care for the temples and festivals were the exclusive prerogative of the pagans (Theodosian Code 12.1.112). Pagans still, throughout the Roman invasion, claimed some power. I share this because we need to learn how one position of faith can exploit and wipe out another one; humans do not tend to tolerate difference well. Oppression can happen when humans become polarised in a viewpoint and lose empathy for the other, as the Romans lost empathy for the pagan community. In embracing our own belief system, we need to acknowledge, accept, and adore the other, not wipe it out. It is the mark of a superior spiritual form when this is possible, when we are not threatened by difference. You may also have similar experiences with parts of you being withheld.

The idea of vilifying others is, therefore, a point of learning, not only for us as humans, but particularly for us as spiritual practitioners. When society loses empathy for others, we need to step back, reflect, and reconfigure. We cannot become consummate spiritual beings if we still engage in hateful, divisive behaviours, not least because of the impact on our karmic imprint. Holding such grudges and antipathy also impedes our mental health recovery. All exacerbated by the perils of social media.

Workbook

Time to pick up your workbook and write some more ideas down.

- **How do you feel about people with different spiritual thoughts to your own?**
- **Could you think about a time when you lost empathy for someone?**

• What was the trigger for this?

• What was it about them that made your loss of empathy feel justified?

• How did you behave towards the other?

• What justified this for you?

• If you went back in time to this period, how could you manage your own process differently?

____

____

The separation of Christianity and spirituality continued. The ancestral, pagan religious rites were restored after the death of Valentinian. However, it was the defeat of Eugenics by Theodosius in 394 that led to the final separation of paganism from the state. Pagan members of the Senate were attempted to be converted by Theodosius, leading to the final separation (Hughes, Philip (1957). However, the pagans either pretended to convert as an obvious method of advancement or remained outspoken in their demands for toleration, but many pagan temples and shrines around the world were destroyed, as was anything that had been written down.

The destruction of the pagan past remains a horrifying move on the part of the Romans, deleting not only a practice in their contemporary times, but also denying much of the legacy of our spiritual history to us today. The blackout was not only about obliterating difference, its effect was to wipe out thousands of years of spiritual practice; our ways of being were just erased.

This deletion is important to be aware of, as when we look to historical spiritual practices, we are often observing them through the lens of others, i.e., the Romans. We only know what we know because of the written accounts of the Romans who observed it, meaning that we learn through a disapproving viewpoint, which inevitably maligns and misjudges what it sees. Therefore, it is vital to remember that whatever we do know about the spiritual past, we should also remember that that past is also largely distorted. This distortion provides another argument to ensure that our current spiritual practices are neither recreating that which we cannot be sure of in the first instance, nor totally ignoring the past context. We need to strike a balance between the two. However, whilst it was easy to obliterate spiritual thinking from written records, it was less so from the mouths of people. And because we modern subscribe to the belief (or pretend we do) that 'the pen is mightier than the sword', we are apt to discount evidence which is unwritten, except where such evidence is of itself conclusive or verifiable from written sources." (Branston, 1957: 38).

There also remains many place names in the U.K. that bear witness to our ancestors' belief in supernatural and spiritual beings. "Grimly and Greenhill in Warwickshire take their first element from Old English (O.E.) 'grim', and mean, in one case, 'the wood', and in the other, 'the hill haunted by a ghost or sprite'. Similarly, a cliff visited by a spectre (O.E. scinna) is Shincliffe in County Durham. While Shobrooke (Devon), Shuckburgh (Warwickshire) and Shucknall (Hereford) stand of rite brook or hills whose visitant is a goblin (O.E. scucca)." (Branston, 1957: 42). Therefore, by closely examining what we often do not consciously acknowledge, we can also understand more from our past.

The British language is replete with words confirming the strength of pre-Christian worship, such as ealh – a temple, Hearh or Hearg – a hill sanctuary, and Weoh, which means 'idol', 'shrine', or 'sacred spot'. Interestingly, the pagan cult names are not evenly distributed across the U.K. – "...the main strength of pagan feeling had rolled like a tide across Kent and the south-east up the centre of the country as far as the north Midlands." Subsequently, we know that spirituality in our history is based in locales, or regions. I think that this is important to consider when situating your spirituality as these regions must still exist.

Anecdotally, the areas of Somerset and North Wales are packed with spiritually minded people, but areas of Yorkshire, as an example, seem less open, in some ways, to spirituality. This might be due to earlier times of living more remotely, in harsher conditions. And in some areas, people are directly hostile towards the idea of spirituality, possibly reflecting the ages' old division between the north and south, with a greater openness to spirituality in the south rather than the north. Inevitably, there will be differences within each region, but it is certainly important, when developing your spiritual practice, to be situated where you are comfortable, connected, and secure.

Workbook

I would like you to research the notion of *Life Story Book*. Find out what you can, and even read some that other people have completed if possible. These are books that contain, usually chronologically, the story of your life. They can be a fairly mammoth undertaking depending on your age or the complexity of your life, but I would like you to consider writing your own. Spend some weeks or months grabbing every photograph possible, every anecdote from your living ancestors, and fill your life story book with them.

Then, I would like you to write a chronology of your life – include all key parts, even those part we would choose to forget. For those of you who have been in care with other people, you may want to also have some much-needed conversations. But be mindful that unravelling the past may offer some surprises, so take care.

Spiritual Figures in the Past; Witches and the Practice of Healing.

Even though the supernatural is exactly that – out of the natural world – it doesn't mean we should not engage with the images, ideas, or feelings associated with such practices. I believe that we can only benefit from reading and exploring the way in which we have approached the supernatural in history. And do not shy away from watching movies that rehash or recreate new supernatural beings for us to enjoy. Supernatural may or may not be entirely created from our subconscious minds, but this does not mean it is less valuable or something to ignore. I urge you to always embrace that which we fear or have triggered big feelings. The subconscious – or spirit – is trying to speak to us within that.

It is equally important to understand how non-religious spiritual practices have been treated historically, as it somewhat explains and contributes to the current ambivalence about having a spiritual practice. Let's not forget though, that Jesus himself engaged in what could now be considered magick, such as arising from death, transfiguring water into wine, etc.

When casting our minds back into the history of the world of spirituality, the image that often comes to mind first is that of the witch. We will begin to look at the idea of the witch here.

Workbook

Before we explore the idea of the witch further, I would like you gather some art materials, electronic or by hand, and reflect on your understanding of the supernatural. Draw the images from your mind on paper, make some lino prints and print them onto anything you like. Or if you are more of a musician, create some music on the theme of the supernatural – choose a wonderful minor key, and let the music speak to you.

The Ways of the Witches

The witch is a being that has always been associated with spirituality, albeit a darker form. We still think of them flying around on brooms, stirring cauldrons, and being immortalised in works such as Macbeth. Have you ever seen a kind, generous and respected witch? Indeed, in areas of the country, the dread of witches was so strong that some buildings were built with square resting places on the roofs for witches to land, as a way of preventing them from coming into the property. However, the witch served many different functions in different cultures across the world and was not always hated or feared. How could they be? They were allegedly around for millennia – could they really have been hiding away all that time? I am intentionally avoiding gender here – we often believe witches to be women, but they were most definitely men as well. Ultimately, given the time they were around, they must have had a use to society in general at some level.

In Western Europe, the witch was often a source of help,

providing herbs and spells to aid people with difficulties. In a way, the precursor to today's doctors and nurses. They would have been called to help with labour and cast spells to ensure abundant crops. They practiced ways of answering the uncertainty in pre-religious life, and served the function of the therapist, healer, or shaman. This role was subsequently taken over by the priest, who became the state approved therapist, advisor, healer, and exorcist. Witches were not always beacons of darkness, out to catch children. However, in other continents, such as Africa, the witch is predominantly still considered a darker force, and stoning continues to happen, inevitably influenced by white Christianity's position on spirituality and magic, as practices such as voodoo are commonplace in other regions of the continent.

To give an idea of how far witchcraft goes back in time, Margaret Murray, in her book The Witch Cult in Western Europe (1921), claimed that Witchcraft has origins in Paleolithic times. Her position has also been heavily disputed subsequently, but Murray's viewpoint was influenced by the belief that there must have been so many questions about nature and the universe in those times. For example, how does the sun come up each day, who makes the seasons turn? An explanation needed to be formulated, i.e., a goddess or god makes this happen, thus when we make a sacrifice, this will ensure us a good crop. Murray provides us with the first reason we may have needed spirituality – to answer difficult questions. Murray's view is probably based on her beliefs rather than 'concrete' historical documents, but I am open to difference here. However, I find that her view provides an accessible way of understanding our ancestors' probable approaches to spiritual matters – humans still have a fear of the unknown, as the unknown is also a potential threat. However, there are more substantial examples that support Murray's view.

As a preliminary example, there are cave drawings from Paleolithic times that show pictures of bison being killed, with clay models of bison being speared. I read about a suggestion that, if the model was killed symbolically, this would lead to success in the field, and the pictures illustrate this. The action of doing something to affect something else is defined as 'sympathetic magick' (Buckland, 2018), and therefore could be deemed a spiritual practice. Other examples of sympathetic magick have survived, i.e., the Mandan Indian's Buffalo Dance, and the Penobscot Indians' rituals, and there is, therefore, a suggestion that people have, since that time, been thinking about trying to change circumstances magically. This is slightly different to something referred to as 'apotropaic magic', meaning if we observe certain practices, we can deflect misfortune or avert evil; the former is trying to create something, the latter is trying to avert something. Magick is a way of trying to manage the two needs.

The witch has always had a chequered history, and even today, there is a gross lack of understanding of the practice and identity of being a witch – I want to be explicit that few contemporary witches will intentionally practice the dark arts, most preferring to be of service to others. There is a belief in the witching community that what goes around, comes around threefold (we talk about this as 'karma' in future chapters). No-one in their right mind would wish to attract something negative to the power of three. I am not naïve enough to think that no one has ever tried dark magic, as inevitably some humans will risk this, but largely, this is just pure myth based on a long history of toxic scapegoating and fear-mongering by the Christian majority.

As a few examples of what early spiritual practitioners faced, in 1484, Pope Innocent VIII produced his bill against witches, and two years later, two monks, Heinrich Institoris Kramer and Jakob Sprenger, produced their Malleus Maleficarum (The Witches' Hammer), leading to definite prosecutions of witches. In 1586, the Archbishop of Treves blamed local witches for a severe winter, and 120 people were burned to death on the charge of interfering with the elements. Consequently, witches were blamed for environmental difficulties despite the lack of any logical explanation. When humans are scared, our fingers point, and we scapegoat, which we continue to do. The role of us as spiritual practitioners is to hold the idea of the causation of historical fear in awareness, subsequently learn from our pasts, and offer different mechanisms that avoids scapegoating, discrimination, and intolerance.

Workbook

- **Can you reflect on a social justice matter that triggers strong feelings in you?**
- **Which person in particular triggers this?**
- **What are the feelings?**
- **Are you able to reflect on how these feelings contaminate your ability to see the person clearly?**
- **Looking in from outside, can you see the limitations in this position?**
- **What are they?**
- **More importantly, what are your options for approaching this differently now you have more awareness of the process?**

Write as much or as little down as fits for you.

In 1951, the last laws against witchcraft were finally repealed, clearing the way for actual witches to share their voices; an incredibly exciting time, marking the arrival of Gerald Gardner and his book, *Witchcraft Today*. I encourage you to read further, not only what Gardner wrote, but also what people wrote about him! He is certainly a character – just imagine people dancing in circles naked, around fires, with incense burning, and you will be somewhere in the right ballpark. The key tenet from his practice appears to be, 'avoid evil and the appearance of evil at all costs'. The Gardnerian practitioners' motto is to 'harm none', and they strive to lead a peaceful, tolerant, and balanced life in tune with nature and humanity. This focus and value persists, and is certainly a value that I both endorse and encourage.

Throughout the 20th Century, Gardner's influence also led to the revival of neo-paganism. A renewed interest in the past happened, and 'pagan' was a term used by various artistic groups inspired by the ancient, natural world – the pre-Raphaelites. Whilst this is not the book to explore this movement in any detail, this period signified a return to nature, natural practices, and a questioning of modernism (a symbolic Christianity). The term attracted different connotations again. Gardner (1955) claimed that the practice he delineated was from ancient practice, and that there have been witches in all ages and countries:

That is, there have been men and women who have had a knowledge of cures, philtres, charms and love potions and at times poisons...At times they were hated, at times they were loved; at times they were highly honoured, at times persecuted." (Gardner, 1955: 31)

Most of what we know about then (pre-medieval times) comes from cultures known to classical antiquity, anthropological field research, and the evidence from archaeological artifacts, but the evidence is inconsistent. Gardner refers to the witch as a 'shaman' though, which is a person who people went to for healing, curing, and support with apotropaic magic. However, we hear of the Witch of Endor in the Bible, Huldah the Sorceress, and of the psychological Cave of Adullan for, "...'emotional women', repressed women, masculine women, and those suffering from personal disappointment." (Gardner, 1955:

33)

The role of the witch in history, then, was as a spiritual practitioner, regardless of the specific techniques they may have employed. Although you may not see yourself as a witch, or healer, or medium, becoming spiritual is an opportunity to connect with the other, the unknown - and the universe - in exciting ways that can feel liberating. However, as mentioned above, the term 'witch', although now a term of empowerment used by witches, was a term of fear and hatred for thousands of years. This term continues to colour our perception, and our psyche is yet to fully clear the negative associations with witchcraft. As a result, I encourage you to step aside from using the term to describe or delineate your spiritual practices because of the notion of 'field theory'.

This a useful juncture to introduce the concept of Field Theory to you. Field Theory refers to everything around you, behind you, and inside you; your beliefs, your influences, your thoughts, your feelings, and those things in your life, such as your family, your friends, and the physical things like clothing and housing. The field is everything. And within this field is the years of absorbing at some level – conscious or unconscious – the negative associations of witchcraft. The field informs the structure of our beliefs and has done forever, both you and society. Being stuck with the term 'witch' simply creates added drama for you. You will spend your life trying to persuade people of your virtues, and dealing with the connotations and projections, rather than the reality. Let's learn from the past, and step aside from what has gone before.

Spirit Around the World

Even though there is, in this book, a heavy Indo-European bias, there are similar spiritual practices around the world. Even with different names and places, practices remain consistent. The world is our field. Shamans could easily be considered witches, as those who commune with spirits, often in an altered state of consciousness (Hutton). The shamanic practitioner clearly has the closest connection to the clearest sense of spirit, but may not embody what we see as spirituality in the West. However, the etymology of the term, has, in my view, more accurately been linked to the Sanskrit word for 'wandering monastic, or holy figure' (Mircea Eliade, 1989). The etymology is helpful to think about – a spiritual practice is akin to becoming a healer, even if just of self. We will certainly be focusing on your healing throughout this book. A healer is a holy figure, a person linked to spiritual practices, outside communities, somewhat itinerant, with ineffable links to paganism and everything non-Christian. The word, healer, could be used interchangeably with witch or seer, and there are probably direct links to northern European practices given the levels of migration and immigration.

Indeed, when we consider wider spiritual practices through history, the role of the solitary practitioner seems central to the practice. In Navajo history, the witch would travel alone, at night, draped in the skin of an animal to 'skin walk', sitting amongst corpses, occasionally having intercourse with them. In Africa, the practitioners are again solitary, apart from coven meetings, and allegedly engaging in incest and other perversions. The theme of spiritual practice being dangerous and dark continues throughout the world. Among the Zande of the Congo and some other central African peoples, the source of this evil-working capacity is believed to be in the witch's stomach, and its power and range increase with age. It can be activated merely by wishing someone ill and is a kind of unspoken, or implicit, curse.

I guess, what I would hope you take from this, is not only the need to be diplomatic with whatever and however you practice, but also to consider that the majority of your work as a spiritual practitioner will be solitary. Being diplomatic is not because of the need to hide, but to remember that being spiritual, wherever you are in the world, can be misinterpreted. In fact, diplomacy is about respect and safety, not hysteria.

I also hope you can take the notion of creativity from the examples of the imagination, the world of fantasy, and our healing requirements, which is an openness to what our imaginations – and our subconscious – is telling us.

Ultimately, history shows us that having a spiritual practice is about service to the self and others. We engage in spirituality to support others in whatever ways we can, beginning with ourselves. We use herbs and incantation to influence the universal rhythms. We use sounds to interact with the universe and think about deities as ways of reflecting on values and connection with others. We remain well read and versed in history and literature and live in communities but on the periphery. Our personalities have a drive to help and support, using characteristics of patience, tolerance, and kindness to connect with others. Subsequently, we learn from the past, and evidence what we do with, what is know from those times. We retain a caution about our identity, and do not quibble with the need for diplomacy in everything we do.

I will talk a little bit about the politics of neo-spirituality here. Whilst I respect many views that do not consider witchcraft as a form of paganism, I do. Paganism is a term used originally by the Romans to refer to all non-Christian spiritual practices. On this basis, witchcraft is a form of paganism – indeed, some Christian practices are probably pagan. If I use the term 'pagan', this is the meaning behind it. However, I also want to drop in the notion of 'Druid' in our conversation about witches. There are neo-organisations that are revivalist in nature and attempt to mimic what they imagine occurred before, which again, is due to the Roman 'cleansing' of paganism. Druids work the same 'magick' as witches, and this is just another term (as far as we are aware) for someone who engages in spiritual practices. There is some suggestion that the practice of a Druid is more inclined towards the earth, although there is nothing to contradict the idea that witches are also deeply respectful of the earth and her offerings. Other terms are Bard, Ovate, and Medium; all sharing lots of similarities, with different preferences, according to personal values. I share this just to help you recognise that history shows us a wide breadth of spiritual practices, and people refer to themselves howsoever they choose. I urge you to do the same, regardless of how deeply your practice develops.

Workbook

- **What does the term 'witch' bring up for you, and what images or stories have you experience of?**

- **Does nurturing a spiritual practice equate with becoming a witch?**

In terms of field theory, I would like you to also take a piece of paper and draw a small version of yourself in the centre. From this, draw lines out to things that figure in your 'field' regarding witches and spirituality – i.e., perhaps you consider Halloween celebrations, or movies. Draw as many or as little as you see fit.

The Issue of Gender

It is pertinent to spend a bit of time exploring the idea of gender divisions in spirituality and the history of spirituality. There have traditionally been differences in how spirituality was applied to men and women, and this is something you may wish to reflect on moving forwards, both in terms of how you view the past and exploring your own preferences. Whereas masculine symbols of courage and strength were seen through the hunting iconography, the feminine was celebrated through the development of the fertility goddess, i.e., the Venuses of Willendorf, Laussel, Sireuil, and Lespugne. There is also some suggestion that the Sheela na gig images we see across the

U.K. were also linked to fertility. If you see these models, they do not have faces, and are depersonalised; seen only through their swollen breasts, enlarged genitalia, and potentially pregnant bellies. The goddesses, though, not only overlooked reproduction, but fertility of crops, and therefore the seasons, and were, in effect, magick. These practices were embedded within the type of spirituality of the times (i.e., Neolithic). Subsequently, it is important to think about how your gender identity impacts your spiritual beliefs.

What I see in the spiritual community is an increasing dependency on one of the gender polarities – either someone is totally into the notion of the goddess and the feminine, or a masculine and godly focus. The problem with single gender – apart from inclusivity issues - is that we become polarised. In reality, when developing spiritual practices to heal, there is a need for a mixture of both the feminine and masculine in our practice and our lives. We need to open up rather than close down. Many of the covens traditionally had females or males at the head, but more recently (thankfully), there is a move to having both male and female energies at the head of covens.

Workbook

- **Has your socialisation as a specific gender affected your openness to exploring the opposite energy?**

- **Are spiritual energies so binary?**

- **How has your understanding of gender changed over your own lifespan?**

- **Does the issue of our focus on gender binaries impact you now?**

- **How could you create your own spiritual practice that**

respects the past, but creates a more inclusive future?

• **How do you feel your identity has impacted your history?**

• **How do you feel your identity will contribute to your recovery, or notion of recovery?**

Ancestors' Reverence for Nature

Our history demonstrates a clear connection between spiritual practices and nature. Indeed, our ancestors were most definitely and necessarily embedded within the earth around us; we depended on the harvest to survive, and the seasons to thrive. Inclement weather had a more urgent, more pressing need for us to respond. Indeed, there is something natural about spirituality that we would all benefit from remembering, and this has always figured in our spiritual practices.

Prudence Jones and Nigel Pennick speculated much about Celtic spiritual practices. In particular, they believed that the celts were animists who believed that all aspects of the early world contained spirits, and that communication was possible with these spirits (Jones et al., 1995). There is also speculation that worshipping rocks, water, and trees was also widely practiced, which is entirely consistent with what we believe to be shamanic. One particular Bronze Age grave was unearthed by Arne Runeberg in Denmark, finding the claw of a lynx for medicine/amulet, bones of a weal to remedy diseases in animals, vertebrae of snakes, horses' teeth to help children's teeth grow, twig of rowan to be used as a charm, and multifarious other artifacts. Gardner (1955) certainly postulated and extrapolated from this that, given some of these articles are still used today in a similar way, there is, subsequently, a wonderful continuation of the practice.

Beginning to consider the spirituality of items, such as water and trees, deepens our connection with nature. The consideration that your house, for example, is alive and receptive to energies within and outside, helps us begin to develop a different relationship with them – I would like to think this is to develop the relationship between ourselves and the world.

I always say hello to my house when I return; I touch the walls and reflect on what they have seen and heard in their 150-year existence. I may conduct short ceremonies thanking my house for providing shelter. When we decorate the house, we always think about what the house would feel comfortable in as well as what we want to see as decoration. We are inextricably linked to the physical. I know the house is not going to talk back to me, certainly not in a way I am currently able to tap into, but connecting with the house in this way helps me respect the property more.

This relationship with nature also presents a need to consider the climate crisis. If we are so dependent upon nature for life, and if we truly believe the concept that we are nature, should this not mean that it is vital to do something differently? Is it not important to think about the climate being us, and that this is somethign we are doing to ourselves?

Ultimately, an important takeaway at this juncture is that it is our ancestors who supported our lives today. It is the ancestors' connection with nature and reverence for nature that ensured our survival. What we see though, is that our respect and care for those of us who have gone before has been eroded, which is highly dangerous. When we ignore those of the past, we open ourselves up to making the same mistakes. We need our ancestors to learn from so we can ensure survival for our own descendants.

People who practice spirituality have often communed with those in the after-life. Cunliffe (1997) proposed that the pagans had a strong belief in the after-life, ascertained through various items being buried with the dead, especially precious goods being buried with those of higher status, and the practice of burial being venerated. The Gravettians (22,000-18,000 B.C.E.) were renowned for their beliefs in the after-life, burying the deceased with full clothing and ornaments and sprinkling them with red ochre to give back the appearance of life (Pike et al, 2012). We also know that Caesar was aware that the pagans believed in reincarnation, transmigration of the soul, and power in the gods and goddesses. There is also the notion of the 'otherworld', a magickal, faery place, where supernatural beings would entice humans into their realm, often felt to be underground (Dunning).

I won't be talking much about direct contact with spirits in this book as, in my view, this is a practice you should undertake in person with an expert. In fact, it is generally more helpful to begin this kind of practice with others around you, primarily people who are experienced and know what they are doing. I am also aware that there is a lot of cynicism out there, and an alleged lack of 'scientific evidence'. Also, there are charlatans.

My position is that the mind is separate to the body, which mirrors the position of the Buddhists. The mind isn't contingent on grey matter, it exists separately and independently. There is numerous evidence supporting the idea that the mind persists after death, not just in terms of past life regression experiences, but including factual information being passed from beyond the grave. I will go further into what this means in future chapters, but for now, I encourage you to have an openness and interest in the notion of spirit, in whatever form. You do not have to pack your bags and move into the house of a medium just yet!

Offerings

It is clear that our ancestors also made offerings. According to Barry Cunliffe, in most cases, deposits were placed in the same places on numerous occasions, indicating continual usage "over a period of time, perhaps on a seasonal basis or when a particular event, past or pending, demanded a propitiatory response." (Cunliffe, 1997: 194). There is also some suggestion of human sacrifice (MacCulloch, 2007). Caesar describes how Gauls of rank would be placed in wicker men and burnt. A range of creative ways of murdering others were used (see Boudica for further examples), such as ritual decapitation. The archaeologist, Barry Cunliffe, believed that the Celts held "reverence for the power of the head" and that "to own and display a distinguished head was to retain and control the power of the dead person." (Cunliffe, 1997: 210), while the archaeologist, Anne Ross, asserted that "the Celts venerated the head as a symbol of divinity and the powers of the otherworld, and regarded it as the most important bodily member, the very seat of the soul." (Ross, 1974). Buckland adds, "With the development of different rituals - for fertility, for success in the hunt, for seasonal needs - there necessarily developed a priesthood: a select few more able to bring results when directing the rituals...these ritual leaders, or priests and priestesses, became known as the Wicca." (Buckland, 2018: 4). I won't complicate our understanding further at this point by talking about the Druids as this is another hotly contested area where some archaeologists rely on information provided by Caesar, which others contest due to bias. Ultimately though, don't Wiccans sound quite similar to what we believe Shamans to be? I also need to be clear that even though some people may still believe that the head holds the soul, we won't be encouraging any ritual decapitation!

Finally, we know much of our past through the Icelandic/Norse sagas, as intimated in the introductory chapter. The Icelandic/Norse sagas are factual stories about family life in Iceland from the 9th-11th century. I am aware that some people and groups consider such communities as Heathen, but again, such terms were Christian and used interchangeably with others, such as pagan, so I will continue to refer to them as pagan for clarity's sake. I also know that, in doing so, I do not account

meaningfully for the plethora of beliefs and practices in all those communities – again, this is not a sociological study, this is background reading, which can be developed for those interested parties.
As Iceland was on the periphery of life elsewhere, their writings were not subject to banning or victimisation from stronger forces. As they were robust farmers, there was plenty of vellum to write on, and the long, cold winters, in a relatively isolated province, provided time to apply themselves to activities such as writing. Psychologically, such activities perhaps also assisted in developing identities and coherence of self during very difficult, trying times. The sagas provide incredibly rich, vibrant insight into pagan lifestyles; they contain information on all aspects of life, and there is much to learn about gods, goddesses, and magic. Women in particular were regularly cited as adept at magic and other spells.

The sagas are probably the main source of historical information regarding the way in which pagans thought and practiced their belief systems, complemented by archaeological findings. Take the example of the Oseberg ship – two women, one 50 and one in her 70s, were buried in the ship. They were surrounded by accoutrements used in shamanic practice such as iron rattle heads, suggesting that both the practice and reverence of such practice, given the importance of the burial. Even though the documents were written in this epoch, the information also pertains to much earlier myths and legends - indeed, some of them have crossed over into other forums, their influence was so great. Dorothy Whitelock adds, "It is often held that Anglo-Saxon poetry is permeated by a strong belief in the power of fate, inherited from heathen times, and some have even seen a conflict between a faith in an omnipotent Christian God and a trust in a blind, inexorable fate." Remembering that we are in the hands of fate, that what will be will be, which it will, is also liberating.

I share the information about the sages, firstly because they hold incredibly interesting insight into past beliefs, and secondly because holding the idea of gods and goddesses helped our ancestors reflect on issues that affected them. Such meditations also helped manage difficult circumstances. In future chapters, we will return to the idea of specific deities. Again, not because I think you will see them on the bus, or because I think they are floating around on a cloud above us. My position is that deities reside in our deep subconscious. Meditation and hypnosis help us access them, and our openness to this practice supports our recovery because invoking the support of deities can help strengthen us, and working with them effectively can help us raise awareness, and capacity for relationships with others. All potential opportunities to support our recovery.

Workbook

We have just taken a brief journey through the different elements of spirituality through history, over different cultures. In your workbook, answer the following:

- **Which parts of historical spirituality resonate with you most?**

- **What feelings come up for you when we think about larger cultures squashing smaller ones?**

- **Write down some of the people you plan to read around in more depth.**

- **What deities are you already familiar with?**

- **What is your relationship with deities?**

To conclude, we have visited various parts of the world, and I have encouraged you to think about your knowledge and experience of spirituality in your life. This is about setting the ground for the actual practices, which we will now move onto without further ado!

3. Eating Spiritually to Thrive

The Magician

I have used the archetype of the magician within this chapter, as it is through our relationship with food that we create a certain magic to enhance our spiritual development. The magician is an archetype that we associate with powerful characters who understand the universe and how to interact with the universe to create change. If we nurture that archetypal magician inside our own psyche, we can develop this magic in our relationship with what we put into our bodies.

For further clarification, if you think about the witches in Macbeth, these are obvious magicians who transform matter into something else. There is also a dark association with these particular magicians, but obviously, we can use the archetypal magician qualities as a way of developing light, growth, and harmony within our bodies. I also see the magician as obvious characters in the Harry Potter series. Dumbledore is an able and creative wizard. However, Gandalf in The Lord of the Rings is another archetype that provides a benevolent influence in what can be a disturbing and settling world. Plus, the way we create magic with our food and a relationship with food helps to also stabilise our own relationships with what can be an alarming world.

In terms of strengths and difficulties, the first challenge with the magician is the risk of corruptibility and arrogance, which is certainly true for our relationship with food as we can often minimise and deflect from what we are putting into our mouths. However, the magician also holds a great omnipotent discipline, and we can nurture the strength from the archetype that serves us well in a quest for recovery and healing.

Workbook

Reflect for a moment on the idea of the magician:

- **What does the idea of a magician bring up for you?**
- **What are your memories of a magician in your childhood?**
- **What are your familial views of a magician, and how have you absorbed them?**

Welcome to the notion of eating spiritually. This may be a new idea to you. How can we eat spiritually in reality, you may ask? I would not be surprised if you thought this was just mumbo jumbo, but there are tangible concepts to practice, all of which can support your spiritual practices in a holistic way. The purpose it to consider food as spiritual nourishment, not simply physiological fuel.

Up until now, your relationship with food has probably been ok at best, problematic at worst. I do not think I have heard of anyone having an unremarkable relationship with food. In fact, so many of us may struggle with over-eating, or purging, and others may yoyo diet, continuously gaining and losing weight. Some of us appear to have found the right amount of food and willpower to fuel their bodies at a healthy level, but this is by far not the norm. The norm is, alas, a very different picture.

In this chapter, then, I will support you in developing a new relationship with food, which will help you attain an emotional balance. This will not offer you a diet, but will encourage you to think differently about what you put into your mouth, and how. It will also be about learning to eat more consciously – many of us with problematic eating approach eating mindlessly. Adopting a spiritual approach helps us to be more ethical in the choice and manufacture of our foodstuffs, particularly in terms of harm to the environment and animals. Even subtly changing our viewpoint towards food in this way can support an important shift in how we function in the world. This is not just about feeling virtuous for eating virtuously, but incorporating a range of eating practices to support a greater spirituality. Hopefully, you will begin to enjoy eating again.

There is also an additional point about food nourishing the brain. Our brain is the control pad of our entire existence. If we don't feed the brain, we don't thrive. If we fuel the brain with artificial stimulants, and deprive it of essential nutrients, we damage it. If we neglect ourselves, this can effect permanent and irreparable damage to the brain. The important also of water is huge. Take a quick look at the scans of chronically neglected children's brains for insight in to potential harm caused. I consider the brain our control pad - do we want to land on rocky land with no support? Do we need adequate lighting to land safely? I would suggest we do.

Workbook

Take a moment or two to find your workbook. Reflect on your relationship with food, and write some observations about your diet:

- **What do you eat most of?**
- **What foods do you avoid?**
- **How do you cook?**
- **How many times a day do you eat?**

Begin to scope out the environment, and we will complete

some more activities shortly.

The Backstory

There is a clear relationship between historical trauma and eating issues. Even though the causes of eating issues are complex, and can be attributable to a genetic predisposition (runs in families, as does abuse), environmental issues such as abuse, trauma and unhelpful feedback about size can all contribute. Eating disorders increased massively during lockdown, especially chronic over-eating, leading to a huge growth in organisations, such as Overeaters Anonymous.

What is obvious to many is that we are all in the middle of an international obesity epidemic with 35% of adults in the U.S. being obese, and many more having disordered eating habits. Even twenty years ago, globally, there were 200 million people who were obese; that number has probably tripled now. When we refer to obesity, it is not just being a bit tubby, but clinically obese. Clinical obesity refers to those whose movement is impaired, their breathing can be laboured, and they can encounter issues with self-esteem and body image. We should all, by now, know that the impact of obesity is horrific – those of us who are struggling with obesity are more likely to get diabetes mellitus, cardiovascular disease, hypertension, and stroke. This is before we begin to navigate the outside world, apply for jobs, buy clothes, or try to find a partner.

The problem is not just on our shoulders though. Our eating habits are impaired by both our history and the power of cheap, fast food laced with salt, fat, and refined sugar, a lethal, yet highly addictive combination for human beings. We probably all know how compelling a burger and fries can be, especially swilled down with a huge vat of sugary pop. Also, our family histories may be replete with enormous family feasts, feeding on highly calorific food and sweets, so over-eating can be in our

DNA. It is also no coincidence that when we go shopping, the cheaper options are also the most processed, which is obviously alarming and bewildering – why are the foods that have seen the most processing also the cheapest? Why do the number of additives increase in the cheaper products? The answer, obviously, is marketing, manipulation, and exploitation. The supermarkets and fast-food joints are out to make massive amounts of money, they want you to eat their products, and will do anything to make sure that their products ping your brains into oblivion. Their food is tasty, it is designed to be, but it will not nourish your body, let alone your soul.

Take myself for instance. I became so stressed before becoming a psychotherapist that I put on four stone in a few years. I worked 14 hours a day in a highly stressed environment. It was when I developed shingles that a GP diagnosed me with high blood pressure and high cholesterol, making me realise that I needed to change. My insides were surrounded by fat, and my arteries were beginning to get clogged. I could not walk very far, could not fasten my shoelaces, and relied solely on my fat pants. I was definitely approaching heart problems, increasing my stroke risk, and generally limiting my life. Also, we know that it is when we struggle with tasks such as getting dressed that our risk of premature death is vastly increased; I could not put my socks on standing up, and rarely found trousers that would fit. Whilst I thought I was coping, (I probably was in some ways), my body had other ideas. I needed this reality check to help me realise that desperate situations required desperate remedies.

Consequently, I trundled out of the doctor's surgery the day after the diagnosis, mortified, ashamed, and went home. I had never been that large in my life. Determined to make a change, I firstly made some practical adjustments to my life. I left my job and began to work independently. Change requires change. I know for a fact that if I had not made changes to my external world, my habits would have remained. I was, after all, eating emotionally. I then made some adjustments to food intake, and I began an exercise regime, which my body did NOT like.

It took some years to really understand from the research, and from my experiences, what worked for me. Most importantly, I realised that my eating habits had lost spirituality. I ate anything mindlessly with no awareness of the origin of my food, and no knowledge of the labour (and exploitation) required to bring the food to my table. But I needed to find out – it is only through direct awareness raising that we can trigger change.

Subsequently, through my spiritual practice, I adjusted my relationship with what I put into my body, not how much. I raised my awareness about the wonder of nature, and the labour and effort that went into producing my food. I studied more about the impact of factory farming, and made changes regarding meat (or rather, flesh). I also studied the various chemicals I had been absorbing, in particular, artificial sweeteners and refined sugar, and I began to cut out various foodstuffs. Nothing dramatic, just the really toxic stuff; energy drinks, takeaways, and sweets. Most importantly, my connection with spirituality enabled me to treat my body with kindness and respect. I thus developed spiritual practices that improved the way I thought about, reflected on, and related to food. And by taking out the high from eating, even though I craved it, my brain adjusted to eating the food it needed rather than craved.

Within six months, I had lost two stone. The ability to fit into old clothes was an amazing feeling, but more importantly, I could get out into nature more often. I could enjoy the spiritual wonder of nature. I felt better in myself, and this supported my own recovery by reinforcing that what I had been doing was right. The more practical changes I made led to greater spiritual attunement, and the growth continues. Currently, even if I gained a stone in weight, I would still be within the normal range, but my fitness would be impaired, I would walk less, have less energy, and that is before we think about the way I feel about my body. So, my practice most definitely continues.

My experiences have led me to believe that there is a relationship between the decline of our spiritual lives, and the increase in the many problems we experience. The increase in social media use, and us gaining weight, are symptoms of a spiritual deficit. As we left churches, synagogues, and communities, we became more insular, less connected, and more prone to over-eating fast and convenient food. And although we have probably always capitalised on others, our spiritual deficit, and lack of empathy for others' plight, has heightened this enormously. And so we are left with food that is obviously also laden with saturated fats, sugars, and additives, needing to pay for water, and becoming dependent on Big Pharma to 'heal' the symptoms that could often easily be remedied through changes in diet and eating practices. And now our obesity leads us to remain isolated, perpetuating the problem.

Finally, before we move into the next part of the chapter, I also want to state that whilst there are parts of this chapter that are worded strongly, my wish is not to alienate anyone. I hope that you are able to understand that I am here to support your entire spiritual development, and how we fuel our bodies is a key component of that. This is about fuel, not a paint job. I am passionate about this, hence devoting a whole chapter. I am also keen to clarify that this is not a diet book, nor am I advocating that you start a diet. Diets do not work; severe food restriction generally results in over-eating, and I am not here to exacerbate any pre-existing vulnerability. I am here to support your growth and help you fuel your brain into long life.

History of Food

Most of human history around the world has been predominantly a period of scarcity and shortage. We have spent our lives hunting food, storing food, and enjoying food, but only the rich have been able to do this to excess up until recently. Let us think about the royal houses during the Middle Ages – we all know of the feasts, even if we have not read about them.

We know about Henry VIII and his size. We also know, through poetry and writing, how those who indulged were often treated by others (think of the Canterbury Tales).

We may also know about the stories of poverty; people dying through hunger. The history in the U.K. alone is marked with chronic issues of starvation. Let's also remember the Great Hunger in Ireland, whereby potato blight, a focus on singular crops, and capitalism led to over a million deaths, and worse, a mass exodus from the country. The potato crisis in Ireland is a distinct, and harrowing example. Indeed, the theme of famine and hunger persists to this date – there are people in Ethiopia and other third world countries who, today, lack sufficient basics such as food and water. The climate disaster is exacerbating this.

In reality, our bodies are designed to withstand certain periods of abstinence, and also abundance. Not famine, I hasten to add. Only in the past few centuries has man managed to get access to consistent food and shelter. We can store fat for leaner times, and also tolerate a certain level of over-eating. Our liver and kidneys are also generally very good at repairing the body from the excesses. It is only through repeated and long-term damage that their capacity to self-heal is impaired.

It should also be said that we have always craved sweetness. Finding a beehive and being able to extract honey would have been a thing of wonder (not to mention bravery), and we would have venerated the bearer of such a wonderful thing. This led to changes in our brain, whereby the pleasure receptors are still wired to 'fire' when we eat sweet things. Sadly, they do not fire so well when we eat spinach, which is because sweetness was an unusual treat, and not readily available, and therefore triggered complex processes within us.

The modern world, however, is such an abundant place for calories, comfort, and other pleasures of life; our brain, unfortunately, has not adapted to such abundance, and there is no wonder we sometimes struggle to manage temptation. Eating the honey that someone found once or twice a year is very different to the temptation on offer every single day. With that being said, our primal physiology is still adapted to living in an evolutionarily unforgiving landscape. Our species have followed the pattern of feast and famine for thousands of years, which is the exact opposite of the situation we are facing right now. We do not need to get more comfortable; if anything, we need to get less comfortable.

Finally, humans have always used food ceremonially. A simple search will produce a range of results. We have certain drinks such as a wine for ceremonies (sacrament). In Korea, they eat sea mustard soup to celebrate childbirth. In Sri Lanka, they eat a mixture of coconut milk and rice called Kirivath, which is eaten for the first breakfast of the month, and any other significant transition. Native Americans are known to drink 'black drink' for ceremonies, which is an emetic made from Yaupon Holly, brewed in a particular way, and drank in special ceremonial cups. I have written another chapter on ritual practice, but food could have been incorporated into any section.

We Are How we Eat

We truly are what we eat. Most importantly, we are how we eat. What we directly put into our body impacts our well-being, like it or not, and how we eat is as significant. I will not try to present some of the research evidence. If, at this stage, you doubt the need for a healthy diet, you do not need dietary advice, but support to help with your denial. But weight problems are not simply just about moving away from spiritual lives.

Ill health can be a sign of stress overload, meaning that there is an inter-relationship between stress and ill-health. Stress impacts the body negatively, which may also not be news to you. Certainly, you may even have experienced some of the symptomatology - fatigue, chest pains, muscle tension, changes in sex drive, upset stomach, or sleep problems. All are well documented. Stress is bad (overall). In fact, the impact of chronic stress over time can lead to heart problems, shingles, raised blood pressure, anxiety, and stroke. It is a killer and needs to be tackled – I will talk more about stress in later chapters. Whilst tackling the external factors is essential, our diet can also support our well-being.

If we are ill, we are anxious, meaning that being ill is also stressful on the body and the mind; we become distracted, preoccupied with the discomfort, and perhaps worried about the future. If we become less mobile, we are less able to do the things we would probably want to do, and thus experience the double whammy of less time doing the things we might like to do, and the knowledge that we would prefer to have been doing those things. We would probably experience more discrimination from the world (this is not about being like everyone else), and it can lead to a terrible downward intra-psychic spiral. Being overweight is not cute, but immensely damaging. I know, strong words.

I just want to also mention a few things about body positivity. When I talk about obesity, I realise that people who have been put into that category may well feel shame, or worse, at the mere mention of the word. I am immensely sorry about that, and do understand how that label can make things worse rather than better, not least by becoming a self-fulfilling prophecy. It is vital that we all love our bodies and those of others. However, if I said there was no problem with obesity, I would be dishonest and lacking in congruence. There is a real problem, and I hope you can hear the care behind this. Let's talk about an example here, HungryFatChick.

HungryFatChick is a beautiful, American woman called Candy Godiva. Candy is a proponent of Mukbangs. Mukbangs originated in South Korea, and are essentially a way to pay someone to eat with you or in front of you, usually on camera. There, it is frowned upon to eat alone, and people pay other people to eat with them. Through publicising them on YouTube, Westerners have bastardised these into horrifying freak shows where people eat grotesque amounts of food in one go. Watching these shows is horrifying but compulsive – Mukbangers often just eat those foodstuffs that we never would, tragically sacrificing their health for clicks.

If I am honest, I am filled with sadness and horror when Candy does another Mukbang because her breathing is so obviously laboured through her being in excess of 600lbs, and she is opening herself to ridicule through eating those foods in those amounts that few would be willing to. And I reiterate that this chapter is not about what we look like, but about maintaining our earthly vehicle to maximise our spiritual development.

You see, the purpose of sharing the story of Mukbangers such as Candy, is that their relationship with food is so far away from any sense of spirituality. They are lost souls, offering their health and wellbeing to clicks. Or attention. This is also about projective identification – we disown in ourselves that which we are uncomfortable with, and in a sense, we watch Candy do what we would wish to do ourselves (or even are), but do not. Candy's addiction (arising from complex abuse and trauma) is so immense, that she lacks awareness of the impact of her endless takeaways (i.e., meat production/packaging) on herself, the environment, and the world. However, this is also about emotional management – Candy eats her feelings down, and has mentioned this in her videos. In gestalt, this is called retroflection, whereby we use food to anaesthetise feelings. I am sure many of you will know that satiated place, whereby you have disappeared into a buffet, and the next thing you know, you have eaten 15 plates of food, not really being conscious throughout.

So, it is important to say that I empathise with Candy's struggle rather than judge. I feel saddened by her helplessness with food, but do not blame her. The food industry is designed to entice, manipulate, and keep us addicted to their products, and what better comfort is there in life than eating a pot of something sweet and delicious. I have been there, so the experience resonates with my own. And we are especially vulnerable if we have had a tricky history, as Candy has. But there is also the issue of having an unhealthy spirit, which is obviously more potentially subjective, with the possibility of less reliable data to support it. However, when we are lacking in spiritual belief, or focusing purely on material matters, we lose the potential for heightened engagement with the universe. Without spirit, you are surviving, not living.

So, this chapter will introduce you to a way of eating spiritually to become fit and healthy again. I will introduce you to some evidence-based approaches which will support you in taking care of the fleshly vehicle you reside in. The unhealthy spiritual practitioner, when satiated, will not win the battle, and it is time for you to begin to nourish and care for the only fleshly vehicle you own! You can only benefit. This is not something I am just proselytizing though – I have been where Candy is, and know that you can make some changes.

Workbook

- **How would you describe your current relationship with food?**
- **What are your weaknesses?**
- **How do you imagine you could begin to have a more spiritual relationship with food?**
- **What are your views on obesity, or even using the word?**
- **Where do you believe your relationship with food altered?**

Eating Spiritually to Thrive

We now understand a little bit more about the challenges we face as individuals. We have also had a brief look at the role of food in our history. We are now going to look at various kinds of practices to support the development of eating spiritually to thrive. I offer them as suggestions to complement and reorder the way you think about and approach food. In doing this, you will be able to revitalise your relationship with food, begin to think about food differently, and slowly imbue food and eating practices with a more sacred, sanctified approach. Again, excusing the metaphor, just adapt whatever you see fit, chew over everything, and spit out that which does not fit for you.

This part of the chapter is divided into three parts – that which you should refrain from, that which you should embrace, and that which you should practice. The three strands will, I am sure, lead to a more positive and helpful relationship with food and your approach to eating. This is all about imbuing everything you do with care.

1. Embracing

You may be the kind of person who sees food as treats, and you may also celebrate everything with food. Do you buy a treat if you are feeling sad, angry, or wanting to celebrate something? Notice the pattern here? You are using food as ways of managing feeling; it is when the two become embroiled that our weight suffers. We have to see food as fuel and healing, nothing else.

There is another issue, that of getting a high from food. I will talk about addiction in another chapter, but getting high from food is addictive behaviour; we anesthetise feeling with food. You will benefit from moving away from this, for obvious reasons. I understand how easy it is to get into this habit, but it is important to move away from using those foodstuffs and drinks – especially food laced with caffeine and processed sugar. When you stop getting high from food, you will become less obsessed with eating, generally meaning you will begin to eat less.

My primary request to you is that you begin to see food as fuel, not as an indulgence. View food as that which will give you strength, and that will provide you with the capacity to heal. In fact, organise your food in that way. Unless your weight is healthy and stable (which means you somehow manage to eat correctly), you will also need to ensure your activity levels are sufficient for the food you eat. I tend to encourage people to avoid weighing themselves.

Let's have a look at some more information from our history – the Spartans. The Spartan society was very self-sufficient, and this shines through in their approach to food. Common foods for Spartans were meat and fish with honey, milk, cheese, bread, figs, and wine. And, naturally, fresh fruit would grow well in the warm Greek weather, providing the Spartans with variety, albeit rather basic. Natural food, grown locally by the helots, was where most of the Spartan diet would originate. Obviously, you may not live in southern Europe, and some of these foods may not be available; the point is about moderation and simple approaches.

I include this example as it can help us in thinking about simplifying our approach to food. Rather than trying to eat every kind of food, focus on the more local foodstuffs to you. Edward Carpenter once said that health in body or mind stems from unity and integration, rather than disintegration. Making sure your food is wholesome and nutritious, even if from a smaller range of foodstuffs is better than a little bit of everything. This requires effort, but the practice is about developing your capacity for care, respect, and connection.

We should also support the local growers wherever possible, as it is more likely to be organic, fresh, and seasonal; a mindful, spiritual practice in itself. By connecting with our community providers, we take ourselves out of isolation and into connection with others. Valuing their products and offering them payment for the toils gives us unity, not only with the self, but with our environment, even if we are not directly digging ourselves. Eating organic is also important for retaining Ki, or prana, in our food – the more processed and refined the food is, the less natural Ki that is there. For those who aren't aware, Ki is the energy or life force that exists everywhere, and which practices such as Reiki channel.

Now, we are all aware of the hefty price tag associated with many organic products in the West. People are often concerned about buying organic fruit and veg, especially from supermarkets. My advice is to steer clear of supermarkets wherever possible. I know this is not an option for most of us, but there are huge problems in the role of supermarkets in our world. They not only wrap everything in plastic to keep it fresher for longer, which further contaminates the environment, but they charge the earth. However, if I do some research, I find that I can eat healthily and locally for less than £50 a week, which is consistent with the amount that people on benefits live on as well. It just requires effort to get out and find those foodstuffs (which is beneficial in itself). Seeking local food is also part of eating spiritually – listening to what your environment is offering you now, searching for value and quality, and accepting and using that which is on offer.

I advise you to find a local organic fruit and veg box provider and get one each week. Use this box as the staple for your diet, providing an interesting part of your week where you discover what foods have been offered, and you decide how to use them to their advantage. Doing this can also help you to organise your time – rather than endlessly nipping out to shops each week, you rarely nip out, meaning you have more time. You could even cook up batches on the same day and save even more time. A substantial box of fruit and veg can be found for £15, and in supermarkets for much less. Add your grains and add your proteins whenever you can so you can nurture your body with wholesome, nutritious food, especially if a good amount of it is raw. Your body will love it, so spend time reflecting thankfully on what is offered, and what you are able to locate.

I also encourage you to eat seasonally, not just buying what is available. By this, I mean that in history we would eat fatty meat and tubers during the long winter months, and feast on leaner meats and vegetables during the summer. Adopt this into your life – indulge more during the winter, and restrict more during the summer; eat starchy potatoes and turnips during winter, but focus more on salads and lean meats during the summer. By becoming more attuned to the seasons, we connect more with the universal rhythms of life, developing more respect for the seasons, and the challenges that face our growers in such times of climate change.

Overall, remember that the food we have comes from the ground we walk on, so try to research how the food in your region is made; what farming methods are used, and how the animals are treated. Remember that the energy and love that is put into farming will be transmitted into the food, and this in turn will impact you, the consumer.

Workbook

In your journal, spend some time reflecting on the food available to you. Write about the blessings you receive from the food you can buy, and the generosity of mother nature in providing this for you. Reflect on what you know about food production and commit yourself to three points that you can do differently, i.e., recycle better, cook less, and preserve more. Also spend time meditating on the role of animals in our food – whilst I would never encourage a particular diet such as vegetarianism or veganism, researching and becoming more aware of the farming world can help inform whatever

decisions you do make more energetically.

Water

Water, not beer, keeps you alive. Water is the most important element on Earth, and without it, you will die. Your brain is 75% water, and when you are hydrated, you will feel more alert, have greater clarity, being able to think more clearly, and your whole metabolic system will work with greater efficiency. You have to drink water, fact.

Another reason for drinking water is that the hypothalamus is a bridge between the nervous system and the endocrine system, which regulates hormones in the body. The hypothalamus also controls body temperature and is responsible for sensations of hunger and thirst. An axis formed between the hypothalamus, the pituitary gland, and the adrenal glands, controls the body's response to stress by regulating the hormone cortisol. Unfortunately, the hypothalamus cannot always differentiate between hunger and thirst, and often when we are hungry, we are actually thirsty. It is, therefore, vital that you are always hydrated. If you are hydrated, you are therefore likely to know when you are truly hungry. Drinking fruit teas throughout the day can help as can always having a water bottle with you. It is also helpful to drink a pint of water four times a day, throughout the day. Try it and see what you think.

As an aside, I used to drink loads of squash, and never drank water on its own for most of my life. Water was 'council pop', and no-one drank it. Plus, squash was nice because it was full of sugar, and tasty. In fact, drinking squash was like a luxury. It is only in the last ten years that I have been drinking pure water, which made me realise just how addicted I had become to sugar, especially squash. Drinking water also made me more aware of the chemicals that go into such products. If you are a squash drinker, try to dilute your squash more and more each day, or even each week. Do not deny the squash, just add more water to it. Eventually, you will get to the stage where the squash does not taste much better than water, and you can make the full switch. You will feel the benefits immediately.

Spiritual beings drink water. Water is one of the secrets to our health and lifestyle.

Fermentation

I advocate as much fermented food and canned foodstuffs as possible, but not to excess. This prevents waste, ensures you have greater spiritual and energetic connection with your food, and gives you a strong connection with the seasons and with nature, given we attune our canning and preserving processes with the seasons. Being spiritual is equated to being careful, not just in respect of people, but objects too. Preserving is offering care and attention to those things, so do it consciously!

Historically, fermentation techniques were used as a way of preserving foods and drinks long before the days of refrigeration. During the process of fermentation, microorganisms such as bacteria, yeast or fungi convert organic compounds - such as sugars and starch - into alcohol or acids. For example, starches and sugars in vegetables and fruits are converted to lactic acid, which acts as a natural preservative. Fermentation can produce quite distinctive, strong, slightly sour flavours. I find them amazing, especially home-made vinegars and kimchi.

The consumption of foods and drinks that have undergone fermentation contain benefits to health that stretch beyond food preservation. The transformation of sugars and starches enhances the natural, beneficial bacteria in food. These bacteria, known as probiotics or 'good' bacteria, are thought to help a multitude of health issues, specifically digestive health. In getting healthier, using these kinds of foods really support not only recovery from some digestive problems, but a more holistic way to health and treating your body with love and care.

Examples of fermented food are:

* Kefir - A probiotic cultured drink, kefir contains multiple strains of bacteria and yeast. Kefir is rich in minerals and vitamins, particularly the B vitamins and vitamin K.
* Sauerkraut - Easy to make at home, this fermented cabbage dish has been around for centuries. It is high in fibre and vitamins A, C, K plus various B vitamins. Sauerkrat also a good source of iron, manganese, copper, sodium, magnesium and calcium.
* Miso - This traditional Japanese paste is made from fermented soybeans and grains consisting of millions of beneficial bacteria. Miso is rich in essential minerals and a good source of various B vitamins, vitamins E, K, and folic acid.
* Kimchi – Spicier than sauerkraut, kimchi is also a form of fermented cabbage and other vegetables. It contains vitamins A, B1, B2 and C and minerals such as iron, calcium, and selenium.
* Lassi – Made from soured milk, lassi has been drunk as a pre-dinner yogurt drink for centuries. They are a popular way of achieving probiotic bacteria.
* Kombucha – A fizzy, fermented black tea. Yeast turns sugar into alcohol and carbon dioxide, and bacteria called 'acetobacter' convert the alcohol into acetic acid, giving it a sour taste. Watch out for the sugar in shop-bought kombucha, you are better off making it at home once you locate a 'mother' to activate the fermentation.
* Tempeh – Another version of fermented soy beans, tempeh is a rich protein source so a good choice for vegetarians.
* Bread – Some breads, such as sourdough, are made from fermented dough.
* Yogurt - Lactobacilli bacteria convert lactose sugar in milk into glucose and galactose, which break down further into lactic acid, giving yogurt its sour taste. Live bacteria remain in the yogurt and provide a valuable contribution to gut

microflora.

The queen of fermentation, Sandor Katz, also a friend of mine, writes accessibly on this, and waxes lyrical about them! But there are also financial benefits of making your own. Not only will you be able to use leftover jars and containers again, but it is so much cheaper. You can make your own kombucha for example, for next to nothing, whereas a small bottle can cost upwards of £4. Also, by developing our physical health, and improving circulation and energy levels, we make ourselves more capable of recovery and healing on a deeper level.

2. Refraining

Your body is the temple of your spiritual mind, capable of great things, such as healing, recovering, and growing. We have the ability to heal illness and can easily recover from many diseases through relatively straightforward changes to our diets. I recovered from high cholesterol, fatty liver, and high blood pressure through such changes. However, so much food is laden with chemicals that alter our capacity to be present and meaningfully engage in spiritual practices. If you have had two cans of energy drinks, alongside a huge fast-food takeaway, your attention will be poor, and you will struggle to concentrate and even sit down, let alone get into a deep state of meditative equipoise!

Thus, firstly, I advise you to stop eating food containing processed sugar. An excess of sweetened foods and beverages can lead to weight gain, blood sugar problems, and an increased risk of heart disease, among other dangerous conditions. There is a difference between refraining and cleansing. Eating sugary foods can become ingrained into our lifestyles and routines. That spoonful of sugar makes your coffee taste better and dessert can feel like the best part of dinner. If you have ever tried to cut back on sugar, you may have realised how incredibly difficult it is. For some people, it may seem downright impossible, which leads us to the question: can you be addicted to sugar?

Sweet foods are highly desirable due the powerful impact sugar has on the reward system in the brain called the mesolimbic dopamine system. The neurotransmitter dopamine is released by neurons in this system in response to a rewarding event. Drugs, such as cocaine, amphetamines and nicotine hijack this brain system. Activation of this system leads to intense feelings of reward that can result in cravings and addiction. So, drugs and sugar both activate the same reward system in the brain, causing the release of dopamine.

This chemical circuit is activated by natural rewards and behaviours that are essential to continuing the species, such as eating tasty, high-energy foods, having sex, and interacting socially. Activating this system makes you want to carry out the behaviour again, as it feels good. We talked about the potential origin of this specific part of brain development.

Dopamine has an important role in the brain, directing our attention towards things in the environment like tasty foods that are linked to feelings of reward. The dopamine system becomes activated at the anticipation of pleasure, meaning our attention can be drawn to cakes and chocolates when we are not necessarily hungry, evoking cravings. Our routines can even cause sugar cravings. We can subconsciously want a bar of chocolate or a fizzy drink in the afternoon if this is a normal part of our daily habits. Now there are fewer receptors for the dopamine to bind to, so the next time we eat these foods, their effect is blunted. More sugar is needed the next time we eat in order to get the same feeling of reward, similar to tolerance in drug addicts, leading to escalated consumption. Sugar can exert a powerful influence over behaviour, making cutting it out of our diets very difficult. And quitting abruptly, or going "cold turkey", leads to withdrawal effects.

In the absence of other things in our life that brings us joy, losing sugar can seem disappointing. Most people would love nothing better than to curl up with a box of chocolates and demolish them. But let's try to think about the balance between immediate pleasure and lasting spiritual recovery. Removing the highs from your life also removes the lows, creating more balance and harmony.

My advice is to set up a withdrawal day. Clear your cupboards of sugar on this date, and stock up on nutritious fruits and nuts. You probably won't be able to clear out everything containing sugar, as 61% of our processed foods contain sugar, but do your best. It is my belief that sugar has contributed to our need to have 'treats', but there is no need for this. Our systems need to be cleaned of this toxin as much as possible. The positive impact on the environment is also something that will be beneficial.

Similarly, fast food is highly addictive, full of sugar and salt and trans fats, and although cheap and cheerful, is ultimately toxic on your system. In eating fast food, you are also supporting the powerful capitalist systems that keep us in slavery. Step out of this system wherever you can. Just shred all those takeaway leaflets, and you avoid temptation. Create that virtuous, loving life for yourself at every level. And just eat three meals a day.

Workbook

Pick the date! Choose a day that will be less stressful and less distracting. Take some medical advice to check for any underlying vulnerabilities. A Sunday may seem tempting as the day to stop, but if you spend a lot of time slouching around on Sundays, it could be easy for your mind to drift into snacking. Spend the week building up to the day, using up and giving away the sugary products you have left, then go cold turkey. You may feel jittery and slightly unwell, but these symptoms will quickly subside. Then get busy. If the going gets rough, pick up your workbook, and write down the many reasons

you are doing this. Also connect with someone who does not eat these foodstuffs so much, and get support. If sugar consumption has been a massive problem for a long time, consider attending a fellowship meeting such as Overeaters Anonymous – this will help support both your spiritual and physical practice for free!

The above process is one of cleansing. The next one is fasting.

Fasting can be controversial to think about, and if you are a food-restrictor, I do not advise that you participate in any form of restricting behaviour like fasting just yet. For you, fasting can be an adjunct when other safe eating practices are in place. For those who eat ok generally, perhaps over-eat more regularly than they would like, then read on.

Fasting is not eating for a set period of time. We have fasted for thousands of years (not in a row!), sometimes as a conscious decision, sometimes not. Hippocrates was an advocate of fasting, and he recommended fasting for certain symptoms of illness. Fasting was also used religiously at least since the 5th century BCE. Indeed, fasting is still prominent amongst most yoga schools, the Jewish tradition, Christianity (Lent), and most other religious practices. Muslims regularly fast due to Ramadan, often for all daylight hours, only being able to eat at nightfall. It seems that the process of withholding that which we need to thrive has also been a test of our commitment to certain processes and beings. The physical and mental sensations from such a practice can be incredible.

Nowadays, there are three main types of fasting; calorie restriction, nutrient restriction, and seasonal eating. Calorie restriction is self-evident, nutrient restriction is more about certain macronutrients, i.e., fats or carbs. Seasonal eating is that mentioned above.

Intermittent fasting seems to be a well-researched entity that provides an important positive impact on our health. Evidence shows that being in a fasted state improves cognitive function, gives the gut a break from digesting, and benefits the microbiome. Fasting also lowers inflammation in the body by reducing oxidative stress. Being in a fasted state also develops our spiritual presence, making us more receptive to spiritual insight and awareness. At its worst, we just feel virtuous for being able to fast.

However, whilst fasting develops our capacity for greater spirituality, we need to exercise caution. Firstly, we need to always eat sufficiently for the days running up to a fast. We also need to maintain the boundaries of the fast. You should take medical advice prior to embarking on any kind of fast, especially if there are any other ongoing issues.

Workbook

My suggestion is that you fast only on the full moon, for the day before, the day of the full moon, and the day after, but just stick to the actual day if that seems more accessible at this juncture. Eat well for three days before. Drink as much fluid as you need throughout the three days, and try to eliminate as many stressors as possible. If you are able, engage in other spiritual practices – this may be a great time to coordinate a fast with a retreat – and get the very best from the practice. My suggestion is for you to spend the time in fast meditating, engaging in journeying, and recalibrating the body through earthing and/or calisthenics. Be extra careful when you end the fast, and try to take the return to food as slow as possible. Maybe have a light breakfast, or shake, and take the return to normal eating from there. Use the workbook to reflect and write down your thoughts and feelings, and any spiritual insights that come up for you.

3. Practicing

The final section of eating spiritually to thrive is to incorporate practice alongside the sections on restriction and embracing. Practice is about altering our approach to food and eating and building on the first two practices as a way of deepening our spiritual awakening. Recovering is also not just about reading what to do, but putting the above into practice.

I encourage praying at meal-times. Whom you pray to, what you say, or even how you pray, is up to you. There is something important in how we energetically relate to the universe (think scalar energy). Taking things for granted only leads to greater indulgence, which results in less awareness of the impact on us. So, I also recommend that you spend a few minutes before every meal sensing the energy from the food; feel thanks for the people who have grown the food, celebrate nature for creating the right environment to produce the food, and be thankful for the positive impact of the food on your body. This attunement with the universal energies creates not only better karmic pay off for you but supports a subconscious containment with what is available for you, and thus switches off neuroceptive anxieties. Your body and your spirit will benefit from this.

Ceremonial Eating

I want to return u to the idea of ceremonial eating here. The world is your proverbial oyster, and the key is to get as creative and open as possible. Consider incorporating a special drink, such as mead, that you make yourself, to celebrate the passing of one season to the next. Perhaps attend a pottery class and make some ceremonial food and drink containers – fill them with marks and designs that support what you do in your practice. The containers will hold your energy and imbue all that you eat or drink with that energy.

Also, think about the kinds of foods you want to eat at different times of the year. You may, at times such as Mabon, have a larger feast with close friends and family. You may want to cook fresh seasonal produce and enjoy them in moderation. The energy and love that you put into the food will also be preserved. You could set up a canning weekend with friends, whereby you come together, share foodstuffs, and prepare them together for storage. I often have a kimchi day with friends, whereby we bring instruments and play music whilst we wait through each stage of the preparation. Those particular batches of kimchi taste the very best.

Using spirituality to recover from whatever happened to you is not only being physically healthy, but is about being frugal, less wasteful, and having a minimal impact on the environment. Becoming more respectful with food and eating, and using food and meals mindfully and in connection with nature and spirit, can only benefit your recovery.

Workbook

Cast your mind back to your ancestors and immediate family.

- **What kinds of food would they have eaten?**
- **What was it like to eat in your family?**
- **Was food associated with big feelings such as guilt or shame?**
- **Did your family over-eat?**
- **Did you push your trauma down with food?**

When we eat, we also are inextricably linked to our experiences of eating growing up. We remember the feasts we may have had with loved ones. We may also remember certain recipes or foods that we ate in our family units. Food may have a range of associations for you. Part of using spirituality to aid your recovery is to become more aware of this. Write everything down. Make connections between what happened then and what is happening now. Your awareness will help you make different choices now if appropriate.

Finally, great food is an amazing experience, and there is no perfect approach. Your approach should be the one that you develop with experience, preference, and insight. The suggestions above are just that, and I hope you can develop your own approach using these exercises to support that.

Workbook

For a final exercise, I would like you to find somewhere comfortable. Complete a supported body scan – there are plenty of good examples on my website and YouTube - and take yourself to a place of deep relaxation. In this space, imagine a white light glowing over you; a light of healing and protection, and sense the light enveloping your body, purifying your system, healing your hurt. Stay here for at least fifteen minutes, absorbing the light's energies. Afterwards, very slowly begin to move your body, starting with your hands, and your head, until you are conscious and back in the room. Over time, practice the same exercise with your foodstuffs, imagining the energy being imbued in the food. And then enjoy!

4. *Sacred Love*

The Lover

The archetypal lover is quite an obvious link to make with this chapter on sacred love. The lover is, indeed, a particular archetype that is guided by emotion and passions of the heart. There is also a certain level of physicality to the lover that supports the appropriateness of using this archetype in relation to sacred love. When I think of the lover as a person, I am reminded of Romeo in the famous Shakespearean play, Romeo and Juliet. I also consider the lover to be represented as Jack and Rose in the Titanic movie, and as Scarlett O'Hara in Gone with the Wind. Obviously, we cannot ever establish a universal archetype for anyone, and so the purpose of sharing a few ideas here is to simply introduce you to the idea and see where your imagination takes you.

In terms of strengths and weaknesses, one of the strengths of love and intimacy can be passion and conviction. However, there can also be risks inherent within intimacy and love, in particular when thinking of elements of naivete and irrationality. Overall, sacred love is about prioritising the notion of love, and viewing it as something profound and precious.

Workbook

Take your workbook and spend a few minutes exploring the idea of the lover, and how the concept relates to you. Do you embody love? Is love, for you, sexual or emotional? Or both?

Even the mention of intimacy can, to the British public at least, trigger major discomfort. We have all seen the 70s sitcoms, replete with prudish, Hyacinth Bouquet types. The British are internationally renowned for being priggish and uncomfortable around sex and intimacy, certainly in public anyway. It seems that the word 'prude' is synonymous with British - if you check the definition, it means a person who is shocked by rude things, especially of a sexual nature.

Alberto Letona, a Spanish author, recently wrote a book on the British, observing that we were either crude and vulgar or prudish; we were overly polite, but also binge drinkers and violent. His book makes it sound as though we should throw in the towel now, but is this really the case behind closed doors?

Behind the safety of our front doors, we know that the situation is often very different. Many of us are really quite liberated, and trying hard to embrace diversity, multi-culturalism, and more unique lifestyles. At this point, I am also reminded of Madame Cyn, perhaps weirdly so. If you are not aware, this was a movie based on the later life of Cynthia Payne, the famous British madame. When she was arrested, there was a line circulating that, when a particular vicar was arrested, he called for his solicitor who, he confirmed, was in the next room. Seemingly, we were all at it!

However, love is that which heals us from our past. It is in the loving arms of a safe, caring adult, that we heal from past trauma. It is through the re-imagining and re-experiencing of our original love - that between us and our mother - that we heal in the here and now. The importance of seeking this relation, or union out, cannot be trivialised.

In addition, there is also importance in adjusting our connection with sexuality and intimacy, as intimacy is an extension of the original love, albeit in adult form and shape. Love is, regardless of the intimate nature, is still often triggering, and we have much work to do in order to begin to use love helpfully within our lives. In short, love is not necessarily sex, sex is not necessarily love, but intimacy is most definitely the way to enjoy loving sexual relations.

Workbook

Let's begin with sexuality. Take a moment to consider how you think about sexuality. Draw yourself in the middle of a piece of paper, and thought shower anything you associate with the idea of sacred sexuality.

My own relationship with sensuality has been, let's say, interesting. My late adolescence and early twenties were marked with shame and withdrawal from sexual relationships; I did not want to be seen, and could not accept who I was, or how I looked. I would have hidden myself in horror had anyone come close.

I then began a torrid affair with a 32-year-old friend of the family when I was 19. I would exclaim to people that all my birthdays had come at once, although she was no Lady Chatterley. The woman in question was, let us say, quite liberated, and would be an encouraging participant at all kinds of debauchery. Whilst we were not fully compatible as people - I was far too immature - I was introduced to the concept that sex could be adventurous, energetic, and gratifying, and it was ok to like sex with others. Sex did not have to be the shameful, furtive acts I had been taught, but I could not yet be intimate. And that is an important point of clarification. Sex was a place where we can meet the needs of the flesh, but not the spirit. And although enjoyable, sex for myself was deeply private, shameful even. It has taken a great deal of work to modify my relationship with intimacy.

When I arrived at university, I was determined to experiment with intimacy. I saw the arrival at university as an opportunity to come to terms with who I was as a person. I attended pubs and clubs, and, let's say, became somewhat generous with my body. My time at university was spent having multiple affairs, and occasional longer-term relationships. Again, even though we were well past the seventies, I had multiple partners, everything was physical, and usually, quick. My physical cravings were quenched, but my soul most definitely was not satiated.

After university, I found myself in a married 'situation'. Whilst there was attachment in the relationship, there was no real love. Intimacy was quickly put in the background after the first year or so as we ate ourselves into oblivion each day. Once the physical excitement left, we realised there was nothing left for us. I entered a period of hermitage; years of very little sexual expression, and even less emotional intimacy. After my rock bottom, I realised that part of my recovery had to include the way I related sexually to myself and others, which was not about creating a false narrative about how I looked, but how I connected with the deeper spiritual self intimately.

As I connected with others in spiritual circles, I discovered ways of bringing feeling into love-making. There is a real connection between trust and love, and I developed my relationships, introducing a capacity for tolerance of love. I also learnt that there were so many groups and movements that made fanciful claims about intimacy and love, but the reality was that they were just as messed up as I was. I started to wonder if anyone actually understood love.

I eventually completed my psychotherapy training, and for the first time, I developed an understanding of what love was. I met the most amazing woman (my trainer), who literally held me for four years, saw everything about me, warts and all, and remained available to connection with me. She never rejected me, regardless of my flaws.

Through this relationship, I learned what it was like to be truly intimate - how to sit, look into the eyes of someone I loved, and to reach heights of intimacy I had never imagined were possible, without getting undressed or messy. I was offered a reparative, healing connection, where I could redress my deficits, and repair my wounds. I could access love, absorb the benefits, and subsequently offer this elsewhere. Our relationship truly kick-started my recovery. I could not count the times I let go of my grief, or she held me; I have wailed like a child in her arms, letting go of my hurt and distress, all of which could not have been accomplished without her. I truly opened up during this time.

And although this was without sexual intimacy, I developed a way of transferring this process to intimate spaces. As I experimented, I developed more experience of what I enjoyed with intimate connections, and developed more capacity to avoid that which I did not enjoy. As I opened up emotionally and spiritually, I understood the factors that complemented intimacy, and rejected the factors that did not.

My extensive training and learning also helped me sift through the plethora of misleading material that exists online. I noticed that people were talking about 'tantric sex', and there was no substance to what they were claiming. Tantra is a meditation practice, and Westerners were bastardising the practice, often in bizarre ways to manipulate and support pyramid selling. I became disillusioned when I heard about 'cosmic intimacy'.

When people were making fantastical claims about their approaches, I was able to cross-reference this with reality and make important choices for myself. I want this chapter to support you in doing the same. There are charlatans out there, although possibly with honourable intentions (some not). This book is designed to help you work out what works for you without moving into a cult or selling all your belongings in favour of an organisation that does not truly value you.

I also discovered over time that the vast impact of my early experiences had an impact on the here and now. I believe that this is also something important for us all to think about as our history can inform or affect the present. For those of you who have experienced violations of your boundaries in childhood through abuse, you will know that your relationship with intimacy in adulthood can be tricky at best. You may be totally avoidant, and consider yourself asexual. You may encounter difficulties with openness to touch, and may present in life as cold and distant. And there can be a huge array of different experiences of love-making. Others may be able to enjoy sexual intimacy, but struggle to manage appropriate boundaries with others, which may look like sexual addiction or a certain level of sexually indiscriminate behaviour. The risk in adulthood of becoming involved in abusive relationships is also very high, and well established in research.

It is important to me that you at least begin to develop your relationship with sexuality and intimacy. Intimacy can be profoundly reparative in adulthood, regardless of our historical experiences, and it can be an important part of being validated as a person. There is very little more pleasurable than a healthy sexual connection with someone you love. Indeed, opening up to our infinite and wondrous sexuality can be transformative.

History of Sexuality

Let's go back to the beginning and think about some ideas on sexuality from history. Pre-Christianity, the evidence is sparse on sexuality and sexual relations. Much of Western Europe's material was destroyed, and we rely upon Roman material to view the pre-Christian lifestyles. We have information on, for example, traditional roles and expectations in other cultures, such as Native Americans (Two Spirit), although, as with everything, there are different interpretations and ramifications. The Romans themselves, however, were clearly enjoying sexual relations.

However, we do know that male sexuality was associated with virility and strength, as seen through the hunting iconography. The feminine was celebrated through the development of the fertility goddess, i.e., the Venuses of Willendorf, Laussel, Sireuil, and Lespugne. If you see these models, they do not have faces, and are de-personalised, seen only through their swollen breasts, enlarged genitalia, and potentially pregnant bellies. The goddesses, though, not only overlooked reproduction, but fertility of crops, and thus the seasons. There was a clear representation and association of femininity and reproduction, and thus sexuality to fulfil this purpose.

But there are lots of other symbols of sexuality in the world. Let's start with the image of the Nymph and Satyr. Both are famous symbols of sexuality and sexual expression. Roman life was patriarchal, we only have male opinions of sexuality; the reality, especially for women, may have been very different. But sexuality was an act of prosperity for the state, and people could partake in private magical practices to support fertility. Prostitution was legal and commonplace, as was male relations with young people of either gender. Same sex female relations were either celebrated or reviled by Roman culture, and there were moral codes regarding hyper-sexuality and male effeminacy. Overall, there is some evidence (disputed) that sex was binary, reduced to penetrated or penetrating, when it may well have been more diverse.

We have very little information on pre-Roman times, sadly, but sexual relations were more likely to have been based on necessity and procreation. We needed sex to have more children. Larger families meant greater chances of survival, especially as so many children died in childbirth.

As Christianity's influence grew around the world, practices became more proscribed. Heterosexual normative practices were enforced, and we all married where possible. This was under the backdrop of various emperors attempting to obliterate various spiritual practices, in favour of Christianity. Theodosius I began his reign in 381, after a period of time as the co-emperor in the eastern part of the Roman Empire. He reiterated a ban on pagan sacrifice and Haruspicy (divination through an animal's entrails). He was also responsible for breaking up some pagan associations and destroying pagan temples. Not content with this, he also enforced a ban on the remaining pagan holidays and refused to restore the Altar of Victory in the Senate House, as requested by pagan senators. However, temples and festivals were still celebrated until the law of 386, which declared that care for the temples and festivals were the exclusive prerogative of the pagans (Thodosian Code 12.1.112). These actions also impacted pre-Christian ways of relating sexually, shutting down difference, and normalising Christian expectations.

The Norse sagas also show a fundamental difference to sexual relations outside Christianity; a lack of shame. All bodily functions were considered natural, and were not surrounded by the same levels of shame as that which we find today. Interestingly, one of the sagas talks about olsa þattr, a cult which involved passing around a huge horse phallus. When the phallus is passed to a slave girl, she talks about wanting to lie with it. The symbolism is obvious.

But gender was also not so strict, with Loki occupying a fluid role, and Odin holding some characteristics that do not fit with a stereotypical role, such as the knowledge of magic. Magic was predominantly associated with women. There is even sexualised imagery in relief in Neolithic artefacts found in

Anatolia, Turkey, with a man holding his penis as two leopard's approach. Whilst we cannot accurately interpret this, we would possibly assume the role of the phallus has always been of concern, let's say. Indeed, the image of the phallus is embedded within prehistoric findings. Phallic paintings have been found from 27,000-19,000 years ago in the Cosquer cave, and an actual 8inch phallus found in Ulm, Germany, dating 28,000 years ago! Truly, our bits, especially male bits, have figured strongly in our consciousness.

It seems, from a brief journey into our history, that sexuality moved from a very open, normal process within human interaction, to a very shameful process as a result of organised religion, particularly Christianity. But this was not just with sexual expression, but also emotional expression, which we continue to struggle with. We most definitely need to find our happy ground again. Let us look at current gender differences in sexual expression before we move more into practices. This will help us understand the role of gender in history, and offer suggestions on how to manage things differently moving forwards.

Gender Differences

I wanted to include a section on gender differences when considering sexuality as there are important differences that we just cannot escape, and should not. Some of us consider that gender is just a construct, but there are important biological determinants that impact the way we relate sexually. It is essential that we understand this and respond to it before we begin sacred sexuality practices. I am open to differences here, and I understand the position that same sex attraction is considered 'genital preferencing' by some, but the reality is also important to consider – males and females are different.

Men and women, contrary to social media gender activists, approach sexual intimacy very differently. Women need intimacy and safety, and more importantly, some kind of relationship before sex can happen; if they are not feeling it, it will not happen. Men do not need (but can enjoy) emotional intimacy, and it is no coincidence that it is only men who engage in sexual activity, such as sex in public sex environments (i.e., tea rooms). These are environments where sex is anonymous, often without any verbal communication, and occurs even in the dark. This is the land of glory holes, and impersonal, furtive encounters with someone you will never meet again. Apps such as Grindr and Scruff have probably positively impacted the need to go into PSEs, but the issue of honesty and relationship still exists. This does not mean that women cannot be promiscuous, but if they choose promiscuity, they go about it differently.

There is the problem of sexual offending. Men are disproportionately reflected in the statistics, and I have never heard of a woman stalking a random man to rape him as stranger. This is not to say women do not have inappropriate sex with minors or the vulnerable, or even use sex manipulatively, but there are important differences.

There are also some important differences in sexual frequency. Generally, for heterosexual couples, frequency begins 3-4 times a week in a relationship, and after a year or so, drops to weekly, and even less thereafter. Most couples engage in 'solitary' activities within a relationship. For lesbian couples, the pattern is the same, but with gay men, sexual frequency is maintained, and they are far more likely to normalise sex outside of the primary relationship. I imagine that both genders would view sexual relations very differently, with different perspectives on what constitutes 'good sex'.

I would argue that it is men who influence women's positions in practices such as dogging, although this is just a hunch and a generalisation. I am going to talk about polyamory very soon, but it is clear that gay men occupy a key position in this practice also. This kind of relationship is often incorporated within spiritual practices.

And intimacy aside, there are differences in how people of all genders approach and process the concept of loving relations with others. What is important is that you find something that fits for you. And remember, although intimacy is a continuum of love, you situate yourself along that continuum wherever feels safe for you.

Workbook

I think it is always helpful to think about your boundaries and their role in intimacy and sexual expression, I want us to practice a short exercise. This will help you think about your boundaries, and hopefully the changing nature of them.

I would like you to take your workbook to a safe space where you will be sure of no interruptions. I would like you to spend ten to fifteen minutes in meditation. Light a candle, and spend the time simply gazing into the light. Think about the light at that which provides sustenance and inspiration. Let go of your daily stresses and frustrations. Begin to tune into your body, and scan your body from head to toe.

Now think about your areas of sensitivity, and where you enjoy being touched. Reflect on moments of enjoyable intimacy with someone else, and also by yourself. Reflect on the highlights, and skim over the more distressing experiences. We do not want to open that up here. Immerse yourself in the times past where you have felt connected and moved by contact with someone else, regardless of the depth.

Benefits of Sexual Health

Now we have had a look at a brief history of sexuality, let us explore some of the benefits of developing and experiencing a healthy sex life. The research on the benefits of sexual health is clear. An active and healthy sex life is known to lower blood pressure, improve the immune system, and promote sleep. Our heart health can be improved, and there are important benefits to our emotional well-being, such as improved mood, better self-confidence, and increased libido.

For men, the most immediate motto is 'use it or lose it'. The more times we get and maintain erections and ejaculation, the healthier our 'waterworks' are. Men who ejaculate more than 21 times a month are less likely to develop prostate cancer. For women, orgasms can improve bladder control, and sex acts as exercise. It is important that we all begin to discover and enjoy our bodies as much as possible, safely. The benefits are immense, and if we have had tricky encounters in our history, working through this successfully, and not letting the rest of our lives be smeared by this, is so important – our abusers do not deserve that much power over the rest of our existence.

Let's move towards processing various sexuality practices, and tap into the benefits. I am going to offer three intensive practices. Please read carefully, practice what you see fit, and reject the rest. All is good.

1. Developing a spiritual connection with your own sexuality

Before we try some exercises, let's return to some practice for a moment.

Practice

I would like you to reflect on your own body some more, and explore the way you experience energy in your body. Find somewhere safe and comfortable where you won't be interrupted. Feel free to go skyclad (naked), and perhaps light some candles and add some relaxing music. Spend some time relaxing first, using breath to slow your breathing, and consciously let go of anything going on inside.

I want you to think about an amazing bright light above you, and imagine this (nwyfre – life force, or chi/prana) spreading love and joy into your body through your mouth. Feel the nwyfre entering all parts of your body, filling every cell with healing, love, and energy. Spend some time here, absorbing and rejoicing in the nwyfre. Try to join your breath consciously with the nwyfre, letting go of all toxicity while breathing out.

After this, move your hands around your body, not touching anything, just sensing the space between your hands and your body. Experiment with different parts. Imagine sending sexual energy to different points, and your body receiving that. Be playful, experiment, and explore what works for you.

This exercise was our first attempt to explore the interconnection between our physical bodies and the universe. We used the power of nwyfre to fill our bodies with light energy and joy. Please spend some time writing in your workbook how this was for you. Explore the differences between how you would normally touch yourself, and what it was like to connect spiritually but not physically touch.

Nwyfre isn't necessarily a sexual energy, but something that exists energentically in the universe Nwyfre can be sexual, but it is most definitely required for love. That glow we feel and sense when we are intimately connected with someone, when we sense they see us fully, is nwyfre. I encourage people to begin to notice that in themselves and in their relationships, and to work out ways to develop this further.

It is time for more practice.

Practice

This time, I would like you to return to the practice above. Create an essential oil mix for yourself; use those fragrances that you truly connect with, and sprinkle a few drops into a small bowl. Take care with allergies, and add a mixer oil, such as any massage oil. Find somewhere safe and comfortable where you won't be interrupted. Feel free to go skyclad, and perhaps light some candles and add some relaxing music.

Turn the heating up if you are skyclad, obviously. Spend some time relaxing first, using breath to slow your breathing, and consciously let go of anything going on inside. I want you to think about an amazing bright light above you, and imagine this (nwyfre) spreading love and joy into your body through your mouth. Feel the nwyfre entering all parts of your body, filling every cell with healing, love, and energy. Spend some time here, absorbing and rejoicing in the nwyfre. Try to join your breath consciously with the nwyfre, letting go of all toxicity while breathing out. Dip your finger into the oil and anoint your brows. Then massage your third eye (the area between your eyes on the temple). As you touch your temple, see the fragrance being absorbed into your soul.

Imagine the energy radiating out towards those you love. Visualise the energy being absorbed by them. This is something we can do even when together, as in reiki.

Then, bring the energy back to yourself. Rub other areas of your body that you see fit, perhaps your neck, behind the ear, or your nipples. This exercise is not about reaching straight for your genitals and masturbating, but slowly, and in a controlled way, attuning to your physical sensations. Avoid the temptation to move to stimulation – this is about sensation and an introduction to touch. You can experiment with touch, going light or harder, but avoiding the genitals for now. Our

current aim is to hold energy inside, not release it.

I hope that the practice above helped connect you to the power of nwyfre, and that you were able to at least visualise something. One of the challenges with spiritual practices is that not all of us are visual – some people work best with verbally recounting something. Just do what works for you. This entire book is about developing your sense of self and understanding what works better for you, so roll with it.

We have done a couple of practices now, both of which are about developing some self-practice. We will now move on to practice with someone else. Now, this may create challenges for some of you as you may be happily single. You may also be on the asexual spectrum, and have no plan on changing this, which is absolutely fine too. As mentioned variously, there are no expectations or pressures here. However, even if you do not have a partner, the following discussions and exercises are as easily practiced with spiritual 'others', or imagined people - the mind is a wonderful thing.

For those of you who have a partner, you may also encounter a situation whereby your partner does not feel open to engaging in some of the practices here. We must absolutely respect this, and do not on any account try to force the issue. This may open up further complexities within your relationship and could be something you wish to process constructively with support. This would be an important process for you to both honour and respond to.

Polyamory

Polyamory is most definitely in vogue. We are reading about it everywhere. Somehow, the practice of sex with more than one partner is becoming de rigour, not just something a few people do. We are also noticing an increase in more liberal programmes, and we have even been shown programmes that display full frontal nudity. Times are a changing, for better or for worse!

There are some possible explanations for this. Firstly, as the world breaks away from organised religion, especially Christianity, the strictly defined expectations on how we live are becoming eroded. Also, as the hard-won battle for inclusion and acceptance from people with diverse gender identities continues, the rest of society are required to adjust and adapt to the new ways of being and relating. The increase of gender identities is also inevitably linked to the increased awareness in relating intimately, and so we enter an exciting time of metamorphosis. We are no longer repressed by religion (laregly), and we can truly identify who we are and what we need intimately from the world.

But what is polyamory?

Polyamory is a form of consensual non-monogamy where one person is open to fostering emotional intimacy and love with several other people simultaneously (Barker & Langdridge, 2010). This is not necessarily a sexual intimacy, but can be. Wikipedia describes it as the practice of or desire for intimate relationships with more than one partner, with the knowledge of all partners. It has been described as 'consensual, ethical, and responsible non-monogamy'. There is obviously an ethical, moral undertone to much of the research.

For some, being polyamorous is as natural as snow melting, and incredibly life-affirming. For others, polyamory is complex; it challenges our concepts of traditional relationships, which is heavily underpinned by conscious and unconscious anxieties around the expectations from religion, culture, and identity. Inevitably, our own lifestyles and experiences contribute to this.

Polyamory is an entirely different beast to polygamy, in that the latter tends to refer to relationships with an element of religious and interpersonal coercion (Porter, 2015). Polygamy also carries significant inequality of power and position, and it has traditionally been considered by some as misogynistic (Strauss, 2012). Others go further and attribute the inequalities inherent within polygamy as a major contributor to civil war (The Economist, 2018). Some proponents of polygamy argue that if we legislate for gay marriage, we should also legislate for polygamy (Harrison, 2015). But the two are not equitable, they are different in most respects, with the former lacking the historical and oppressive power structures that the latter is imbued with. However, for the purposes of this book, the focus will be solely on polyamorous relationships, between consenting partners, with or without marriage.

As I have already intimated, the interest in polyamory is increasing. Research recently demonstrated the magnitude of the correlation between 'consensual non-monogamy and web queries', with a significant increase in web searches using words and phrases such as 'polyamory' and 'open relationships'. Curiously, 'swinging' as a search term has declined in frequency (Moors, 2017), perhaps due to the ethical and moral concerns that such a practice attracts. Swinging and dogging are somewhat different practices to polyamory!

Polyamory, on the other hand, is certainly increasing in visibility, acceptability, and accessibility, although alternatives to 'the couple' are largely overlooked in law, organisations, and employment (Moors, 2017; Robinson, 2013). Proponents of polyamory wish the term to become recognised as an additional descriptor of sexual orientation, believing sexual orientation should not be based solely upon the gender of sexual attraction (Tweedy, 2011; Klesse, 2016). Indeed, that it should necssarily mean sex.

The term is frequently misconstrued, however; some believing it is consensual non-monogamy, with people rendering its similarity to monogamy as a means of making it more palatable to critics (Brunning, 2016). However, the term is far more complex than this, and as spiritual practitioners, there is a need to understand, engage, and relate to those of our clients who choose to accentuate their life with this choice(s) (Holmes and Witherspoon, 2017).

Workbook

Spend a little bit of time thinking about the idea of polyamory. This may well be a new term, and that is ok. I would like you to write down the pros and cons as you see the practice. Do not get too caught up in what the practice triggers for you, more just the objective benefits and issues as you see it.

You may also be wondering why I have been talking about polyamory. Firstly, I share it, and offer an understanding, because it may be a new term. I also offer it - especially the part on differentiating different practices - because there are lots of similar practices within the world, especially connected to spiritual communities and tribes. I am by no means implying that every spiritual community are polyamorous, but at some point, you will encounter someone with these practices.

Learning more about polyamory from this book could help you to develop your self-awareness and capacity for relationship with others. Primarily, sex with strangers aside, polyamory is a way of fully getting what we need from the world - we may have a partner that we love but are not sexually interested in. We may need someone to go out and explore the world with, but keep our primary partner at home. Ultimately, polyamory is not about sex but about ensuring you are able to meet your emotional needs, from more than one person if that fits for you.

My particular interest in polyamory is around emotional intimacy and love with others. When we are able to practice this and develop our capacity for emotional intimacy with others, we also develop emo-diversity. This is a fairly new term that means emotional diversity, or an increase in the variety of emotional expression that someone can achieve. I think, therefore, that such a practice - within your boundaries, and 'safe' - helps our brains develop that evolutionary capacity to develop with the changing world.

So, how can we consider polyamory in terms of our spiritual practices? Firstly, connecting with someone in an intimate, relational way, is spiritual. There does not have to be any physical intimacy in polyamory – we can love without sex, and it is ok to have both. There are few things so beautiful than a rich connection between one person and another, on whichever plane you can connect.

I recall times when I have met truly magical people - people with such a powerful aura, that others were drawn to them. I remember meeting my yoga guru many years ago, and it was clear that we were going to connect on a powerful level. I recall being mesmerised by his presence - he was such an astute man, confident and intelligent, and a consummate expert in his field. I remember sitting in workshops with him, hanging onto his every word, knowing that, for this moment, we would interconnect on more than just a material plane. We were not lovers in the carnal sense, but we were definitely connected on a higher level. And the impact on me was enormous; I felt more aware, more attuned, and impacted by his presence as well as his knowledge; the unknowable, just the sensation. He took me to a magical place of connected awareness that left me stunned by its level. Those moments are ones that we never forget, and I will never forget Yogi's impact. He is one of the men I love, and have been impacted spiritually in incredible ways. And this is the key to enjoy spirituality and intimacy – there are grades, but connection with self is just the first time.

Workbook

Think back to a previous time when you met someone who triggered a strong, positive reaction in you:

- **What were the feelings you experienced?**
- **What was the kind of connection?**
- **Did the feeling last?**

Now that we have explored the impact of others on us, let's think a little more about how sexuality supports spiritual practice. Firstly, let's look at how to connect with others - we have already done many practices that support connection with self. We need to now move out of what I would call the 'self-contact boundary', the space where we connect with self, and move towards a space where we offer ourselves to connect with others in order to get love, and thus benefit from its gift.

When connecting with others spiritually, we need to consider what we bring to the table. Are we defensive? Are we painfully shy? Do we deflect from contact with others to combat the self-consciousness? There is a theory called Gestalt that has some meaningful connection to spiritual, eastern practices. When we think about this, we can really develop what we bring to the table so we can have more meaningful relationships with others.

Firstly, the theory encourages us to think about the ways in which we interrupt contact with others. What this means is the kinds of things that we do that get in the way of accepting or offering contact, or love, to others. We can do this in a range of ways. I will mention the key methods of interrupting contact, but there are more. Let's begin with projection. Projection is when our historical experiences are overplayed to contact with others in the here and now. We may have a strong reaction to someone we have never met before, but when we think about our history, they may remind us of something that happened to us previously. The person may have the same colour hair, or a smell that is triggering. It is important that we are always seeing someone as clearly as we possibly can, and often need support with pointing out how we project and when. This is where a spiritual guru can be immensely helpful. Also, some of these interruptions may not resonate with you, and that is also important to honour.

The next interruption is deflection, which happens when we crack jokes to avoid discomfort, or blame others for what is happening in our own space. We all deflect at times, but when it becomes chronic, we need to really address what we are doing. We all know someone who constantly makes jokes, and they can get a bit frustrating to be around at some point. People can easily begin to feel unheard, or distant from us when we do this.

Another major way of interrupting contact is through something called 'retroflection'. There won't be any examinations for you on these terms, but they are important to think about in terms of what we do and how. Retroflection is when we put a lid on big feelings. We may feel rage towards someone, but for whatever reason, we are unable to share it. We may sit around, grinding our teeth, wanting to say something but never doing so. As iwth most things, there is a time and a place for retroflection - who would want to say absolutely everything going on inside us at any opportunity? Whilst we may want to say how much our boss makes us angry, we probably should not share it as we could end up losing our job!

The final interruption I will share for now is something called 'introjection', which refers to the messages given to us from the world that we then generously incorporate into our psyches. When a kid at school calls us ugly, we begin to believe we are ugly. When our mother told us to not be so greedy, we begin to believe we are greedy and develop an unhelpful relationship with food. When our headteacher calls us stupid, we introject this to believe we are indeed stupid. Introjection can lead us to having a whole pattern of unhelpful and stressful beliefs and ideas about who we are and how we function. Spiritual practices are a way of addressing some of these toxic messages. However, some of us are able, perhaps intuitively, to chew over the messages and spit some of them out. This is the way we process and work through the internal stuff.

Workbook

I would like you to write a paragraph or two about each of the interruptions to contact. Think about the people who you retroflect around. What messages have you introjected about yourself? Spend time in meditation thinking about them. Most importantly, think about how they get in the way of you connecting with others, and work out ways of doing things differently that feel safe to you. Also, how do the interruptions limit your capacity for intimacy?

Now that we have explored how we connect with others, we should have also worked out some ways in which we can do things differently in the relationships we form. Our histories may well make relationships feel very difficult to us, which is why it is helpful to understand how we function and do something different. Now is the time for transformation; seize this moment.

The way we relate to people in the here and now may well be more about our past contaminating the present. But hopefully the techniques above will help you to develop ways of doing this differently. And if we are with a partner who does not meet one of our needs, negotiate a way of having that need met elsewhere.

Let's move on to connecting with others intimately.

Union with Others

Once we have a better grasp of the ways we let ourselves and our histories get between our relationships in the present, we can begin to develop intimacy with others. An idea I would like you to consider is that of Awen. Awen is a Welsh, Cornish, and Breton word that means 'spiritual inspiration'. Awen can also be referred to as 'spirit energy' that is the essence of life. Sexual unity with someone else has the potential to help us reach the heights of Awen, which many of us can only dream of. Sexual expression helps us to heighten Awen through maximising the sensation of life in the here and now. Sexual expression is about living, about connection, and the union with another human being maximises the Awen. Think about the physiological benefits as an extension of what happens spiritually.

Fantasy and Experimentation

Too often, we become ground down in our intimate relationships. However, once we see the spiritual potential in our encounters with other people, we can develop our approach to sexuality more robustly. Fantasy and experimentation can be two components to this.

Fantasy, as opposed to Phantasy, is the process of imagining those things which turn us on. We do not have to tell anyone about our innermost fantasies. Fantasies might be a way of thinking about kink, or considering intimacy with other people. I encourage you to spend time reminiscing about times you have made love in the past, and also opening our minds to what may be pleasurable to incorporate into our future interactions. If there are practices you have not considered, consider them. If you have never used toys, buy some. If you have fantasies about certain types of cloth or clothing, invest in some. There is no time like the present. Get the food out, and just pour. Or buy those oils you have always fantasised about. One of my close friends has a massage table, which he apparently uses frequently. Having special sex furniture can really transform the experience.

Another key term is that of enhancement. Do not be afraid to experiment - the worst that could happen is that you do not like it, in which case I imagine you will not want to be doing it again, and that is fine. I would also encourage you to buy books such as the Kama Sutra, and read about other practices. If you are an introvert without much interest in other people, buy erotic fiction. This will help you to develop your imagination, and also understand what can be possible with other people.

The key thing with all sensual practices is to identify the blockages and remove them. Return to the concept of interruptions and remove whatever is getting in the way for you. There is no maximum age limit on sex between consenting adults (other than the minimum!), and as I have mentioned above, the more you use your sex organs, the healthier you will be. And I assure you, once you have experimented with other people with whatever need, you will widen your viewpoint immeasurably. Whilst some practices will never be a fit for you, others will be, so do your homework, but most importantly, try to get yourself out of your comfort zone and connect with others where possible.

5. Profound Physicality

The Explorer

I have selected the archetype of the explorer for this chapter, given that we often associate the idea of an explorer with strength, vigour, and an openness to growth. The explorer archetype is recognised as, in some ways, relatable, and found in everyday life. However, the explorer is not an Everyman. Indeed, we find strength and power in physicality in all areas of our life. In fact, physicality and strength is a requirement for us to survive.

In terms of literature and famous examples in popular culture, I always associate the explorer with protagonists such as Dante in the classic, *Inferno*. As Dante wants to discover his own spirituality, his exploration takes him to the pits of hell and paradise. It is also possibly helpful to correlate the explorer with characters like Indiana Jones and Captain Kirk in Star Trek. These are also obvious examples, but it is sometimes helpful to specifically pin our imagination and our subconscious on these examples.

Like other archetypes, there are positives and negatives with this. As the explorer is a character who is driven to stretch the boundaries of any status quo, one of the strengths are that the explorer is also curious and motivated by improvement.

However, in a quest for self-improvement, particularly physical improvement, we can develop an element of restlessness and feelings of never being satisfied. There is therefore a need to remain vigilant within physicality, and to always be clear about this.

Workbook

Take your workbook, and begin to reflect on the idea of the explorer.

- **What does exploring mean for you?**
- **What have you achieved in your life that could be consistent with exploration?**
- **What risks have you taken?**

Spirituality and the body may not, at first glance, seem to be automatic bedfellows. Spirituality has connotations of an ethereal, unseen world. Physicality seems very grounded, pragmatic, and real – and more easily assessed. The former is also associated with healing, whereas the latter often requires healing! Nevertheless, welcome to the chapter where we will explore physical practices to support our developing spirituality.

Throughout the chapter, I will talk you through some of the key practices that can benefit your health, often in profound ways. As in previous chapters, I will talk about the evidence behind each one, leaving you to make informed decisions regarding what you choose to practice. I will also offer various workbook exercises so you can have opportunities to develop your awareness practices further.

The key point I wish to get across right now is the concept that our minds and bodies are linked. There is something called the 'vagus nerve' that travels from our brains to all of our major organs in our body. This is important because it is the vagus nerve that offers an inter-connectedness of our emotional and physical worlds.

A couple of years back, researchers in Finland completed some research into the relationship between feelings and the brain, and discovered that people actually experience feelings in similar areas of our body – as an example, people feel fear in our bellies, and we feel anger in our jaw. This does not mean that it is identical for everyone, just that we do experience physiological sensation alongside feelings. There is a universality to where we are feeling, and a need to remember the importance of the body in recovery. In fact, it is tricky to see how we can recover emotionally without any attention to the body.

Even though the mind is non-physical (and we discuss the mind elsewhere), our mind also still exists. When the body dies, the mind ceases to exist in its current format. This chapter is about trying to bring a unity and cohesion to both parts.

The Importance of Physicality in Healing

Let's talk a little about my experiences with physicality in healing. I have had a fairly chequered journey with physical practices at different times. If I do not see immediate or obvious results, I can become disinterested. However, I know that with practice and tenacity, the benefits of the practices I will introduce you to can be profound. Certainly, once I found clarity in my spiritual practices, my physical practices benefited. The physical practices benefited my spirituality, and the cycle of inter-relatedness moved towards completion.

As I have mentioned in other chapters, I have experienced complex trauma, as many of you have. Surviving such experiences is immensely trying for lots of different reasons, and one of the ways in which we can struggle is polarising with exercise. Sometimes, we may need to exercise three times a day for two hours, which can then look like self-harm as we put our bodies through gruelling, harmful regimes. At other times, we may struggle to get out of bed, and we over-eat. The combination of over-eating and lethargy becomes a cycle, and we can end up more depressed and withdrawn. This is not inevitable, but can be prevalent.

Survivors of complex trauma are often beset with various health conditions and issues, and the evidence suggests that survivors are either ill all the time, or never. If I unpick this, the impact of trauma on the body in childhood can be so enormous that our immune systems are known to be impacted significantly. The outcome from this is that survivors often end up experiencing multiple illness and are seemingly always ill, or they seem to never be ill and enter a state of readiness.

I recently re-read some material I had written on developmental trauma a few years ago, which reminded me of Pavlov's dogs, a study into something called 'classical conditioning', namely a way of changing behaviour through reward. Basically, an additional finding was that the dogs used in the study could be aggressive and would attempt to bite the scientists. At first, they could not understand why the dogs were so aggressive. The dogs were often caged and were not provoked, but the researchers soon realised that the dogs were in fight or flight mode. They were being traumatised by being caged, and this led to them acting out in self-defense. We can extrapolate from this with confidence in terms of jails. When people are locked up with limited exercise, studies have shown that aggression can also increase, albeit not inevitable.

Some of you will never be ill, but others will be ill all the time. If any of you have been removed from your birth family, you will know that this removal from the primary attachment figure creates an additional level of complexity specific to children in care. The combination of removal from primary attachment figures, however inadequate, and the placement in local authority care with strangers, has a corrosive impact on children's welfare. In fact, attachment is said by some to eclipse trauma (Maté, 2003). The issue of complex developmental trauma is becoming increasingly prominent in the U.K. especially (Mind, 2019).

When humans are house-bound, a similar mechanism occurs, that being Cabin Fever. I am sure most of you will have seen The Shining, starring Jack Nicholson, based on a book written by Stephen King. If you have not, a family travel to a remote hotel to 'babysit' the building over the winter months. The hotel is cut off during winter, and the father steadily begins to deteriorate, become paranoid and having alarming delusions. Eventually, he becomes psychotic and tries to murder his family before running outside and freezing to death. It is a truly horrifying film. However, the phenomena is well understood for people living remotely. Again, this is probably due to a lack of socialisation with others, the impact of being alone (loneliness is a bigger killer than smoking), and being cooped up without the capacity for our bodies to discharge stress hormones.

This is important for lots of reasons. If you consider animals in the wild, most animals will physically shut down when caught by a predator. Usually, and this is key, when they are released, they reactivate their nervous system by shaking their body. The process of shaking the body is a way of clearing the system of stress hormones that have shut the animal down, preparing them for escape. Humans no longer operate in this way, so the hormones are left to fester in our system. We sometimes shake when startled, as a remnant from the past, but we do not recognise the importance of this mechanism for spiritual and physical health. It is no wonder that humans – once the prey for many predators – also benefit from such a practice.

Workbook

The next time you have encountered a stressful situation, I would like you to find somewhere private where you won't be disturbed. Find some music with a vibrant beat and turn up the volume. Then slowly begin to shake your hands, then your arms, building in intensity. After that, shake your feet and your legs, until your whole body is shaking energetically. If you are not mobile, shake what you can, where you can. There is no right or wrong, just an opportunity to release stress! Afterwards, in your workbook, record any differences or sensations that you have observed.

My Story

As I have said previously, I once ballooned in weight to the largest I have ever been due to being depressed and in addiction. I threw anything down my throat to suppress difficult feelings, and had no energy to walk to work, let alone exercise. Let us remember that certain foods can be addictive, and it is easy to get stuck in this rut. But again, this is not just a chapter about exercise, but the physicality of spirituality. I was doing no spiritual practices for my body, so the cycle worsened until I made a choice for myself that I wanted to live differently.

Thus, I began to get back on the yoga mat and gradually build up my physical strength. I walked more and developed the practices in this chapter. The journey was so hard – I would roll about on the mat, like lard, sweating profusely, wondering why I couldn't even touch my knees. I would attend classes and be consumed with envy at the people who were fitter and more supple than me. I felt as though I was dying at times, but there was something inside me that continued; I could not quit on myself. Determination is a quality that I would urge you to nourish in yourself - your physical health is no one else's concern but yours. When things are rough and difficult, it is this care of self that will support your determination to continue. And thus, benefit from the practices.

After a while, I turned my attention from others and looked inside. I used the mat to assess my physicality, but also my emotionality. When we just sit, our souls cannot help but open up and release whatever is there. Even though our physical discomfort may seem more obvious, physical practice opens up the rest. I realised that my physical yoga practice helped me to heal and let go of the difficult feelings building inside. Movement, even if just a stretch, released the deep stuff. I am minded of what we know from movements such as Bioenergetics, and the interconnectedness of the body and the mind.

Over the years, there would be times when all I could do was sit on the mat and let the tears come; that is all I could tolerate, all my body required. At other times, I felt broken, and needed different processes to support me. I complemented my practice with deep massage, but kept returning to the mat, accomplishing whatever was available in that day; never trying to force myself into difficult spaces, but offering kindness and compassion for wherever I was.

As I felt uncomfortable getting undressed in front of strangers, and not wanting a stranger to 'oil me up', I gravitated towards Thai massage practices. These are practices whereby you remain clothed, and the practice is quite challenging with hard pressure rather than strokes. The massage helped clear my chi and improved the circulation in my body. Really deep pain shifted over several months and my awareness of my process improved.

Once I felt strengthened and flexible, I incorporated the wonders of other practices, such as Qigong. In fact, I have experimented with most things, but it is most important to maintain optimum physical health wherever possible, and use physical practices to support and complement spiritual practices. Currently, I still practice yoga (thirty years in total) and walking every day, usually with my faithful familiars. I also practice Qigong every week and try to pump some iron at least weekly - there is something helpful for me in discharging aggression through weights. I have monthly massages and also offer massages when possible. I will also, if time permits, attend local yoga classes as well. Solitary practice is helpful, but there are benefits from being with a teacher, primarily because they will notice things in you practice that you cannot.

Moving forwards, this is one chapter where I won't be going backwards to explore the history unless there is a historical context for a particular practice, i.e., if something has a past, I will explore what we know about it. If not, I won't because a key element of our historical relationship with physicality was simply staying alive. We ran to evade threat, and we ate what we could because there was always a scarcity of food. Times have changed since then.

I have divided this chapter into groups of practices. Firstly, there will be a section on those practices that help us assess where we are up to. Then we will move into practices that help us heal and recover. Finally, we will move onto practices that help us maintain our health. Enjoy!

Workbook

Before we explore ways of assessing our physicality, let us start with some workbook exercises. I would like you to sit in a comfortable position with your workbook close to hand, and a pen, preferably on the floor, but if this is not available to you, then sit in a chair. Spend a few moments relaxing, slowing the breath, and noticing what is happening for you. In your notebook, start writing sentences in the present tense, beginning with 'I notice...'. Then write what you notice in your body. Write anything that comes up for you – whether it be

a churning stomach, tightness, knots, whatever. There is no right or wrong. The purpose is for you to become accustomed to what is happening for you physically.

---

1. Assessing Physicality

For those of us who have experienced trauma, particularly, complex developmental trauma, you will understand that the body is a wonderful and bewildering thing. Our bodies can hold us up and break us down; they can offer surprises, both positive and negative. Many of you will spend a lot of your time in fight or flight, reacting strongly to things with very little provocation. This is down to the amygdala. The amygdala is a special little part our brains, which is our internal fire alarm - it activates the adrenaline release to turn on the sympathetic nervous system. As we go into fight or flight, cortisol activates the parasympathetic nervous system. In therapy, we sometimes call ourselves 'amygdala whisperers', as we need to appeal to the amygdala and 'soothe' it during our work.

Some of you when assessing your physicality will notice much pain and discomfort, which you may live with on a daily basis. A few of you will have a diagnosis of conditions such as fibromyalgia, which is where the physicality and emotionality can have the wires crossed, and you physically feel what is happening for you emotionally. As counsellors, psychotherapists, and psychological therapists, the field is beginning to recognise the importance of understanding the impact of complex developmental trauma on the way people function as individuals (Maté, 2003). This grave problem is multi-faceted, complicated to formulate, and costly to treat (De Bellis and Zisk, 2014). Subsequently, the topic of complex developmental trauma is becoming embedded within both the thinking and practice within the U.K. (DfE, 2017), and there appears to be the aim to provide consistent and high-quality interventions to vulnerable children and young people who have experienced complex developmental trauma by the government (DfE, 2015).

Finally, whether we talk about the impact of trauma or abuse, the fact remains that the impact on the brain and body is the same, regardless of the origin. This is inevitably why there are so many similar problems in victims of complex developmental trauma, such as psychopathology, depression, P.T.S.D., and conduct problems (Gustafsson et al., 2009). And more importantly, there is much scientific evidence to support this understanding. What we need to do is bring together the different thinking to create a more cohesive model of understanding that serves everyone's needs. We also need to develop a personal understanding of what is happening for us inside our bodies and minds. It is only through awareness that we can begin to heal and recover.

In addition to the physiological processes that happen to us, there is the question of the spiritual element of being hurt by someone else's energy. A simple way of understanding this is remembering that the body has a flow of energy. There is a biological basis for this – the body using chemical energy, or fuel, to do biological work, namely adenosine triphosphate. These are molecules produced by mitochondria, or the body's cells, in the most basic terms. Practices such as massage release and free up the flow of energy in the body. Some cultures refer to the energy as Chi (Chinese), others as Prana (Indian), Kundalini (Asian), but here in the West, as mentioned above, we refer to the flow of energy as nwyfre. The simple equation we use is that optimum flow of nwyfre leads to awen, or spiritual insight. Our assessment of our bodies is about attuning to the flow of nwyfre and incorporating practices that support a better flow.

Workbook

Let us take a minute to put the book down and spend ten minutes scanning the body. I would like you to begin with the breath.

- **What is happening?**
- **Is your breath long or short?**
- **Where do you experience it? In your throat?**

From the top of your head to your toes, gradually and systematically scan the body downwards. Notice what is happening in your head, your face, your neck, and so on. As soon as you notice a sensation, practice letting go - releasing tension, letting go of knots, and loosening tightness.
This should become a central part of your daily self-care, particularly at times of distress. This enables you to manage your process differently and take yourself out of fight or flight, allowing you to take control of how your body reacts to threat.

These two practices should begin to support you with the practice of awareness. By tuning into your bodies, you will notice what is occurring for you on a gradually increasing level. At first, you may struggle to hold your concentration, or very quickly drift into sleep, but over time, with perseverance, you will be able to hold your attention, and tune into deeper intra-psychic, spiritual processes. We can also become aware of material that may have been hidden through our defence mechanisms, which is released through the increased flow of nwyfre. Massage is a powerful spiritual practice, whereby the energy from one person merges with that of another, and their hands – strategically placed in energy centres along the meridians of the body, release, attune, and support a better energy flow.

As we let go, and explore our internal processes, we can sometimes reconnect with old memories. Sometimes, a word or a touch can result in powerful unravelling. So, as always, if you doubt it, do not do it – your instinct is always right. And if something comes up that you had not been aware of previously, process it with someone – see the shaman or healer, or just have a chat with a friend and consider the new awareness a blessing. During my first Thai massage, the waves of release from someone laying their hands on me in a safe, supportive way, was tremendous. I became deeply attuned to the grief that flooded my system, and as I returned to subsequent sessions, my experiences grew immensely. My energetic flow increased, I felt fitter and more connected with the world. So, although massage can be triggering for some – and in those instances, I definitely suggest some caution when considering massage – it can be a beneficial practice.

Whilst many people enjoy massage and find the process helpful, the practice is not for everyone. If we can tolerate the process, it can be an incredibly healing experience as part of our self-assessment process. Also, there are easily accessible treatments, such as act-pressure and acupuncture, which all act on the pressure points and meridians in the body that conduct the flow of chi through the body. In fact, this may feel more accessible than other practices, so develop what you love and enjoy!

Workbook

I would like you to now find a massage therapist and just have a massage. If you struggle financially, find someone who is willing to offer some massage, such as a friend or family member, perhaps as an energy exchange (you do something for them in return). Try to arrange an unhurried session, where you will have the opportunity to be there for at least

an hour or an hour and a half. During the massage, practice the 'I notice' exercise again. Try to notice every sensation, especially the interface between the masseur's body and yours. Obviously, you will need to do the writing part afterwards. Just take your time and do what you can.

---

2. Healing

After a period of time practicing the above exercises, you should have started to develop a greater awareness of your physical self. Massage may have released old ache and pains, or at least brought them to your attention, and you may have reflected more on that which ails you. You may have noticed subtle changes happening, be them blocks or growth. Hopefully you will also have tolerated touch better and have spent more time just being at one with your body.

We will now explore additional processes we can practice to support ongoing changes in our nwyfre levels. I know 'nwyfre' is an unusual term, but it is an important one to embody when we are thinking about spirituality, particularly in terms of our mortal vehicles. Nwyfre appears in Middle Welsh as meaning 'sky', but over time, it has come to mean 'life force' or 'energy'. At the basic level, nwyfre is about stressing the importance of staying as alive as we possibly can and enjoying the physicality of being alive, whatever your limitations. As the Celtic languages were squashed by Christianity, the use of words and concepts, such as nwyfre, were also taken out of use. Dr. Alan Jones talks and writes about nwyfre more thoroughly in his book: *Nwyfre*.

Herbs

Firstly, let's have a chat about herbs. I need to be clear – I support anyone and everyone going to their GP if they have an issue in their body. I am not 'anti-vaxxer', and I do not support people putting themselves at risk of harm. This book is all about what we do, not so much what we do not do. When I talk about herbs, I talk about them in respect of complementing mainstream practices, not replacing them. And I do not hold any negativity towards those who do choose to focus solely on herbal approaches to illness and disease. We are all adults here, and we can all make whatever decisions we see fit. In fact, if you already take any pharmacological treatment, please check with your GP before using any herb.

A lot of you may not have a clue where to go with this element of recovery, and I need to be clear that this small section of the book will not offer you a comprehensive insight into using herbs to heal. But it will be a start, at least to let you begin your own journey of discovery, and perhaps open yourself to possibilities.

Firstly, it is important to find out the known impact of different herbs and tinctures. Do some reading and find out for yourself. There are numerous books and courses out there if you want to learn more about this exciting topic. For myself, let's just focus on ten keys herbs that, when used respectfully, can impact our health positively. I also want to return us to the idea of organic food – we want plants and herbs that have been loved and nourished, not exploited. You should all by now know about the impact of TLC on plants – plants will thrive in the right conditions, as we will, and simply growing some of the below plants will help you develop your energetic connection with nature, growth, and healing. And if you lack the capacity to grow your own healing herbs, get them from a stockist who offers the right energetic care that will support your own healing. A supermarket is probably not that place. Anyway, without further ado, let's look at some herbs.

Chamomile – A very easy plant to grow in most climes, which helps with anxiety and relaxation. Consider plucking some before bed or mix a spoonful of dried chamomile into some tea with a touch of lavender. Or add a spoonful to a cup of water and gently boil it for a few minutes to let the herbs infuse. Immediately try to notice a difference in your relaxation levels. It can affect the way the body uses some medicines, and can cause drowsiness, so be careful. Test it yourself.

Echinacea – The roots, staff, and leaf can be used to prevent colds or infections, and for healing wounds. Studies have shown benefits from upper respiratory tract infections. Only use echinacea short term though as studies also show that it can affect the immune system. Again, gather some dried echinacea and mix into your tea, or buy some echinacea tea already prepared!

Feverfew – Traditionally used to treat fevers, but unsurprisingly, it can also help with mouth ulcers or migraines. Do not use with warfarin or other anticoagulants. feverfew is a lovely herb to pick and dry at home, which you can then use to brew a tea, as above.

Garlic – Renowned for using in cooking, garlic has powerful anti-cancer and anti-inflammatory properties. Again, do not use with warfarin. I love garlic with other strong spices such as chilli and ginger in a watery broth. My own witches' brew when under the weather, but you could develop your own!

Ginger root – This is known for easing nausea and motion sickness. It is also being tested for roles in surgery and anti-cancer treatments. However, ginger root can cause bloating and heartburn for some, so take care. Ginger root is usually just grated into a cup of water to make a ginger tea, but it is nice to have honey and lemon added. Amazing on a cold, wintry night.

Gingkgo leaf – Traditionally used for fatigue and bronchitis, gingkgo leaves can improve your memory and other brain disorders. Never use Gingkgo seeds as they contain a toxin that can cause seizures, and in large amounts, death. Again, avoid using gingkgo leaves with anticoagulants and tricyclic antidepressants. Probably best to buy from a health food store.

Ginseng – This can be used as a tonic and aphrodisiac, or even as a cure all. It is hard to research as 'quality of life' and 'vitality' are challenging to study, but again, be careful with steroids or anticoagulants. Ginseng is also plentiful in health food stores.

St John's Wort – This herb is a common treatment now for depression. It has a small effect on mild to moderate depression over a period of about 12 weeks, so it can be helpful in the short term. However, it can cause sensitivity to light, but only in large doses. It can also cause dangerous reactions to certain medicines, so again, please consult with your GP before using.

If you are at all concerned about how to use herbs and tinctures, then please go directly to a herbalist. Speak to them about your needs, and they will 'prescribe' something for you. Similarly, a Chinese herbalist will offer the same service. Safe experimentation is the way forwards!

Finally, it is important to remind you to develop an idea of what works for you, and experiment (within reason). Try something you have not used before, but not if it is considered unsafe – learn from others' learning!

Workbook

Let us conduct a short study of our own. I would like you think about a condition which ails you, and for which you are not receiving any treatment. Pick one of the above herbs that could be of use to you and begin to take an amount each day. For example, if you have a chest infection, take an echinacea supplement for two weeks, and notice any changes. Record them in your workbook. If you have been experiencing low mood, take St. John's Wort for four weeks, giving the herb time to build up. If you are taking supplements from a health food store, ensure they are organic, with good origins, and

even better, try to grow your own!

Earthing

Over the past few years, you may have come across the word 'earthing'; most of us have. You may have an idea that this is about walking in forests barefoot (that was my presumption), or generally being a bit of a hippy. Well, it is possibly all of that, but definitely much more. I came across this concept through spirituality, but then found that the actual evidence is immense and high quality. There is some high-quality research out there, often gathered from the medical world's gold standard of randomised control trials.

So, as a bit of background, earthing is also referred to as 'grounding', and means the same thing. The clinicians tend to gravitate towards 'grounding', whereas the freer, more integrative souls tend to refer to 'earthing'. The basic belief system is that the earth is a reservoir of free electrons. Without a connection to this reservoir, it is believed that our bodies are unable to deal with electron-deficient free radicals. The effect on 'clumped' blood cells is well documented – scans of blood have been taken before and after earthing sessions, showing a dramatic de-clumping of blood cells. Such findings have been replicated, evidencing efficacy. Studies have also been conducted on sunflowers, showing that they thrive better when grounded. Truly, the range of research is incredible – from the vagal tone of infants to blood urea and creatinine responses. There are many scientists, such as cardiologists like Dr. Stephen Sinatra, who speak widely about the benefits of earthing.

This is because our bodies are exposed to a wide spectrum of electromagnetic radiation – from the likes of computers, mobiles, Bluetooth, power lines, and domestic wiring even. By earthing, we greatly reduce the levels of these induced voltages, and are then effectively shielded by the earth's large electrical mass. There are also beliefs, perhaps on a less tangible level, that earthing helps carry information from the Earth, thus improving the connection with and intelligence of our planet.

Let's now have a look at some techniques – they do not need to be complex or convoluted to get the proper benefits.

Earthing techniques

1. The most universally accessible way of earthing is by going to the earth – a forest, a field, a garden – take your shoes off, and stand. I believe that, if you love the place you earth in, the benefits will also be increased. Go to that special place! If your mobility is impaired, sit with your feet on the ground. Close your eyes. Slow your breath. And notice the sensation of your feet on the ground; what do you sense? Stay there for as long as you can tolerate – say five or ten minutes at first – and then return to the car/house. Record your experiences. At times, especially if you live in the U.K., it may be raining, snowing, or both at the same time. Try to persevere and keep up the practice. The benefits will begin to render the practice invaluable in your overall journey.

I first practiced earthing in Austria. Some friends and I were in the mountains, and we were able to practice earthing at the top of a huge ice cave. Whilst I don't recommend starting on icy cold surfaces for obvious reasons, the cold most definitely heightened the benefits from the practice. If you gradually build up your tolerance, you will develop a range of additional benefits to your immune system.

2. The next step is for those who are mobile, and the same rules apply. Firstly, remove your socks and shoes and get ready to walk this time. Connect with the earth, feel the ground beneath you, and slowly and deliberately put one step in front of another. Now, for this practice, you need to be on ground that won't cause much difficulty for you, so try to avoid areas

where there is a lot of gravel. Grass is perfect, but if the grass is in built up areas, also be vigilant to hidden 'surprises'. Again, start in accessible ways, nothing too arduous or extreme in temperature. And record your experiences – what do you notice physically, emotionally, and spiritually?

I first practiced this on the Isle of Iona. My associates and I had made a huge circular maze trail of stones in the sand. I remember the wind flowing, and a deep connection with Mother Earth. We stood on the sand, sensing the ground, and slowly and deliberately followed the trail of stones, allowing us to sense the energy from the ground upwards. Now, we did this in bare feet, and this is an important element of the practice. Rubber soles and insulated sleeping arrangements prevent full contact with the earth. Work out a way of developing this, and again, write about it!

3. Finally, there is a way to earth differently without even going outdoors. Firstly, you can put a metal rod in the garden, tie wire to it, sufficient for the end to come indoors, and hold the end. Your connection with the ground is ensured. There are also a range of products that you can buy to practice earthing. However, to develop our spiritual practice, we need to become more in tune with the earth, not less, and buying more disposable items will diminish this. Although, I have to say that the earthing sheets made of organic cotton are rather appealing as they can be plugged in when you're asleep. But ultimately, try to just get outside wherever possible – the ground is free to step on! Let me know how it goes.

Workbook

Try one of the above exercises this weekend, regardless of the weather (as long as it is safe – try the exercises even if the weather is not pleasant, but avoid if there are gale force winds and flooding – use common sense, depending on where you are

in the world).

Crystals

People use crystals to heal, recover, and protect, amongst other uses. Many people wax lyrical about their benefits and walk around with crystals in their bras and handbags, although others are less fanatical. Unfortunately, the research into crystals shows that they only have a placebo effect. There is no known positive impact from using crystals as far as science can determine. Now, before you throw this book out the window, I want to explain a few reasons behind this.

Firstly, there have not been many studies conducted, so if we have not studied them extensively, can we truly say they are only placebo? Also, do randomised control trials truly study what they claim? You may not have answers to these questions, but as an academic researcher, I would say the jury is out. Also, even if there is only a placebo effect, it is known to have a positive impact on people. If you believe in something, it is more likely to be true.

Personally, I do not use crystals. I have some crystals that were bought for me by others, and which I keep with respect and because I like them. The harvesting of crystals is, to me, unhelpful to the Earth, and I do not support the crystal trade, which is often exploitative and unhelpful to the environment. This does not mean that you should also avoid crystals if you personally find them useful.

Therefore, consider exchanging crystals from those who already own them instead of buying new ones. Give them as gifts, and gradually help to stop the crystal trade. We all know they are pretty and lovely, but we already have enough. Perhaps your spiritual practice in terms of crystals could be about how they are safeguarded and protected rather than exploited?

Workbook

Think about your relationship with crystals. Also, think about sites that promote the use of crystals, and the comments used with regards to them. Write some lines on your view on this. Do the views seem over-rated? Are they based on fantasy rather than reality?

3. Maintaining health

In the previous section, I discussed some powerful practices that can help to reduce the levels of electromagnetic radiation in our bodies. I also offered the idea of developing a relationship with herbs and herbalism as a way of healing and recovery. In this section, we will talk about the concept of maintaining health, avoiding addictions, the role of stress, and respecting sobriety. We will also introduce the idea of avoiding addictions as a way of maintaining spirituality practices. Let's begin with weight.

Weight

We have talked in previous chapters about the importance of physical health, and using food to support health rather than impact health negatively. Your relationship with your body needs to be of paramount importance – if you are making yourself unwell, this needs addressing, and in a timely way. So many of us do not even consider our bodies, and just respond to health issues with apathy as though we have no role in this. I have news for you – we most definitely do have a role. Your body is your supreme vehicle for spiritual practice and recovery. Unaddressed physical issues, such as obesity and deteriorating joints etc., will negatively impact the flow of nwyfre, and get worse rather than better without action.

Trusting mainstream medication that will fix our ails is fine, but it won't get to the root of disease. If you are not taking any vitamins or minerals in your bodies through a varied, healthy diet, any number of supplements will only ever be supplements. Get to the root cause of your deficiency rather than finding and using quick fix approaches.

The link between weight and spirituality is also important. A suggestion to support your weight is to walk. There is no need to invest in gym memberships or costly classes, just go out of your front door and walk. If you can only manage a few minutes at first, then just manage that. But gradually increase your steps. An hour a day walking is probably a good limit, but on weekends, the world is your oyster – experiment with longer walks, perhaps going higher and through fields and valleys. Use the walks to connect with nature spiritually – feel the air on your face, touch the leaves and trees. In particular, hug the trees, as doing so increases the oxytocin levels. The oxytocin hormone is responsible for feeling calm and encouraging emotional bonding. Use nature to maintain your health and recovery.

Thus, we should spend time and thought trying to maintain our optimum health, not just for healthiness' sake, but for spirituality's sake.

Workbook

Develop an achievable plan of walking that can include some time spent barefoot on the ground (not concrete). Spend at least a minute with your feet on the earth, breathing, absorbing the energy, as a tree absorbs nutrients. As you stand, grounded, imagine your body filling with nwyfre on inhalations, and exhaling negativity. An amazing practice at sunrise!

Avoiding Addictions

Many of you struggle with addictions. Whilst I could write another book purely on addiction, the key principle to think about here is that of addiction being a process of desensitisation of feeling. Using whatever we use to anaesthetise feeling also has the adverse effect of anaesthetising our capacity for spirituality and recovery. Whilst we may believe that drugs or alcohol improves our ability to connect with spirituality, when in reality, makes it worse. Even if we believe that taking drugs or alcohol is not ok while also being addicted to sex or compulsively eating, the itch is still being scratched.

I support a life devoid of addictions wherever possible. I say 'wherever possible' because if you have struggled with addiction in the past, you will know how easy it is to get caught up in another. This is again, definitely not about judgement, but understanding empathically with a view to making different choices. Personally, I have experienced many addictions, and will probably have other challenges through my life. The issue is not having an addiction, but how we deal with it, and how our denial prevents us from taking action. And let's face it, most of the addictive behaviours have their reward, even if just a feedback loop.

However, within spiritual circles, there are belief systems that romanticise intoxication and addiction (the two are not always shared). I think this is a helpful place to mention the role of Shamanic Ritual. I wanted to include this because many of us will have heard of the term, but not exactly know what it means or entails. I hope to elucidate this a little right now, but you can read further if you so wish.

We have conducted shamanic rituals for thousands of years. As mentioned in a previous chapter, a shaman is a person who interacts with the spirit world through an altered state of consciousness. There is a plethora of information out there if you are interested in reading more about shamans or shamanism. The key issue with shamanic practices is that the person, as indicated above, alters the state of consciousness. Many people accomplish this using hallucinogens such as peyote, ayahuasca, or mushrooms, depending on where they are in the world. Whilst it may be enticing to gets loads of tattoos and travel to Mexica to take Peyote, there are numerous inherent risks, and I do not advise you take any mind-altering substance. Obviously, you are an adult, and can make the decision to take mind-altering substance, but I clearly and unequivocally do NOT recommend any substance misuse. On the contrary, I recommend the opposite – complete abstention.

Whilst I am not critical of shamanic practices per se, there are tremendous risks which I personally do not support. Indeed, when we are looking at recovering from something, we need to minimise chances of relapse or other difficulties; dealing with the impact of something also inhibits the wider recovery opportunities. There is a clear correlation between using drugs and subsequent mental health problems (and a raft of different views supporting that). A 2019 systematic review and meta-analysis by Murrie et al. found that the transition rate from a diagnosis of hallucinogen-induced psychosis to that of schizophrenia was 26% (CI 14%-43%), which was lower than cannabis-induced psychosis (34%) but higher than amphetamine (22%), opioid (12%), alcohol (10%) and sedative (9%) induced psychoses. Transition rates were not affected by sex, country of the study, hospital, or community location, urban or rural setting, diagnostic methods, or duration of follow-up. In comparison, the transition rate for brief, atypical and not otherwise specified psychosis was found to be 36%. Hallucinogens can be dangerous, and how could someone unequivocally state that their experience was spiritual or a result of the hallucinogen, therefore chemically induced? We do not need to pretend to be spiritual just because we have had a good trip. Even the pro-hallucinogen movements are clear that the area is still relatively untested, albeit developing steadily (Sanabria and Talin, 2017). More importantly, for people with histories of complex developmental trauma, we will always be prone to addictive behaviours, and it is vital that we look after ourselves as much as possible, and I would not want hallucinogens to be the next addiction for you. Thus, stay safe, and enjoy rituals that create harmony and recovery rather than more problems for you to manage.

In fact, there are other ways to alter your consciousness, and there are many rituals you can engage in within the U.K that., whilst not offering illegal substances, can offer a different experience, i.e., drum circles, or cacao rituals. There is no need to contaminate your body with toxic drugs or alcohol. In fact, bonding with others, recalibrating yourself with breath, and developing a greater level of intimacy with others can have similar effects. I would suggest that even cacao rituals can be incredible – to sit with others, consider the drink with reverence, and enjoy it can be immensely powerful. Also, being in an enormous drum circle with friends and associates can give an unrivalled experience that does not involve putting yourself at risk. You truly do not need to trip the light fantastic to experience a reverential ritual.

Workbook

I would like you to attend a drum circle. There are plenty online or in person. You can even watch a YouTube version, and play along, using headphones, although in person is better. Then write down what you experienced. Go into detail about the physical sensations, and then your thoughts. Also describe anything higher you noticed - such as images. Then try to make sense of this and perhaps treat yourself to a cup of hot chocolate afterwards!

Stress

I want to talk a little bit about stress because it is often underrated as a toxic force in our lives, especially the way it impacts our bodies and minds. We routinely minimise being busy at work, and we often, because it is so common, think that work is stressful and difficult, but because everybody else is putting up with it, we sometimes take responsibility for being the problem, when actually the problem is not us. We are just working in highly toxic, corrosive environments, and it is time for change, albeit for a different book. When I left my job, as I said, I immediately felt much better. My sleep improved, I felt more alive, and I really engaged in those creative processes that were incredibly rejuvenating and restorative. As I relieved myself of the toxic stress, my body and mind woke up rather than doubting what I had done with my job. I realised that it was actually the stress that was steadily killing me.

As a brief primer, when we experience stress at a lower level, we might find this quite pleasurable. We might feel strong, more alive, and more alert. However, when the stress response keeps firing, day after day after day, we begin to see how it can negatively impact our health, leading to significant and serious health risks. We can experience a whole range of issues. Headaches resulting from stress can trigger increased tension, and chronic stress can also lead to an increased risk of depression. We can also experience issues such as heartburn, whereas stress increases the production of stomach acid, which also can lead to issues with our digestion. Stress is also corrosive on the brain, impacting all areas of our functioning.

Stress often leads to issues and concerns around insomnia, whereby you cannot sleep very easily, and we either find it hard to get off to sleep or wake up in the morning. Sleep, of good quality and for sufficient length of time is, as you probably know, vital. Sleep is where our brains recalibrate, process the day's events, and help us repair what was harmed during the day. Chronic sleep deprivation is massively problematic on weight, mood, and overall wellness. We can also find ourselves with issues around rapid breathing, which can leave us breathless and with a weakened immune system.

Long term stress in particular negatively impacts our immune system, and we can find ourselves becoming ill with a lot more minor ailments, like colds and flus, and make us vulnerable to other immune-deficient issues. On an even more serious note, chronic stress can lead to heart attacks, high blood sugar levels, and high blood pressure. Even if we are not always experiencing a pounding heart, it can really impact our health on a more subtle level, which is an issue.

There are also reported studies that look at the impact of chronic stress. As an example, I understand that lots of families who have not been able to conceive children have adopted. However, once they have the adopted children, they feel less stressed and more rewarded, and their stress levels reduce (and different ones emerge). They can then sometimes suddenly find themselves pregnant with their own children. This is a really interesting and important thing to think about, especially if you are hoping for children yourself. We can also experience issues around missing periods, a low sex drive, and this in turn can negatively impact our relationships. Overall, stress is corrosive, and I would urge everybody to definitely not minimise or deflect from the seriousness of this.

Alongside the impact of chronic stress on our lives, there are also issues more generally in the way society is developing. We are finding ourselves more isolated, and as we are engaging more on social media, and less in the real world, this leaves us feeling isolated and disillusioned with life. Also, the lack of exercise and abundance of food also negatively impacts our health levels. It is not any coincidence that we also now praise organisations that celebrate issues such as body positivity, when in reality, they are supporting people making unhealthy and problematic lifestyle choices for themselves, which impacts their emotional and relation well-being even further. I need to be clear that I am not fat shaming; I see us all as intrinsically and inherently different and wonderful, but I do think that when we support unhealthy lifestyle choices, we get into tricky territory. I also believe that we do have choices here, and we can make different choices for ourselves once we feel empowered and have the right skills to do this. I also speak about myself here. When I struggled with obesity, I was incredibly unhealthy, lacking in energy, libido, and felt doubly despondent because of my appearance as well as what I had been doing to myself. I did not need to be supported in that; I needed a way out.

Stress is corrosive on the system. In families, if someone is acting out violently, the stress is corrosive for all family members. Asthma is an illness that is linked to stress, and the treatment is a medication that directly replicates the hormone, cortisol. Chronic disease is also linked to 'helpers'. Much research has been conducted into conditions such as ALS and the impact of people feeling responsible for others. Helpers can end up with acute risks of physical issues. I add this specifically for adoptive parents, who are often feeling responsible for children's complex behaviours, which tend to result from early trauma, not parenting

The challenge with stress is that we often need to make radical, yet practical changes to our world. We need to assertively manage the stressful things - change the job if it is killing us, and end those toxic relationships. We need to be clear, definitive, and energetic in deleting the things that are destroying our health and well-being. This often just requires a quick look at our lives, but sometimes, it requires some deeper digging to source out the root. There are plenty of exercises throughout this book that can support us here.

A further practice to help manage stress is cold water immersion, which is growing in popularity. I am sure all of you have now heard of Wild Swimming. One theory suggests that the immersion into cold water causes vasoconstriction, leading to lower localised blood flow. It is thought that the temperature-induced reduction in blood flow around the damaged tissues, caused by strenuous exercise, reduces oedemas and inflammatory activity. We definitely need to be brave before we take a dip, but this could well also support our recovery from stress.

Workbook

Write a list of troubles that contribute to stress in your life. Be honest with yourself, and list everything. Then take a step back and reflect your list.

- **What factors could you drop?**
- **What could you change?**

Imagine what your new life could look like devoid of these factors.

6. Retreating from the World

The Sage

The sage archetype is a character associated with wisdom and knowledge, or qualities we associate with a mentor. I have used this archetype in respect of our chapter on retreat practice because I feel that retreats are specifically designed to nurture and develop wisdom. Therefore, this archetype is a healthy fit with that element. In popular culture, we see the figure of the sage in Shakespeare as Gonzalo in The Tempest.

More widely, we see sages as characters such as Atticus Finch in the famous book To Kill a Mockingbird, or as Jiminy cricket in Disney's classic, Pinocchio. Also, in Star Wars Obi-Wan Kenobi. It is also quite interesting that many of the characters in Star Wars resemble different archetypal figures.

The sage is, therefore, a wise figure with knowledge for those who enquire. The strengths of the sage include the ability to nurture wisdom and experience. However, they could also be cautious and hesitant to pragmatically join any perceived action. I think this is particularly pertinent for this chapter, because whilst we want to develop wisdom within retreat practice, becoming overly dependent upon it can lead us to develop limitations in the way we relate to others.

Workbook

Take a few minutes to reflect on the idea of a sage. Write down any associations you have with the concept.

- **Does the sage reside in you?**
- **Are there elements of your life where you have brought this energy into focus?**

• **How could you use these qualities to begin to get what you desire in life?**

Writing about retreat could seem counter-intuitive. As humans, we tend not to equate healing or recovery with isolating ourselves. Healing and recovery are concerned with improving and increasing our capacity for relationships with others, not reducing it. Indeed, most things I have practiced are about putting myself back in contact with others. Improving our capacity for relationships is truly a great thing, and in other chapters, we have revisited the importance of connection with others.

The image of a retreatant, or someone engaging in a retreat, may not seem immediately accessible to you or your lifestyle. You may see such a practice as a bit weird, or eccentric at best. You may love lots of contact with others, and you may enjoy talking every moment of every day. Your job may entail working with clients or customers throughout your shifts, and you may love this part of your job. That is a valuable thing to recognise in yourself. However, there are immense benefits in retreats. Sometimes, during our darkest depressive episodes, retreating can be the perfect antidote to our struggle – going inwards rather than outwards spiritually can be a gift to both your body and mind. Let's start with a little internal work.

Workbook

We are going to draw a mind map. If you are not familiar with them, they are just a way to get some ideas down on paper. Start by taking a piece of paper in your workbook and allowing your mind to free-associate. Begin with the word 'retreat' in the centre and write everything connected to it that comes to mind, without censoring. Afterwards, in an adjacent column, write your observations of your process.

My experience of retreats has been varied. Retreats have been the most illuminating times of my life. I have attended Buddhist retreats, Christian retreats, Tantra retreats, and those I would refer to as generic 'spiritual' retreats. During these retreats, I have been amongst gay men, 'straight' folk, and everyone from all types of identities. What these retreats all have in common is that most experiences were mind-blowing – I often felt more deeply moved, more connected with spirit, and more alive than I have ever felt amidst the distractions of everyday life.

My favourite experience was two weeks spent at a house on the tiny Isle of Iona in the Inner Hebrides off the coast of Scotland. I travelled there with a group of five women and one man, all complete strangers, all new to Iona and the house, Traigh Bahn. I spent idyllic days walking the beach and travelling on foot to the magical well of eternal youth. I spent time recording the sights on the island, and have sketches of the birds, and even whale bones washed up on the shore.

At first, we were all anxious and disconnected, and a tad defensive with one another. Other participants were in conflict a lot of the time. I noticed meal-times were difficult, and people were not pulling their weight in the kitchen. Attendees were spending more time separately, and I too began to retreat into myself. This was not necessarily a bad thing, but I was intrigued by the group process. I realised what was happening and began to cook for everyone. By providing warm, nutritious food, I helped to lighten the mood, and encouraged people to come together, at least for the purpose of seeing each other, even if we were all in silence. The increase in proximity seemed to support change.

One day, we made circles with pebbles on the beach. I found it rewarding to collect the large pebbles, and order them, mindfully, in circles. We meditated several times a day, often looking out into the ocean, starting in the early hours each day. We would have a candle burning, and it was haunting to look into the ocean for hours on end with the light of a naked flame. Gradually, we settled and opened up to our internal world. We cooked and ate together, still in silence, and our troubles lifted. I would play the harp for everyone each morning, and I was pleased to be able to offer some distraction for everyone. I noticed that a peace came over the house, and by the end of the retreat, we spent all the time in total silence. We were left in a deep state of connected awareness. I have rarely found such a state of happiness and contentment since. I will always consider the role of Iona, itself a historic place of hermitage and retreat, as pivotal in my personal development.

However, this was not always the case on every retreat I have attended. I have also attended retreats that have been an utter nightmare from the minute I left my car. One particular event was promoted as an advanced mindfulness event, so I imagined long meditation sessions, connection, and nourishing food, but in reality, let's just say things were very different! I will talk more about this further on in the chapter.

Workbook

I would like you to create a space in your home where you can sit, uninterrupted, for periods of time. Call this your meditation or ritual space. Clean it and dress it in ways that work for you, perhaps using cushions and candles. You do not need to be fancy, just meaningful. I would like you to go to your meditation space, and light a candle. Try to sit as upright as possible and focus in on your breath. Look at the light; do not stare, and just let your gaze rest there. Breathe, and let go of any distractions, very gently, without effort. When your mind becomes distracted, again, gently bring your attention back to the candle. Let your mind associate with the notion of light.

- **What light do you need in your life?**
- **What would light represent for you?**

It is also helpful to commit to a certain length of time. Perhaps you could begin within ten minutes, then gradually progress in time. I like a good hour where possible, and when on retreat, will meditate for several hours at a time, releasing my grief and my distress.

Retreats do not necessarily have a positive reputation. Thinking about retreat, we may conjure up images of monks in silence. We may also reflect on biblical stories of people retreating from the world – Jesus himself retreated for 40 days and 40 nights in the wilderness. The thing which links most of the images we have of retreat is a level of darkness and struggle due to the many thrillers and crime stories set in retreats. It is almost as though the idea of retreating triggers something deep and painful for us, as if the retreat unleashes our dark side. I believe that these misconceptions about the need to stay triggers the unconscious to be unleashed, leading to projective identification from the darker parts of our mind.

The movie and literary world are replete with images of people in retreat. Just think of novels such as And Then There Were None by Agatha Christie, or both movies titled, The Retreat. I have never seen a retreat movie that celebrated the positives, but the darker side has certainly occupied the human imagination. Recognising that retreats are not always blissful is important. On the retreat I mentioned above, one person in particular significantly struggled with the silence. She began to eat less, communicate less, and was visibly distressed much of the time. I remember her saying that my harp playing helped her through. My own experiences on retreats have also had darker times. I have, at times, felt strong and deep emotions come to the surface, and have sometimes felt isolated and disconnected from others, even on a small retreat. I have wondered about the safety of others, especially when they have presented as so visibly distressed. It seems as though the silence and retreat unbuckle the subconscious, and we tend to project this into the silence around us. Whilst this is such a perfect process for a psychodynamic retreat, it can often be painful and difficult. If we have lots of unprocessed material, and if the organisers lack the fundamental understanding about interpersonal relations, this is a recipe for difficulties, and at worst, dangerous.

Retreats can be extremely difficult, raising up unconscious processes, frequently without the normal support we would have in the outside world. I know of various people who have had psychologically damaging experiences during retreats, and the experience has been traumatic for them. So, whilst we want retreats to be positive and restorative, if they are not managed well, they can become acutely difficult. We will come back to this issue later. I am now going to start exploring what retreat practice looked like in history.

History of Retreat

Pre-Christianity, the idea of retreat was always treated with horror, certainly in the West. The idea of removing oneself from that which nourishes us and keeps us safe – i.e., society – has always been treated with amazement and suspicion. I recently read an article about a man who has retreated in the highlands of Scotland, two miles from any path, and twenty miles from any neighbour. He is now considered a hermit and is being studied with a morbid interest by journalists. When I read this article, it reminded me of Hannah Hauxwell, an old lady who lived in the middle of nowhere in the rough Pennines without running water or central heating. She described herself as living in summer and surviving in winter. Once she was 'discovered', she became an object of public interest, and was featured in a TV documentary. She eventually moved off the farm when age became too much of an impediment. I share this because the idea of retreat continues to be curious and strange to society. Indeed, when I tell people that I go on retreats, I am often met with wide-eyed astonishment.

In terms of Christianity, the idea of incorporating retreat into religious practice began with St. Ignatius of Loyola. Ignatius devised various spiritual exercises and formulated a comprehensive approach to retreat. His ideas and approach came as a result of spending time on Montserrat in Catalonia, and being introduced to the exercises of Garcia de Cisneros by the monks. The retreat took place over four weeks – retreatants would spend the first week exploring and praying on sin and God's mercy; the second week moved to examining specific episodes in the life of Jesus; the third week saw the retreatants explore the passion of Jesus; and the final week explored the resurrection of Jesus and God's love. Each day was split into three sessions, and each theme was examined during each one. The stages naturally linked to a process of wholehearted commitment to the service of God. There was also a specific focus on not giving advice to retreatants, but to let the wisdom of God emerge organically in the retreatant. Some exercises were very specific, requiring questions such as 'What do I see?', or 'What do I hear?'. The overall purpose was to support retreatants in following God more closely.

Christianity has not been the only source of retreat practice. Islam also places importance on meditative retreats in Sufism, the mystical path of Islam. In Sufi terminology, khalwa is the act of total self-abandonment in desire for the Divine Presence. In complete seclusion, the Sufi continuously repeats the name of God as a highest form of remembrance of God, in the form of meditation. This is a high level of commitment and devotion to the practice of Islam.

Buddhism also utilises retreats, and is known for its three-year, three-month retreat, which entails a complete withdrawal from life for an extended period of time, usually guided, and involves the participants literally living in a box for a period of time. My hips growl at the mere thought. Such a retreat has slightly different connotations depending on the particular Buddhist lineage, but tends to focus on transforming karmic energy into wisdom energy. In short, this means improving our karmic predisposition. These retreats are designed to have four meditation sessions each day, and group chanting in the morning and evening. All practices, like the Islamic practices, are designed to devote body, speech, and mind (three vajras) to the transformative practices of the Vajrayana (Vajrayana is one of the three methods of achieving enlightenment).

Throughout history, different retreat organisations have been set up, including those such as 'Sword of the Spirit', an organisation founded on Christian principles, and is vehemently opposed to Islam, feminism, and gay rights. I find such retreats to be deeply problematic in terms of their values and approach towards the uniqueness of life. A retreat of this sort risks exposing us to potentially limiting thoughts and belief systems, or at least conflict if we openly challenge this. Some retreats are also 'dark retreats', meaning that the retreat takes place in darkness to promote 'visionary yogas'. I would liken this to hallucinatory experiences triggered as a result of sensory deprivation, although I am open to other views.

In terms of the Church of England, spiritual retreats were introduced by priests of the Anglo-Catholic society of the holy cross in 1856. Firstly, the clergy participated in the retreats, and then the laity. These retreats typically lasted for five days, in secrecy. This practice was then spread by Anglo-Catholic priests, such as Alexander Forbes and Thomas Thellusson Carter. The Oxford Movement then further spread the practice of retreats to many devout men and women, borrowing upon Catholic practices. These retreats typically lasted 3-4 days and featured much silence and prayer.

The practice of retreat continues, and even the likes of American actor, Jared Leto, recently went into the desert for 12 days, only to emerge and find that the world had been shut down due to the pandemic! But you do not have to be a celebrity, and nor do you need to have specific beliefs to benefit from a retreat. Nowadays, you can retreat as a Christian, a Muslim, a Buddhist, or whichever denomination you choose. There are various non-denominational retreats; Findhorn is a good example. Findhorn is a spiritual community in the north of Scotland, originally set up by three spiritual pioneers, Eileen Caddy, Peter Caddy, and Dorothy MacLean. The space holds one of the largest spiritual communities in the U.K., and even has its own Press. Here, you can retreat without specific religious doctrine, although there is a clear Christian influence in terms of using singing material from the Catholic Taizé chanting practice. However, to participate, you need the financial resources to sign up as such retreats are not free. I do, therefore, believe that organised retreats are largely for the middle classes, unless an organisation offers a reduced payment scheme. However, the needs of the working classes are very different to those who do not live in adversity. Some places understand this and offer 'pay what you can' or state that 'NOTAFLOF' (no one turned away for lack of funds'). However, this is not a widespread process. But the problem of retreat tourism remains – people are being charged extortionate sums of money to be on retreat. There is a need to be acutely aware of what you are getting for your money, even though there are many wonderful, high quality retreat centres around the world.

Whilst an individual retreat is not for everyone, it can be an important component of contemporary spiritual lifestyles. We can retreat when things are tough, or simply to just recalibrate each year. The retreats I offer are simply this – time to refresh, rethink, and reformulate our life and our life choices. But what are the health benefits of engaging in such practices? The science is clear.

A systematic review was completed in 2018 (Naidoo) where the reviewers explored 23 studies, involving 2592 participants. Most of these were randomised control trials, non-randomised control trials, and nine longitudinal cohort studies. The evidence suggested that retreats had health benefits, specifically for people with MS, cancers, and HIV/AIDS. Results showed that positive changes can be achieved in metabolic and neurological pathways, loss of weight, blood pressure and abdominal girth, reduction in health symptoms, and improvements in quality of life and subjective well-being. The additional finding that retreat experiences can lead to sustained and significant, wide-ranging health improvements long after return home, is truly heartening.

Mindfulness retreats in particular show that there is a positive effect from attending such events, and this is supported by evidence. By a positive effect, I mean that the participants reported a positive change in their well-being, or something similar, as a direct result of the retreat. A study into Vipassana meditation (a special form of meditation practice that encourages us to look at our attachment to things, e.g., money, or belongings) displayed that a one-month retreat yielded improvements in mindfulness, well-being, and personality, even in experienced meditators. There is a suggestion that the idea of non-attachment might facilitate psychological improvements (Montero-Marin et al., 2016). By reducing our attachment to stuff, reducing the value we place on it, we can achieve improvements in the way we feel. Another study was completed into the impact of a six-day spiritual retreat on immigrant Catholics from Nigeria, proving that they experienced a significant stress reduction overall. Regardless of the kind of approach or ideology of the spiritual retreat, positive impacts were reported. Even more general yoga retreats have a positive impact us; much of the evidence confirms that even if engaging in yoga practice daily, the retreat helps improve physical health, supports inner peace, and helps you 'rediscover' yourself.

Christian and many other religious retreats also report positive outcomes for participants. In 2017, Thomas Jefferson University completed a study into the impact of spiritual retreats and they found that serotonin and dopamine (neurotransmitters that help our mood) levels were significantly increased as a result of a seven-day retreat. In 2021, Blasche et al conducted some research that found a difference between 'meditation retreats' and 'vacation retreats with meditation'. Namely, the former averaged 33.8 hours of meditation per week, compared to 3.4 hours in the latter. They also demonstrated short term and longer-term effects. The short-term effects showed improvements in awareness, emotional well-being, and fatigue, and the meditation retreat resulted in maintenance of the results for longer.

Overall, the results suggest that we can experience significant changes as a result of a retreat, although better, longer lasting changes are made when the retreat consists of meaningful meditation practice. There is, subsequently, much to be said for including, wherever possible, meditation as part of a retreat.

Workbook

Take time to complete a body scan meditation. If you are unfamiliar with this practice, take a moment to search on YouTube and find an appropriate meditation for the length of time you have free. Try not to rush, just systematically let go of tension in the body. When you are in a state of relaxation (or meditative equipoise, your shout), let your mind gently settle on the idea of retreat. Pick up your pen and paper, and associate everything that comes to mind. Again, try not to censor the flow, just write the words, thoughts, and feelings that come up in respect of the concept. Then take a moment to compare your thoughts from the first exercise.

Words of Warning

I have talked about the wonders of retreat practice the scientific evidence that supports such a practice, which is a vital part of our recovery and growth as human beings. However, there are also cautionary tales to think about prior to jumping in and signing up with someone.

Firstly, consider the kind of retreat. Some retreats are based around the use of drugs, illegal or legal. Even if some retreats do not openly declare there will be drug use, this can often be happening, albeit in the background. As an example, there is a notorious LGBTQ organisation in the U.K. that sells itself as an inclusive, tolerant organisation that encourages people to meet in gatherings, or retreats. However, there is a known problem with drugs, and people are silenced and ostracised when about talking about it. I know from my experience that dealing drugs is taking place covertly. This organisation even makes 'space cakes' that they distribute without necessarily telling anyone, so please, please, be mindful. Even the retreats where you knowingly attend to partake of drugs such as ayahuasca, be vigilant.

We hear lots about Ayahuasca, a potent psychoactive 'brew' from South America, typically originating from the rain forest. Evidence of its use has been found as far back as 1,000 years ago in Bolivia. It has been associated with intense spiritual experiences, including out of body experiences. Such retreats underpin the recent growth in psychedelic research, but there is a misconception, particularly with ayahuasca, that natural means safe. However, this is simply untrue. Whilst I would not join the Christian missionaries of the 16th century in vilifying the practice, I would urge caution. Science tells us that ayahuasca decreases the parts of the brain associated with anxiety and social phobia, which explains why people feel that it is beneficial, but there is no way of telling how you will react. A number of people have died or got into major problems during ayahuasca ceremonies, usually because of undiagnosed heart conditions, but often due to interactions with other drugs. As the events take place remotely, getting medical help can be challenging at best. There is also the issue of serotonin syndrome, which is a cluster of symptoms likely to occur when people are already taking antidepressants. These symptoms include diarrhoea, sweating, and confusion, which can also be potentially fatal, and if you have a pre-existing mental disorder, such as schizophrenia, there can also be severe side effects.

Many people using ayahuasca, like author, William Burroughs, approach the drug because of other substance abuse problems. This is important to think about in terms of who will be joining you on your retreat, or where the retreat takes place. Problems have been reported in places like Mexico with drug cartels; there are multiple movies and documentaries highlighting this, but even if such problems are not apparent, there are risks of sexual exploitation. Many shamans are male, and there are numerous reports of rape and sexual assault during ayahuasca retreats. Guillermo Arévala, a well-known healer, was notorious for both his work on sustainable development and his sexual abuse of vulnerable participants when under the influence of ayahuasca. This creates a range of risks that far outweigh any benefits. However, it is not just the ayahuasca retreats that we need to consider with caution.

Take Tantra, for instance. Many people who operate tantric retreats do not understand the concept of tantra at all – most would probably look blank if you asked them about the higher Vajrayana tantra practices. They have sexualised the term, and their retreats are often poor excuses to support groups engaging in sexual activity. I am not questioning the value of practising sacred sexuality – I have written extensively about this myself, I am questioning the integrity and honesty of some of the practitioners. It is fine to celebrate sexuality, but not pretend it is something that it is not. There is a big difference between engaging in safe, consensual sexual activity with a loved one at home, to being pressured to undress and engage in touch with strangers.

I am minded of a practice called 'Sex Magick', a type of retreat in which people sign up to daily 'Heart Circles' where all participants sit in a circle, open up emotionally to themselves and each other. This is perhaps a reductive explanation, but the practice does result in people gradually removing clothing, before engaging in sex acts as a group. There is a consensus that sex does not happen unless everyone agrees – if you do not consent, the group does not have sex, but this has the potential to create massive problems, especially for people who are same sex attracted and/or trans. If you did not know this, and you signed up expecting something else altogether, you could find yourself in an uncomfortable predicament. I believe that 'Sex Magick' proponents would normally be open about the practice beforehand, but human nature being what it is, I would not say this was inevitable.

I once attended a well-known Tantra festival for men, unsure of what to expect when signing up. Being an ardent Buddhist, I had imagined it would be about meditation practice, and because it was for men, I hoped it would allow me to meet other men join in meditation practice. However, the disco music immediately started, and we were expected to dance with each other – definitely the realm of the extrovert, not, like me, the introvert. I was then told about the 'Love Temple' – which I understood to be a place where some of the men would have sex, like a sauna. There was also lots of 'entertainment', which was essentially sex workers selling their wares. Everyone was glossy, slick and under 30, as was the venue, and I was freaked out. I stayed for 24 hours, avoiding the sessions like the plague, rushing to my car to get me home as soon as it was safe. Whilst it was a well-organised and lively retreat, it was most definitely not for me. The retreat, for me, was neither spiritual nor safe.

Without breaching confidentiality and maintaining anonymity, even one of the yoga teacher training I attended as part of a yoga retreat had its shadow side. Whilst the teacher was amazing and I was in love with him spiritually, I found out that there had been lots of people relating from their shadow selves at different times. One woman reported him visiting her at her home, and it getting 'awkward'. Another participant stated that during a previous retreat, she was plied with cannabis, and it left her in a near psychotic episode. There were suggestions of even more issues lying underneath the surface. So, even the more 'respectable' retreats have their challenges. This issue is symptomatic of what can happen in cults with leaders exploiting their members, as the retreat was organised around a charismatic leader.

There is light at the end of the tunnel though. There are many wonderful retreats that do not fail to amaze, The Omega centre in New York state being one of them. This is an enormous camp, offering various retreats at the same time in breath-taking surroundings, offering sumptuous food, and with spiritual gurus at the top of their game. But most importantly, it is safe. I attended a workshop with American Psychiatrist, Brian Weiss, and although Omega felt isolating due to its sheer size, I never felt unsafe. This is another important aspect to consider – different cultures in the world relate differently. The retreats in America often are full of Americans (naturally) – their world is far more sociable and communicative than places such as the U.K., and if you are not a natural extrovert, this may also be uncomfortable. But they are also full of warmth, care, and often extremely high quality.

My own intensity during retreat was especially around being alone and separate to the perceived other, even if the group is not as 'together' as you would imagine. This is also linked to the question about whether it is more beneficial to go alone. What if you had even gone to great lengths to ensure your safety, and suddenly they started practicing something that, even though quite innocuous, was difficult for you? What would you do? I remember attending a retreat where they started with the Happy Clappy singing sessions. Whilst this was not threatening, I became rigid with discomfort as it was way out of my norm. I urge you to think about your own comfort zone and do your own research.

If you are not doing a solitary retreat and are taking part with other people for some or all of the time, consider the idea of participation with care. There are people you may have never met before, so you need to think about whether you would feel comfortable being on a remote island that only allows you to disembark once a week. What if these people have triggering ways of being that you struggle to manage? What will you do? What is your safety net? Think also about the purpose of the retreat. Is the purpose of the retreat being with like-minded people and taking support? Do you, and should you go there with someone you know well? This will definitely be safer, but few participants do this – they take a big risk, especially abroad, in engaging in retreat. Being alone amongst people is the key – you are going as an individual, and this can add to the intensity. If in doubt, go with someone else.

I share this section because it is vital that we all do our research into a retreat before we attend. If things are at risk of going wrong in a remote place with people with complex needs, it can be problematic; potentially dangerous. It is advisable that we meet up with attendees or organisers before parting with our hard-earned cash. We need to do our homework, and sometimes ask the questions that others may shy away from. Be aware of your boundaries, and if an organisation offers shorter workshops, try one of them before you dive into a retreat.

Workbook

Think about your own boundaries for a minute. If you were to go on a retreat, what would your boundaries be? Be specific and tap into your own needs as well as you can. Would you need it to be substance-free? Single gender? Specific topic? Location? Write your list and stick to it. Do not compromise on your own boundaries – it is better to be clear at the beginning rather than finding out something when it is too late!

Practices

As mentioned above, organised retreats do cost money, some costing more than others. You can retreat to Richard Branson's island for a reported $77,500 per night, or to Banwa Island in the Philippines for $100,000 per night. You could stay with the Radical Faeries for free if you found the right Faery to stay with, but you may find it basic at best. I was almost bitten in the face by a Cottonmouth snake when I stayed in a centre in Tennessee and I had not even been told there were snakes in the area. Would you want to go to the toilet in a wooden outhouse? Ultimately, however, you do not need to re-mortgage your house to get the benefits of retreat, and I am now going to present three retreat practices that should not cost you a penny but could bring you immense rewards.

I want you to answer the following questions honestly and courageously before you practice any of this:

a. Are you truly grounded enough to withstand a period of time alone?
b. Do you have sufficient support around you in case things become difficult?
c. Do you have the basics to survive? I.e., food, a phone, clean water, a plan in case of an emergency?

If your answer to all three is 'yes', then by all means carry on. If you are unsure about anything, please return to retreat practice when you are feeling less vulnerable. Retreat practice can be challenging, and it is vital that you are in a strong place before you start. Please bear in mind that retreat practice is highly likely to destabilise you for a while.

The following practices are designed to help you plan and complete your own retreat. The tools for success are, perhaps unsurprisingly, about avoiding too much specificity. They need to just be clear and general. In fact, the planning and preparation is important, but everything must work for you. Listen to your own voice within this. I have not written a template for a specific retreat, just the principles to consider when planning your own.

Finally, the length of retreat is important. Just dip your toe in the water at first. Try a day or two, tops, then gradually build up to longer periods of time. I do not recommend a retreat longer than five days alone. Even the three-year, three-month retreats are highly supervised, and there is a real risk of cabin fever developing for longer retreats, so please, stay in touch with your guide, check in daily, and spend that time opening up.

1. Clearing the Decks

For a retreat to run as successfully as possible, we need to think about context, or venue. Will you (can you) retreat at home? Will you camp somewhere remote? What about choosing a rural hotel where you won't be disturbed? Do you have a friend who will let you stay in their caravan? Make connections, and then decide on your venue in a way that meets your needs. Whilst a home retreat may not seem salubrious, it should be safe. I have conducted powerful retreats in my own home – there are also advantages of managing disturbances and having total creativity on what you want your retreat to look like.

Once you have decided on venue, we need to think about timescale, which may also depend on work commitments, and possibly on other people's diaries. Negotiate what you can. Even half a day may be beneficial – if your day is usually so full that you have no head space at all, such a time will be helpful. For a beginner, it is helpful to start small. My suggestion would be, if possible, to set a Saturday and Sunday aside. Prepare to work from rising until going to bed. If you can manage no contact with your phone or social media on those days, that will be highly beneficial.

Please make sure that you can spend the retreat time entirely undisturbed. Take the kids to the grandparents, send your partner anywhere other than home, and even think about how the pets will be cared for – my partner helps with mine, as they see me reaching for my meditation cushions as an opportunity to get stroked. The pets (not my partner). Turn your phone off, lock the front door, and shut the curtains. Remove anything else that might be distracting. Once you have cleared the house of specific distractions, it is time to home into the practice.

Think about cleaning the house in preparation as we would for ritual practice – really get your mind, body, and environment ready. You may also want to think about the run up. There are benefits in avoiding all intoxicants for a few days beforehand, and consider fasting for a day before, or during the retreat. Also think about your cleanliness, and even what you will be wearing. Do you want to wear symbolic clothing, or go skyclad (naked)? How about the area of your environment that you will spend the time? Is there a panoramic view you can observe? I think it is nice to set the tone by lighting some candles. Create a mood of calmness and tranquillity. Light some incense to invigorate as many of your senses as possible.

If you are planning a solo retreat at home, you will need to think about the length of time you have available. As we saw above, the research supports a retreat of at least five days, and the evidence suggests the longer the better. If you can get this time, even if on leave, then do it for yourself.

2. Structuring the Time

So, you should have cleared the decks, and are ready to begin the retreat properly. We need a timetable of activities. I will suggest one, but by all means, change it or devise your own.

07:00 - Wake up in silence.
07:00-08:00 – Walk, preferably outdoors. Try taking your shoes off at some point to connect with the earth. Walk where your heart takes you in silence and without your phone.
08:00-08:30 – Have breakfast, if not fasting.
08:30-10:30 – Session 1.
10:30-11:00 – Snack time/break.
11:00-12:30 – Session 2.
12:30-13:00 – Have lunch.
13:00-14:30 – Session 3.
14:30-15:00 – Take a break.
15:30-17:00 – Session 4.
17:00-18:00 – Have an evening meal.
18:00-20:00 – Activity 1.
20:00-21:00 – Activity 2.
21:00- Bedtime.

You will notice from the above that there are four 'sessions', and two activities. It is important that each retreat day has a considerable amount of meditation/reflection/thinking time to get the maximum benefits. However, a full day and night's worth of 'work' is too much. We need the evening to consist of activities that require little attention or focus so we can process the day's work. I use activity time to play a musical instrument, sometimes I might draw, and other times, I will make something with my hands, such as sewing.

At other times, I just want to walk, breathe, and do nothing. All are fine, no need to get too caught up in the activities – the purpose is most important, just time to disconnect, without desensitising. This allows the brain to have useful processing time and recalibrate the experiences.

You need to meticulously plan the safety net. Line up someone you can contact in an instant should things become tricky. Have your phone on charge, even if it is turned off. You may also want to have someone as a retreat leader; someone who is fully aware of your whereabouts and agenda and will be available to check in with you each day, more or less frequently. They should be someone who knows you, and who will be able to offer support or guidance if required. Again, this is unlikely, but we should always be cautious. This person might also be an experienced retreatant. There is also the possibility of doing a joint retreat with a close friend, and you check in with each other every day at the same time, even if you are in different locations. This would be the optimum arrangement, particularly for a first retreat.

We will now talk about what the sessions could and should consist of to get maximum benefit.

Session Contents

I would strongly recommend that the sessions include a good level of meditation time. There are two main kinds of meditation – placement and analytic meditation. Placement meditation refers to calming meditations; those meditation practices, such as counting the breath, which calm us physiologically. The analytic meditation is where we reflect on a particular concept or idea. We might also use some of this time to write and reconfigure any realisations. I would recommend that session 1 and 4 have some time spent in placement meditation, perhaps half an hour, or a full hour if doing a body scan variation. If you are not confident in leading your own meditation, listen to one of my meditations on YouTube or check the ones I have on my website. If you are not confident, now might be a time to practice. Here are a few placement meditation practices I would suggest:

- Counting to four on an in breath, and four on an out breath. Repeat.

- Counting to four inhaling, holding breath for four, and exhaling for four.

- Noticing. As you breathe, notice, and scan the body for any sensation.

- Letting go. As you breathe and consciously relax, let go of any thought that enters your mind. You want to develop the practice of not getting distracted by your monkey mind.

- Counting whilst imaging that you are descending a staircase. Count methodically and intentionally, ignoring distractions from the monkey mind.

- Sitting in front of a candle. Light the candle and hold your vision on the light. It feels as if you're not doing much, but just let your mind go where it needs to go.

These practices can be sustained for different periods of time, depending on where you are in your spiritual practices. If you are a novice, five minutes in any practice may feel too much. So, you may want and need to integrate several practices within each session. Use the time as you see fit for yourself.

How will you use the other sessions? My suggestion would be to practice analytic meditation. The world – or universe - is your oyster here. I will offer you some suggestions, but by all means, analyse whatever you see fit. It may be a problem at your work, or you may have a question about your loved ones. Immerse yourself in the meditation and allow the answer to emerge. Here are some more suggestions. Once you are physically calm, open up to these ideas – writing some of the insights may be beneficial. Always end with another placement meditation to support your body in recalibrating and relaxing.

Phase 1- There and Then

- Begin with your history. What is your there and then?
- Who were the key players?
- What was your role?
- Analyse any primal hurt you have experienced, regardless of how insignificant it seems.

- Meditate on the person who did the hurt(s) to you.
- Open up to the experience of what happened there and then.
- Consider what you learnt and also what you lost.
- Spend a session on letting the person go. They can no longer hurt you.
- Spend a session on forgiving.

These may all be separate sessions. Following sequentially may be more beneficial.

Phase 2 - Here and Now

- Who are you now?
- Are you more than what happened?
- What does your life look like?
- Who is there for you?
- Who is not there for you?
- Where do you need to grow?
- What do you need to let go to thrive?
- What do you believe in?
- How much do you value yourself?
- How do you experience your feelings in your body?

Phase 3 – The Future

- What would life look like if there was a miracle overnight, and all your wishes were fulfilled?
- Who do you want in your life moving forwards?
- If you died tonight, what would you miss from your future?
- What do you need to get yourself where you want to be?
- What do you not want in your life moving forwards?
- How will you manage your healing as you continue to grow?
- What role will spirituality have in your life?
- Is pure existence simply enough for you?

Key Pointers

It is vital that during the retreat you plan for yourself, you separate yourself from social media, your phone, and your normal life. A retreat, to maximise effectiveness, requires you to go inwards, not outwards. It is a concentrated period of time where you offer yourself an opportunity to heal from whatever it is that has happened to you.

And that does not have to be anything life-changing or massively transformational – you may struggle with an incident at school, or a workplace issue that you want to focus on throughout your retreat. And that is fine. Do not create stories or narratives for yourself. Sometimes the biggest thing can mean little to us, and occasionally the smallest thing can have the most enduring impact. Just be where you are.

I also want to suggest that there are other options besides the standard meditation and reflection exercises. You may – and rightly could – offer yourself specific treatments to support your retreat practice. These may be on offer if you attend a retreat centre, but if you are at home, experiment with offering yourself something – try a face mask, perhaps that you have made yourself. Really absorb yourself into the idea of healing and recovery.

Your retreat should, naturally, go without a problem. You could find amazing insights on the retreat process that you have not realised before. You will, if you have followed the above process, begin to focus inwards on the things that matter to you, in a structured way.

Workbook

Spend some time planning a day long retreat. Detail the venue, the date, and anything else practical. Then systematically select reflection questions from the above three phases and add them. Choose only those which are a fit for you and work within the relevant timescale. Then try it out!

---

7. Mastering the Mind

The Creator

The creator archetype is associated with a visionary character, and someone who creates something significant. I have used the creator in this chapter on the mind as a way of remembering that mind is a creation. In literature, we recognise the creator in characters such as Victor Frankenstein in Frankenstein, but also Willy Wonka in Charlie and the Chocolate Factory. The creators make wonderful and mysterious things, which I liken to our mind and how we begin to articulate and talk about it. Also, the creator creates something original; we cannot get more unique than our own minds. The key element of virtual practices is that whatever we create, it is something original, specifically for ourselves.

In terms of strengths and difficulties, the creator is associated with creativity and willpower. We need to believe in what we are achieving in order to achieve it. However, that single-mindedness can create isolation and sometimes a lack of practical skills. Therefore, whilst we endeavour to understand and navigate the map of the mind, we also need to do this with care and caution.

Workbook

Take out your workbook, and begin to reflect on the idea of the creator. You may associate the creator with God or the

Universe. Try to identify elements of yourself that has created, or even showed the potential to create. Begin to consider how you can use this quality to develop elements of your own life.

This is a somewhat curious chapter for me to write; in a way, every chapter I have written has been about the mind at some level. Indeed, even the very physical practices, such as earthing, are designed to positively impact the mind, and the mind is typically central within most spiritual practices. And we have, by now, explored a range of ways in which different spiritual practices can support the development of the mind, its healing, and its recovery. We most definitely have not been engaging in practices that are intentionally harmful. We have just explored ways we can develop our spiritual practices, the ultimate beneficiary being the mind. Given this, one must ask why we should explore the mind some more?

Primarily, it is the mind that takes a hit when things happen to us in childhood. It is the mind that takes a hit when things happen to us in adulthood. It is the echelons of our mind that takes a hit from the pressure and stress we load ourselves with even now. However, and I say this carefully, the mind is not a physical thing. The mind is not the grey matter between our ears. The mind is not something we can measure, photograph, or objectively scrutinise. In fact, the mind is the thing that exists outside of our sensory, physical experience. It is the mind that endures after death, and it is the mind that forms the basis of our spiritual practice. It is also the mind that we will visit next to maximise our chances of recovery.

We are talking about the mind because it exists outside of us, and this is the core concept of spiritual practice. If you are open to this, there is a possibility that this could also positively impact our future existences.

Workbook

Let's do a quick recce on your current knowledge of the mind. Take your book and spend some time free-associating (refer to the previous chapter where I introduced the concept). Write 'The Mind' in the middle of your page and draw anything that springs to mind when thinking about the word. Do not consciously think, just write those images and ideas that come to you as quickly as you can. No censoring (just yet), simply a stream of consciousness on the paper. After you have completed it, check through the terms and words you have written and develop each of those further. Go as far as you want, just let your mind open up to wherever it wants to be. In a manner of speaking, this is an opportunity to open up the spider web of connections by branching out as far as you see fit.

Defining Terms

Before we continue, I thought I should confirm my sense of some of the concepts we will visit in this chapter. Whilst the chapter will explore the meaning of the mind, there are concepts such as 'the brain', 'the ego', and 'the soul' that would also benefit from some clarification.

Firstly, the brain is the physical grey matter inside our skulls. When I talk about the brain, I refer to all the neurons and cells that make up the grey mass. I use this term as the mind is often thought of as the brain, but this is definitely not the case. We will also talk about the ego. Now, the ego is most commonly associated with Freud, and refers to one of the three constructs of the personality. Freud referred to the ego as the part of us that seeks to please the primitive drives of the id. The ego is directly modified by the world. If you think of the mind as the sandwich filler, the ego is the bread – the stuff that absorbs the flavour from the world, but is ultimately not where the true value lies. There are other meanings of the ego, such as self-opinion (e.g., they had an inflated ego). I do not use that specific meaning in this chapter. The ego is that which consolidates life and the world, but it is the mind that exists in its own right; the mind can observe the ego, but not vice versa, i.e., 'I know I am hungry' is the mind observing the hunger of the ego. The soul, on the other hand, was originally a Greek term that refers to the mind, or the essence of being. It was later taken up by Christianity, considering the soul to be the actual self. My position is that the soul is the mind; the timeless essence of your being.

My experience of the mind is predominantly through Buddhism. It is through years of courses and study that I have acquired a fair understanding of what the mind is. My learning is supplemented by the likes of Eckhart Tolle, a fine proponent of mind practice (but not mindful – he thinks we should be emptying it, not filling it). However, my learning has been consolidated by reading more widely, and understanding how other people have attempted to make sense of what can be an ethereal concept. This is vital for us all to do – in formulating your own understanding, read as widely as possible.

In this chapter, I want to explore some of the ways our mind can be adversely impacted through abuse and trauma. We will, consequently, need to have a look at the neuroscience briefly – you do not need to become a neuroscientist, or even remember the terms, but it will be helpful for you to have a rough understanding of the processes. It will also help us understand the intersection between the mind and the brain. I also need to share some of the key ideas from around the world of philosophy, giving you a flavour of how we have approached the subject of the mind throughout the world. Whilst I won't be focusing in on too many specific philosophers, more their ideas, I will be encouraging you to think about their ideas of what the mind is, or at least, how the mind is considered by them.

The philosophical thought has permeated all layers of our thinking and practice as psychotherapists, whether you are an existentialist or humanistic practitioner, and we will soon see how much our lives can be enriched by such knowledge.

Understanding and working with the mind is also important for maintaining our health and well-being in the here and now. It is immensely important that you understand which part of your brain is impacted by different kinds of trauma and/or stress. Once you know, you cannot help but make changes in the here and now to your life. Also, since we are here for a spiritual journey, we need to consider practices that support the growth of our mind. Not just for this lifetime, if you are open to that concept!

Definitions and Ways of Thinking About the Mind

Consciousness

Imagine relaxing with friends in the Tennessee countryside and suddenly getting bitten by a snake. You would probably freak out at first, possibly panic, and call for help from your friends. They may well help you get some treatment (if they are real friends). In terms of the pain you will inevitably experience, this is what we call a 'private pain', as it is yours. And this pain, because it is private, is entirely unknowable by your friends. You can talk to them, and try to relay how it feels, but it will only be known by you.

Your pain is your pain because there is something external to that doing the experiencing. The external part is that which experiences the pain in the here and now. You are not just experiencing the pain, you are noticing the pain from an external vantage point, which in turn causes an experience. It is the mind doing the noticing, the ego is doing the experiencing. The two are separate. The brain is that which triggers the ego.

The pain will also be physical in origin, but your mind observes and experiences this sensation too. Your friends may have a reasonable perception of what happened, or is happening, and they may have even experienced a snake bite in the past, therefore empathising with the experience. However, it is only you who has the private experience; even if you share your sensations, it won't fully relay the private sense of what it is like to be bitten by that snake at that moment in time, in your body. This is what is referred to as an epistemic mind state – meaning that access to your mind is direct, private, and infallible. Your personal trauma is also only accessible by you, which is important because we also use epistemic mind states to relate to others – we share our experiences of others through this process, and we can never get our epistemic mind state wrong – it is ours, and no one can tell us that it is 'wrong'. The outside can only be correct about the non-mental cause – i.e., if they thought the bite was actually a spider.

This form of mind state is also only conscious. In that moment, you are not accessing the subjective unconscious states, but both exist, just not necessarily in tandem. This is also important to remember because we tend to think the unconscious is sometimes working independently in the background. It may well be, but we can only access it through the conscious mind. We can do lots of things to help you understand each term independently, but the two states do not co-exist together.

If you have ever studied 'Gestalt', this is about the Figure and Ground, meaning that our conscious is figural, and the subconscious is the background, including repressed desires, for example, where you lack the privileged epistemic access. In fact, people such as John Searle (the philosopher) believe that a mental state must be conscious to be a mental state at all. If we are not aware of it, can it be a mental state? If you are not aware of something that happened to you, how can you mentalise it?

The notion of conscious or unconscious states are important

because they are the mechanism through which we understand and relate spiritually to ourselves and others. Being spiritual happens in the mind, consciously, and involves relating to others sometimes. We all have our own unique, conscious representation of our spiritual beliefs and practices, although, we should never ignore that which may not be consciously present for us.

Workbook

Open your journal and draw a chart with three columns and ten rows. In the first column, list examples of epistemic thinking. In the second column, write what the mind observed. In the third column, write what the ego experienced. Do not be afraid of revisiting the definitions.

Intentionality

Mental states refer to, or are about, objects. We feel cold and worried about a storm happening; our ego holds the fear, the mind observes the fear, and the object is the storm. We may feel angry and sore about an injury we sustained on the rugby pitch. The ego is the internal process happening about the rugby match, and the pitch and everyone on it is the object(s). The mind is that which maps out or represents your worldly experiences.

If you have written a journal entry for every workbook exercise, you will have a group of writings that map them out. The entries are the objects, but the way in which they are represented is the mind, and the way you process and explore them is also the mind. The mind is separate and existing in itself.

My mind represents my own world as experienced by the ego and the objects in them. If I believe that there is a present for me in the kitchen (there is not, unfortunately), I represent the world in that way, i.e., I might say to people that there is a present for me in the kitchen of my home. The present in the kitchen doesn't represent anything itself. As another example, a lamp does not have a mind, even though it exists outside of my mind. You, however, as a human being, also have a mind. There are slight problems with this idea, but we won't complicate our understanding just yet.

Sometimes, people are delusional and represent things that do not exist to the outsider. They may be doing this intentionally to manipulate someone into believing something, but then again, they may not. This may reflect where they are at the time, and how they are representing objects through their mind state as experienced by the ego. This is important, especially in terms of spirituality. Some people perceive things in the real world that others cannot experience, perhaps due to pure delusional behaviour. It may be that the person's mind state is accessing something we cannot. The world of spirituality is often full of people who are hallucinating, or worse, making it up. And some practices tend to encourage that kind of mystical thinking. I encourage concrete thoughts, actions, and descriptions of mind states, whichever 'realm' a person is on. That, you see, will be the key to work out who is in reality, and who is not. I have seen so many people end up sectioned when beginning a spiritual practice, when their already tenuous sense of reality becomes delusional. Stay, wherever you can, in reality, whilst retaining an openness to the universe.

Staying grounded is a particularly important concept for us to think about in terms of spirituality. We talk about and process our spiritual beliefs through our mental state, but sometimes, we may have a somewhat spurious grasp of reality. In these instances, we should work with a spiritual teacher to ensure that we are supported appropriately.

Workbook

Think about the room you are currently in. Have a look around and note the objects within it. Are the objects looking back (dogs not included)? Are they thinking anything? Are you? Where is this happening? If someone else came into your room, would they view the objects in your room in the same way? How would they process the objects?

Behaviourism and Functionalism

Behaviourism and functionalism are two words with complex meanings; that mental states are the way we are inclined to engage in publicly observable behaviour as a reaction to external stimuli. To break this down a little, we react to stimuli. For example, I reacted to Athena's presentation (with horror). Any observer would have seen my open mouth and the shock as I spoke with her; my mind observes the ego reacting.

The important part here is about observation. Our behaviours are inextricably linked with our mind. I reach for the glass of water because I am thirsty, and you can observe me reaching for the glass of water; but you may not know why. My clients may well see me in a supermarket and make deductions from what they observe in their own mind state. This is the same in therapy – as I sit, although I am no longer a blank screen, my clients scrutinise my every move intently. If I sip my tea, I know they see that. If I gesticulate, my client observes this, and again, makes inferences. We do not just observe, but we then infer from that observation. In your life, you will inevitably have also processed objects and behaviours with your own mind.

Workbook

Think about a time when you have been seen by someone you know, maybe at work, or in another venue.

- **How many times have they said something that was not a fit for you?**
- **Have they ever said they thought, for example, that you looked sad as you picked up something slowly, when in fact you felt fine, maybe just a bit aching from the gym?**

Think also about how you may have done this to someone else.

This process is akin to projective identification, another psychodynamic term that refers to a defence mechanism that protects us from shame. Projective identification happens when we rid ourselves of an unwanted part, and project that part onto another person. As an example, we may dislike how we can bully other people, but to avoid feeling shame about our actions, we see other people as bullies. We bump into an old friend in a café and perceive their behaviour as bullying. We might even get big feelings about what we think we see, and act on it by asking the person to stop bullying us, who either spits out the belief and refuses to own it or internalises your request and generate the idea they are a bully. You did not get it wrong as such, you saw in them what you were disowning in yourself.

This concept is acutely important for our spiritual practices, as, with compassion, we often want to help people because we want to be helped as well. We see people as needy when it is our own need that we observe. We end up offering care and compassion where it is not wanted. It is vital for your own spiritual development that you begin to work out what you need, and to not put people into places they do not want to go.

This does take time and understanding, but practice makes good.

Faculties of the Mind

What can the mind do? There are some neuroscientific explanations for some of this, i.e., we remember because certain parts of the brain 'fire'; we can think, we can remember, and we can imagine.

We can also think. You and I can both make sense of our world. We can read things, you can read this, and you can formulate ideas and opinions about what you read. If I talk to you about your history, you should be able to relate your own story to me. You could ask me about mine, and I can think about that as well. I have asked you throughout this book to record your ideas on various concepts, and you have, I imagine, been able to do that overall. You can probably think about more complex ideas quite competently and are probably thinking about the ideas on the mind that I am presenting here. Thinking happens in the mind, but attachment happens in the ego.

We can also remember. There are various kinds of memory, but you can probably remember things from your childhood, as you can also recall from last week. Hopefully. These are examples of long term and short-term memory. If you have just been to the supermarket and I asked you what you had bought, you could probably revisit the journey through the supermarket and recall most, if not everything, you purchased. The brain is incredible.

Imagining Stories

We can also imagine – you could make up a story if I asked you to, and you could probably draw something from your imagination if you tried. It may not be a Michelangelo, but it would emerge from your imagination. In my practice, I use puppets therapeutically – they are potent tools to create projective stories. If we sat down and I gave you my puppets, you could probably work out a story for yourself. The imagination is also caught up in the act of imagining. If you made up a story for me, this may also bear much resemblance to your current life or experiences – children often play out that which is happening to them in their lives through symbolism. This act of story-making will often take place in the here and now (in the Gestalt sense), but refer to actions in the past (the puppet was naughty when it went somewhere), or about the future (the puppets are worried about the storm coming), because the ego holds the imaginings, while the mind holds the observation. What is incredibly important but often missed, is that nothing exists in either the past or the future, the experiencing only happens in the here and now. And therapy requires us to become more present, more here, more able to process different time states right now. Because we do not experience the old traumatic mind states in the present, our ego imagines them. Our mind is the vehicle that is present, and it is that which observes the ego's imaginings.

Stories exist in conscious states even though the characters may emerge from our subconscious. We have been telling stories for millenia, and we are still telling stories. We tell stories everywhere - on the news, in movies, within families, and in therapy. In fact, in therapy, our currency is stories; the therapist has to help the client untangle their content, make sense, and support the client's growth from the content. People offering such a precious gift of their story is a gift, something invaluable and commending deep respect. In that, I recall Finnick Odair in the novel, The Hunger Games, a character who is supposed to be ravishingly beautiful and sells himself to people to hear their stories and secrets. He describes himself as having a currency of stories. I would not necessarily equate beauty with people wanting to share their stories, but we definitely look for specific qualities in that person we want to connect with.

Storytelling predates writing; we could talk before we could write. There is some suggestion that rock art may have served as a form of storytelling for many ancient cultures. Certainly, the Australian Aboriginals painted symbols on caves as a means of helping the storyteller remember the story. The story was then told using a combination of oral narrative, music, art, and dance. Tattooing has also served as visual reminders of stories and includes information about genealogy, affiliation, and social status. Once we learned to write, we developed ways of recording on stable and portable media. We have used anything and everything; carving, scratching, printing, on wood, ivory, pottery, and skins amongst others. Oral stories continue to be popular and are delivered by impromptu storytelling, as well as being passed from generation to generation. Oral stories also enable us to hear about different time states in the present.

Historians in particular have always been storytellers; they reconstruct factual knowns (as far as possible) into a tapestry of colour and life to help us understand and reflect on the past. Politicians use the past and future to manipulate and control. Hitler was a classic example of a manipulative storyteller. He used the fear of what would happen to contaminate and control the present, whilst wiping out the past. But the point is that, even though we talk and argue that our stories are the most poignant, and the most relevant and accurate, we all present our stories from a highly subjective, intertextual position.

I would argue that any text is a story, regardless of how factual or scientific it aims to be. The 'facts' are strung together through narrative. Our lives could be full of rich narrative story-telling; from our own families, work, school, and television. We also attend the theatre to watch stories being enacted. Clients come to us to deliver their own stories, and children in care are particularly encouraged to tell their story (Kerr, 2019) to move on therapeutically with their life. As you begin to unpick your spirituality, you will relay your story, possibly, to others, in the ways described and perceived above. In fact, I would recommend attending places where your stories are cherished and encouraged.

Philosophy of the Body and the Mind

The brain, in animals, is the epicentre of the central nervous system. Our brains are where everything happens. Everything fires from the brain; we do not walk unless our brain enables us to; we do not eat unless our brain allows us to, and most animals have a brain. Primitive animals, such as sponges, do not have a brain, however; they are thought to exist much the same as plants. The human brain is also extremely complex, and we are known to have around 86 billion neurons, each linked to as many as 10,000 others. We used to say that people only use less than 10% of the brain, depending on who you talked to. However, we now know that humans use up to 100% of the brain, and we have needed to revise our understanding of this complex system.

Philosophy, as intimated above, continues to be concerned with understanding the relationship between the body and the mind, a challenging problem, for obvious reasons. In short, there are three schools of thought regarding this: dualism, materialism, and idealism. There are important differences in all three of these ideas, and I will endeavour to make sure these concepts remain straightforward.

The first one, materialism, claims that the mind is a result of neural 'firing', i.e., our mind is only our mind because of the grey matter firing. This means that without our brains firing, we would not exist, which is quite a pragmatic way of viewing existence and the mind. I like to think of it as the lights on a stage – without the lights, or the brain firing, we do not see the show. Idealism, on the other hand, asserts that only mental phenomena exist, meaning means that nothing exists without the mind, and that we only experience anything because of the mind. Idealism is not concerned with something existing in its own right, but the way in which reality is represented, and how we talk about it. Finally, dualism asserts that the body and mind both exist but are separate. The mind is non-physical, and thus a non-spatial phenomenon. If it does not exist physically, it cannot be measured in the ways something physical can be. I understand this as the mind being existent in its own sense, independent of everything, though seen through the eyes of the ego, which is produced by the brain. More of a triplicate sense really, but honouring the duality of mind and body. Those are the main points. There are multiple tomes out there that explore these concepts in more detail should you be interested.

However, although the three schools set out their stalls clearly, an important point to think about is that of traumatic brain injury (TBI). If the body and mind were entirely dissociated, TBI would not, logically, impact the mind because they are separate. However, what happens with TBI is that the physiological process of the ego being activated by the brain shuts down. When the ego is not observing and reacting, the mind has nothing to observe. Because it is not consciously observing, it does not mean that it has ceased existing. However, there are also contradictions within the case material. One example is that of the French civil servant.

This was the case of a 44-year-old man who was missing 90% of his brain. With so much missing, you would think the mind and ego would cease to exist, but he appeared to function normally in the world (https://qz.com/722614/a-civil-servant-missing-most-of-his-brain-challenges-our-most-basic-theories-of-consciousness), albeit with some minor impairments. There are other dramatic cases of people suffering TBI, and although physiological functions were impaired, their minds remained, although this is clearly not inevitable. Even Descartes could not explain complex thought and language in terms of the physical brain alone.

I share this because we need to understand how information is absorbed, and the processes that occur inside us, or outside us, depending on whether we are talking about the mind, the ego, or the brain. It is also important to take a position from the three to at least use that as a starting point for contemplating your spiritual practice.

Personally, I am a dualist. I believe that you should be whatsoever fits for you and that the mind and body are separate entities. Let me explain a little from the Buddhist perspective as this supports what I think. The Dalai Llama asserts that the mind is the ultimate source of our happiness and suffering. The first principle behind this is that we are sentient beings, which is anyone with a mind who is not a Buddha. Animals are also sentient beings. However, everything that biologically exists is not necessarily sentient, such as bacteria or viruses. They exist, but we do not know if they have a mind. In a similar vein, we know that computers are capable of artificial intelligence, but they do not feel things such as fear or pain.

However, movement does not make one sentient either. A Venus flytrap can detect a fly, and respond by shutting its trap, but it is not sentient. There is no evidence that they experience pain or pleasure, even though plants can respond with better growth when humans talk to them. Overall, the brain is material in nature, but the mind is not. Science is not yet able to measure or observe the mind. For me, it is science's failure to measure the mind that leads to the widespread scepticism of what it is; because we cannot put it into a box, we deny its existence. This says more about the human intolerance of the unknown rather than the existence of the mind.

I would argue that mammals also have a level of consciousness. My dogs are clearly aware of what is happening around them, and they know that if they do certain behaviours when I ask them to, that they get a treat. They can remember small things and consequences so change their behaviour. They get treats without doing that, but that is a different story. They seem to know what they like and how to go about getting it. I share this because whilst there are different views on the capacity of dogs, they have consciousness, as do we.

There is a belief that the mind is impermanent in that it changes moment by moment, but also that it exists after death and is thus eternal. We will return to this idea shortly. The Buddhists believe that the mind is defiled through things such as attachment, and the practice of meditation leads (perhaps) to enlightenment, and Buddhahood. There is also a belief that the mind is eternal, and karma dictates how we are reborn. Others also believe that the mind slips in memories from previous existences, and the brain responds. The mental function comes first, and the brain/body follow.

Events at the time of death also lead me to question if our mind always depends on the brain. At least, I am found asking if the body's demise leads to the mind needing to exit. There is an abundance of interesting scientific evidence for this point. Shortly after death, all brain functions stop, but there are numerous stories about people coming back to life after death, sometimes after considerable amounts of time. The Dalai Llama talks about various incidents. A monk in Dharamsala once died, and seven days passed, yet people noticed that his body had not started to decay. He was found to be meditating. Scientists once attempted to measure what happened in experienced meditators once they had died. A Ganden Tripa (spiritual leader of the Gelug tradition of Buddhism) subsequently died, and his body remained fresh without decay for three weeks. He was measured and recorded, and electrodes were placed on his head, leading them to believe that there was a subtle energy that does not depend on the body that might exist. Scientists themselves now recognise that it is only after death that the cells inside the body begin their own death process, suggesting that there is a split between the mind and body, and the two processes in death happen separately.

In terms of the near-death experience phenomenon, this is also inaccurate. The term does not take into account that lots of people have actually biologically died and returned. No-one seems to have tried to understand the process that occurs when someone returns to life after death. It is as though the mind left and returned, and although the body remained impaired, the mind was not. During this death state, people report similar experiences, including judging themselves and realising why their actions were either good or bad. Many also claim to see the downstream consequences of their actions, which is obviously important in terms of how we conduct our lives spiritually. Do we want to die with regret? Do we want to use this knowledge to fully interact with the world in caring, loving, and respectful ways to die without regret? This is an opportunity to fully use knowledge to improve our existence now and in the potential future.

Sam Parnia (MD) calls these occurrences an 'experience of death'. Many people who die report a sensation of being pulled toward a type of destination and review their lives. This is based, interestingly, on their capacity for humanity, not what they achieved. They report re-experiencing and re-living these experiences, and also reflecting on the consequences of their actions.

It is pertinent to explain my own viewpoint on experiences of death. It is simplistic to just shut them down because we do not see the evidence the experiencer saw, but I believe them. I believe that what people recount when they awaken is that which they experienced. There are far too many similarities between unconnected people to discount them. Our real challenge is to locate a method of investigation that can access them – just because we have science, does not mean we have all answers for all problems. I recall an experience at the age of fifteen. I was in bed, restless, and noticed a glow in the corner of the room. The glow grew and began to represent the arms of an angel reaching out for me. I panicked, tried to discount it, and hid under the covers. As I came up for air, the presence continued to grow until I could no longer tolerate the fear and threw my quilt up in the air and dived into my parents' room. I remember my mother waking up in panic, and me just saying I had had a bad dream. I did not have a dream, I had been awake the entire time. I do not know what it was, but it was definitely something I observed.

Workbook

Think about your own actions in the here and now. Can you honestly say that you bring as much care and love to life and those around you that you are able to? Are your actions as valuable and rewarding as you want them to be? Such practices give us an opportunity to make changes now rather than wait until it is too late, and to die with regret. I would like you to write an obituary on yourself. Write, honestly, what you have achieved in your life. Write how you feel people experienced you. This is the template for your exciting change process, and a way to develop a life where your obituary is full of love, respect, and commitment.

I want to now talk a little bit about the phenomenon of past lives. The Buddhists believe, as I have mentioned above, that each individual forms its own continuum with one moment of mind producing the next moment of mind. This is continuous, including the transitions from one life to the next. Most people would refute this idea because they have no memory of past lives, however, not perceiving something does not negate its existence. My dog smells things that I cannot, but does this mean they are not smelling it? Absolutely not. Let's look at the work of Brian Weiss for some more ideas of past lives.

Brian is an immensely popular psychiatrist in the U.S. who offers international workshops on something called 'past life regression'. He has written widely about the subject and seems to refer to the mind as the soul, which is a slight difference to what we have been talking about, but with the same meaning, obviously with a more Christian slant. As the Buddhists believe the mind is that which exists after death, the soul is the same phenomenon; we are not talking about different entities. Brian has not only written voluminously on the phenomenon of past lives, and trained people internationally in the regression techniques, he also trains therapists how to work therapeutically with this for those trained in therapy. I was fortunate enough to train with Brian in New York State some years ago and was blown away by the whole experience. Whilst I was not a complete believer of everything I heard or witnessed – even in my own mind (and nor should you be) - there was lots of incredible things happening. And a lot of what he writes about is evidential.

As an aside, events like Brian's should carry a warning akin to retreats. In fact, they are actually retreats. I want to share a short anecdote. One day, woman spoke about going for a Native American naming ceremony. She described herself as sickly sweet, and she was often bullied for being so sweet. She said she dressed in floaty clothing for the ceremony, so convinced that she would be named something like 'Butterfly Blossom', or 'Radiant Lily'. The Indian actually named her 'Skunk Piss'. The woman said she recalled a frozen moment where she felt floored, and then, quickly, realised that the name was a blessing. She needed to find the skunk piss inside her to deal with the bullying and problems she often encountered. This is also, despite being hilarious, a great indicator of the mind, and how our mind wanders into fantasy, and is based on the objects around it to exist. Back to Brian.

Brian has presented hundreds of case study material about people remembering events with remarkable detail from past lives; his books are full of them. His patients report names, places, and events. He is definitely convinced of the veracity of what he writes about, but he is not the only one – Dr. Jim Tucker has studied past lives in children for 20 years. He has completed numerous pieces of research and is an expert on the phenomenon. If you are interested in this topic, I would also advise you to read the work of the late Professor Ian Stevenson, Reincarnation and Biology: A Contribution to the Aetiology of

Birthmarks and Birth Defects. This book is a classic, and Weiss cites Stevenson variously in his work. We are not in the realm of cranks and wannabes – these are very real, measurable, and quantifiable issues.

Workbook

Think about your early childhood.

- **Did anyone in your family report you knowing things that you could not known about?**
- **Did you sense spirit around you?**
- **Have you ever had any experience that would fit with the above?**

If you cannot remember, ask your family about it.

I have also been regressed. It happened by chance, as such, in Glastonbury, my personal spiritual Mecca. I had been pottering around, thinking about having one or two 'treatments' in the town. Whilst I take everything with a pinch of salt, I am also open to most things, and am fascinated with how people work their own kind of magick. During the day, I found myself looking around the shops, and came across a notice advertising the services of a past life regression therapist, Atasha Fyfe. I impulsively phoned her and went for a session. Her house was near the Abbey, and she lived in a little granny flat, which took me aback at first. I think I expected a grandiose consulting room, but I did not get one, which forced me into reality. However, I went in, and I vividly remember her presence; she was calm, with gravitas, and clearly experienced in the practice. I say this because we often imagine such practitioners stinking of incense with neck scarves, beads, and floaty clothing. She was totally the opposite.

I laid on her couch and submitted myself to the regression,

excited for what was to come. In no time at all, she regressed me, and I journeyed through several lives, providing lots of intriguing material for me to later reflect on. I had been thinking that I would never be hypnotised, but in reality, hypnotism does not make you unconscious to your surroundings; you remain conscious, able to hear and respond to instructions. The stage variety of hypnotism is something else altogether – hypnotism is a process to calm the body whilst the mind drifts elsewhere.

The whole experience was revelatory for me, and left me feeling much safer than I imagined. In fact, I felt out of my body for a short time afterwards, having experienced something truly profound. I found the experience so transformative that I went back to my hotel, packed up, and immediately left for home. My whole life had been revitalised, and all the questions and concerns I had for my life left me. I had a new-found clarity, I was now determined, and I knew where I was going.

Now, do not get me wrong, I also wondered if the 'lives' were simply my subconscious imaginings accessed through projective techniques, but was this just my subconscious? I remain open to that as a possibility, but also open to the possibility that my mind retrieved memories, which helped me link the past experiences with the present, leading to a greater awareness. And that is the key, do not discard what you do not fully understand.

Now, I know that the latter scenario is more open to questioning, but it remains my experience, and that of many others. By closing ourselves down to the possibility, we limit our sense of experience and opportunity for growth. And by ignoring this as a possibility, we inhibit our capacity for reincarnation, and impede the journey of our soul. My suggestion would be for you to simply try a regression yourself. You may be surprised.

A couple of years after my regression, I was curious about

Atasha. I felt a pull to find her, but unsure why. I returned to Glastonbury but could not find her posters. I searched online, in vain, and could only find copies of her book. I wondered if she had passed herself. Perhaps unsurprisingly, I have a friend who works in Glastonbury, and they managed to locate a record that confirmed what I had feared; Atasha had passed. I was filled with grief – even though I had met her only once, she was completely unaware of the impact her work had on me. I felt such a strong connection with her that I could not even explain. I knew nothing about her, but here I was trying to find her, distressed with the loss. I definitely felt something more than the here and now – I wrote a long article about her on my blog. I hope she reincarnated somewhere amazing.

Ok, so we have run through the philosophy and science of the mind, and linked this to the concept of past life regression. We have also explored the various conceptions of the mind. It is now time to knuckle down for some more practice. It is important that we assimilate our learning into practice. You do not need to do all the suggestions at once.

Workbook

1. **We have already done some unconscious practice in terms of free association, but let us do some more. I would like you to write the three primary models of mind and list the pros and cons of each for you. Make a choice.**

2. **Search Brian Weiss, or myself, on YouTube. Find one of our past life regression meditations, and let go. Make sure to record what you experienced immediately afterwards.**

3. **Search Jon Kabat-Zin's body scan meditation on YouTube. Again, immerse yourself in the practice and try it a few times over a week. Make sure to also record what you experienced immediately afterwards.**

4. Jump onto my webpage and listen to the lemon meditation. I know, it sounds bizarre, but it will actually give you another amazing opportunity to experience the split between body and mind, but also the power of the mind to conjure physiological sensations.

5. Read as much as you can. Pick up books or articles on the above concepts and formulate a comprehensive idea of what the mind means for you. Write about how you can incorporate your knowledge into your spiritual practice and explore what this means for you spiritually.

8. Ritual Practice

The Outlaw

I have chosen the archetype of the outlaw in respect of this chapter on ritual practice as a way of thinking about rituals, as I believe that currently in the world, practicing rituals is seen as quite subversive. Indeed, the archetype of the outlaw is a rebellious character who acts outside social conventions or demands. I guess, in a way, we need to nurture that outlaw inside us to develop and grow our own ritual practice. In popular culture, I see famous outlaws being characters such as Han Solo in Star Wars. I also see an interesting phenomenon in most country and western movies. In these movies, even though the central protagonists are resident in the movie, they always represent themselves as outlaws to the world in which they reside. It is, perhaps, no coincidence (albeit unconscious) that the Europeans were actual outlaws in the way they inhabited the Americas.

Specifically, in terms of strengths and difficulties, the outlaw is the rebel who won't abide by society's demands, often unavailable to us all. We sometimes need to nurture this archetypal quality within us. However, when we are able to do this, the strength of the outlaw is that we can nurture and develop independent thinking and that need to owe nobody favours. However, the role the outlaw can also become self-involved, and potentially criminal, so we need to exercise caution. I share this to ensure that our ritual practices do not breach the laws of humanity, or expectations within the world. Practice rituals, but safely.

Workbook

Take your notebook, and like previous chapters, regulate your body and begin to meditate on the concept of the outlaw.

- **How does the outlaw operate in you?**
- **How has your outlaw behaviour changed at different times in your life?**
- **How could the development of the outlaw impact your future life positively?**

Welcome to the world of rituals. I imagine many of you have heard the term but are not entirely clear about what rituals entail. You may think that practicing 'ritual' is taking you into the realms of witchcraft and other unusual practices, or you may already use ritual practices comprehensively in your life. Others may be perfectly familiar with the term, and you may already use rituals in your life. My sense of the meaning of 'ritual' is an activity or remembrance of something we do at specific times for specific reasons. The activity could be celebrating a birthday with a party, or just wearing the same clothing every time you go to a certain place. A ritual can be a one-off occasion, or something we do regularly throughout the year. Rituals can be a way of managing difficult feelings or acting a way to prevent an action.

In this chapter, I will be offering a range of accessible ways you can undertake and practice ritual in your lives. I will also be talking about the benefits that a ritual practice can bring. Furthermore, you will also receive some suggestions about what to do and how, with some exercises to help you think creatively about incorporating ritual practice into your life. My aim is to help you develop your own approaches rather than parroting someone else's because you need to develop rituals that work for you. By way of further research, if you want to consolidate the learning from this chapter, I encourage you to watch the Grayson Perry documentary on rites of passage, which is a useful documentary to feed into what we will think about in this chapter.

Rituals are often connected with organised religion, but my approach is exactly the opposite – I encourage people to choose the ceremonial practices they want to undertake themselves, without judgement, and without pressure. I also suggest that people change their practices as needed, according to the demands and commitments in their life at the time. The aim of the chapter is to support you with ways of effectively utilising rituals to support recovery, growth, and healing. The journey into rituals will become personal to you and does not need to be impacted by anything other than your own needs. In short, your ritual practice should be tailored perfectly to your needs as an individual, and you should remain cautious of aping someone else's practice. This is not the place to be dictated to by anyone else. Whilst I will offer suggestions, you are free to modify/miss out/incorporate anything that doesn't fit for you. Please trust your instinct.

Workbook

I would like you to draw a mind map to represent any rituals you already participate in. Start with drawing something to represent yourself at the centre of a piece of paper; this can be a squiggle or anything. Try not to get caught up in producing a wonderful piece of art and try to avoid comparisons or criticisms. Write down – without too much thinking – those things you do which could be considered a 'ritual' and link each item with the central image of you, drawing something to represent the connection. As an example, a broken line could represent uncertainty, a line with arrows could represent a two-way connection, or drawing a line through the line

could represent something you no longer do.

____

____

Let's now look at how we define ritual, and how cultures around the world approach traditional practices.

Understanding Ritual from the World

The dictionary definition of ceremony is, "...the ritual observances and procedures required or performed at grand and formal occasions, e.g. 'The new Queen was proclaimed with due ritual'" (OED, 2021). This suggests that ceremonies are ritualistic; in other words, a ceremony is a ritual. Rituals are associated with life-changing events, such as marriages, funerals, and births, but also less personal events such as equinox celebrations. Rituals are truly global phenomena, and we are as likely to engage in rituals here in the West compared to those who follow Eastern traditions.

All the evidence from international archaeological findings indicates the importance of rituals to humans since time immemorial. But what does a ritual look like in pragmatic terms? What purpose do they fulfil? "Healing rituals involve a drama of evocation, enactment, embodiment and evaluation in a charged atmosphere of hope and uncertainty." Rituals are powerful mechanisms for helping humans deal with and resolve stress arising from change. Research suggests that engaging in rituals has been reported to reduce anxiety symptoms. Mike Norton, at Harvard, studies the role of rituals in life, and confirms that rituals make us, "...feel less grief, rituals with families can make us feel closer, and rituals with our partners can reinforce our commitment to each other".

Rituals can be both solo activities and ones we share with others. More of the research suggests that, perhaps surprisingly, our rituals – particularly those involving grief and loss – are more likely to be introverted and take place alone rather than with other people. Researchers of Marathi religious practices in Mauritius noted that anxiety levels were reduced when people practised rituals in a solitary way. It is important to recognise that the performance of a ritual does not have to be useful for the issue at hand, the utility of the ritual is not related to its practicality. We may light a candle to celebrate the end of a relationship even though the action of lighting a candle bears no impact on the actual relationship ending.

Anthropologists, such as Jane Derges, study our ritualistic behaviour particularly in respect of disasters. Jane studies recovery in post conflict Sri Lanka, and from her findings, it is clear that extreme circumstances in life lead us to become more ritualistic rather than less. Ritualistic behaviour increased during the recent pandemic as people found ways of marking time or establishing a routine during the days or weeks in isolation. The ritual behaviour appeared to support people in feeling safe, and some rituals appeared to prevent something bad from happening.

At some level, the governments provided us with our own ritual behaviour through mandatory mask-wearing, social distancing, and vaccinations. Obviously, there is some evidence that these processes would be helpful in reducing transmission of the virus, but I found that my routine in pandemic life was more structured. For example, I took the dogs out at similar times each day, ate at the same times, and became more ritualistic about which foods I bought and where from. It was as though my own behaviour became more ritualistic.

So, what do rituals look like? People are infinitely creative. In its simplest incarnation, rituals can be something linked to an everyday routine. Rituals can be little celebrations every morning; we wake up, give thanks for another day, and eat an amazing meal to celebrate another opportunity for life. A ritual can be as small as the way we make our morning coffee, or as grand as holding the most splendid wedding with thousands of guests. There does not have to be a spiritual connotation, although enjoyment and blessings can be increased threefold if a spiritual component is included if you feel so inclined. There is certainly an element of religiosity about rituals without necessarily a connection with formal religion.

Rituals can often be physical, emotional, or practical, incorporating practices such as sitting still for two minutes every evening, or they could take up a full day (or longer) embracing a special occasion in our lives. Rituals are way more than meaningless action stripped of context, and can be seen as a social strategy, or a way of being in the world. We may prepare, say, a marriage ritual for many months beforehand, but celebrate the moon's fullness on a whim. The range of options are limitless, but the rewards are vast.

Rituals can also be the times when we come together with others, sometimes at ceremonial sites such as Stonehenge. They are opportunities for us to celebrate (often with food and drink), connect, and review situations and circumstances. Most importantly, they can be opportunities for us to remember our ancestry, and consider future plans. Ritual practices can be both ethereal and practical at the same time; challenging and soothing. People conduct rituals to energise, purify, and release energies such as in Feng Shui practices, or to bless germinating seeds to generate a bumper crop. Most spiritual people will also cite a love of dressing up in ceremonial clothing, and reconnecting with our inner self when conducting rituals. I believe that the practice is integral to our recovery.

I have, over the years, engaged in numerous rituals, as I am sure you have. I have been baptised by the Mormon church and have myself baptised people in the church. I have been married, divorced, and obviously, I have been born. I was christened, and confirmed, and have attended a range of funerals over the years, including for my mother, my brother, and many family members. I have also attended solstice rituals regularly, and indeed, conducted my own. I have also attended rituals in my own home, and been in some of the most awe-inspiring venues in the world – Stonehenge, St. Paul's Cathedral, and York Minster being just a few.

The things I remember from these are the environments, the splendour, and the special feelings that such events evoke; even if those feelings are tricky ones, such as grief. Most rituals I have attended have offered an opportunity to re-remember and re-kindle connections with other people. The majority of rituals are designed for other people to connect, see, and witness; all very powerful occasions, and all very memorable. I am sure you have attended your own, even if you did not consciously consider them 'rituals'.

The History of Ritual

Throughout history, we have sought assistance from an unknown force, such as God or the universe, to help support that which we do not fully understand ourselves. Humans have engaged in various ceremonial rituals since time immemorial: celebrating gods and goddesses; practicing rituals prior to combat; developing processes to encourage fertility, and undertaking different practices to heal from trauma, loss, and famine. We also created rituals to accompany the process of justice or carry out punishment. Until 1964 in the U.K., large crowds would gather to witness public hangings.

Some of these ceremonial practices were handed down to us, and we have been under pressure to 'comply'. We often undertake rituals that have been developed by others, most obviously seen in Christian, Jewish, and Muslim cultures. Organised religion sets out how and when to pray, encourages us to attend religious venues, and offers guidance on how to live our lives. Rituals can often be heavily influenced by tradition – we do what our ancestors do but tweak them slightly. If you look at a spiritual centre like Stonehenge, for example, we still visit this site, probably for different reasons, but still to connect with what our ancestors have done in the past.

If you are a member of an organised religion, and enjoy these practices, please continue, especially if they help your life have meaning and purpose. There are many benefits, and I have attended many such beautiful ceremonial occasions. However, this book is about developing a unique expression of yourself, and to widen your perspective of what rituals could look like in your life.

Marriage

The word 'marriage' comes from Middle English, and was first seen in 1250-1300 CE. However, the ancient institution of marriage likely predates this. The first recorded marriage was in Mesopotamia in 2350 B.C. (The Week, 2007). At this time, marriage was a business deal designed to bind women to men as belongings. By the eighth century, marriage was widely accepted in the Catholic church as a sacrament, or a ritual to bestow God's grace.

Marriage is celebrated differently around the world. In Buddhism, marriage is considered a secular activity, therefore, people are encouraged to follow the customs in their own community. For Hindus, marriages are still often arranged, although this is gradually changing, and marriage has lots of spiritual beliefs associated with it (e.g., karma). Hindu weddings are often extravagant, taking place over many days, and involve the chanting of ancient mantras and the use of ceremonial fires; celebrants are dressed in their finery, with families coming together perhaps for the first time.

In pagan communities, 'handfasting' is their alternative to marriage, which involves a creative, ceremonial rituals in which a symbolic or actual knot ties the two people together. Handfasting ceremonies are unique, and entirely responsive to the individual couple's needs and desires, including chosen songs with participants often dressed in traditional clothing with opportunities for feasting afterwards. Some people incorporate spells and chants to reinforce their belief system.

The world approaches the union of two people differently according to culture, geography, and spiritual beliefs. The legalisation of gay marriage has also brought about a rethink of traditional ceremonies and alternative ways of forming relationships, such as polyamory.

Workbook

In your workbook, begin to have a think about the following ideas.

- **Do any of these images of marriage resonate with you?**
- **What are your experiences of marriage rituals?**
- **What was your experience of your parents' relationship, if any?**
- **Do you have any traumatic connections with the term?**
- **Do you have any religious expectations with regards to how you view marriage?**
- **Do you have experience with committing to a relationship that is considered a non-Christian 'coupling'?**

Death

There is a saying that growing older is not for wimps, which made more sense to me as I got older, and people around me began to pass away. As we grow into adulthood, we generally experience people being added into our lives – new siblings, new partners, new friends – but when we reach a certain age, the tendency is more for those we love to fall away. Funerals have always been deeply upsetting for me – my brother's funeral, in particular, found me absolutely inconsolable, as he passed so young. My mother's funeral was different in that there were more obvious family issues in our maternal side. I recall feeling a deep rage towards my family, which unsettled what should have been a moving ritual. Humans' capacity to act out in sanctified premises is always a source of astonishment to me. Ceremonial rituals can sometimes bring out the worst in people.

A funeral is the most well-known way of participating in a death ritual, but there are many, international variations. For example, funerals in the Bahá'í Faith are characterised by the fact that they do not embalm bodies, and they prohibit cremation. They also use a chrysolite or hardwood casket and wrap the body in silk or cotton before burial, which must take place no further than an hour (including flights) after the place of death. As the person is buried, they place a ring onto the deceased's finger stating, "I came forth from God, and return unto Him, detached from all save Him, holding fast to His Name, the Merciful, the Compassionate." Various Christian denominations perform different rites, but they tend to include burial or cremation, with prayers, and sometimes music. Ancient hymns often accompany the lighting of candles and the burning of incense, with priests dressed in robes, and people dressed in formal attire. In Judaism, funerals follow specific rites, although they are subject to variation in custom. Halakha (Jewish law) calls for preparatory rituals, involving bathing and shrouding the body, accompanied by prayers and readings from the Hebrew Bible, and then a funeral service marked by eulogies and brief prayers; they then lower the body into the grave and the filling it with earth. Historical practices in Ancient Roman times included the oldest male trying to take the last breath of the dying person, followed by pouring libations on graves and feasting.

Death is, for us in the West at least, often highly anxiety-provoking - we spend our lives attempting to ameliorate the anxiety provoked by death. We all have death anxiety in varying ways, and it contributes to our thinking about and preparation for death (and indeed, life). In psychoanalytic thinking, we use the term 'Thanatos' or 'thanatophobia' for this anxiety, after the Greek god of non-violent deaths. Thanatos can be seen in how we try to be fit, well, and live the best lives we possibly can before death erases us.

Rituals for Suicide

Trigger warning, I want to take a moment to talk about suicide here. If that will be too difficult, please move to the next chapter. Suicide triggers shame and/or isolation, and can create great difficulties in talking about what happened. There are important historical reasons for this. The Archbishop of York in 740 ordered priests not to give Christian burials to anyone who had committed suicide (if it had been proven that they were sane at the time of their death). There followed the practice of burying suicides at crossroads, a Christian practice enduring from Anglo-Saxon beliefs. It was believed that burial at a crossroads would confuse the ghost of the deceased (which was also why it was a punishment for criminals), as the ghost would not know which direction to travel. The ghost would thus be stuck waiting at the crossroads forever.

Even for the pagan communities pre- and post-Christianity, the impact of suicide must have been huge – if a parent died and left their family, they would certainly have experienced much hardship. In Medieval times, committing suicide meant that you denied your Lord of the Manor your labour, and thus the Crown could and would seek recompense by taking ownership of any property or belongings left behind. Religion and the need for survival have combined to make us judgmental of suicide.

This is a long way from the Japanese practices around suicide. The European world certainly did not share the beliefs of the Japanese practice of seppuku. Suicide, assisted or not, was a form of honour and highly ceremonial in nature. But we are gradually morphing from the Christian view of suicide being a gross sin, with eternal repercussions; no longer do we need to fear being sent to the seventh circle of hell, alongside the murderers, blasphemers, and sodomites, if we end our life. However, suicide still brings the pain of guilt or regret.

It may be that you have an experience of suicide in your life. In extreme circumstances, you may have thought about ending your own life (many of us have). You will be aware that raising this issue can be triggering. If this is the case, it is even more important to develop a ritual to celebrate the passing of your loved one in this way, especially if the original funeral ritual was marked with shame and avoidance.

In the reference section, you will find further sources of support should this discussion trigger something in you.

Workbook

In your workbook, answer the following questions:

- **What funerals have you attended?**
- **What are your experiences of death?**
- **How do you feel about Thanatos – do you believe your lifestyle is impacted by any thoughts about death?**
- **What rituals have you found most helpful with regards to death?**

Births

Up until contemporary times, giving birth was a highly perilous activity. High numbers of mothers died in childbirth; children also often died before the age of 5. Childbirth was also perilous for midwives - in 1481, the English midwife, Agnes Marshall, was accused of using quasi-magical incantations during one birth: clearly the impact of earlier pagan times still endured. Whilst not strictly a ritual, in 1441, the Norfolk woman and prolific letter writer, Margaret Paston, asked her husband to wear a protective ring that she had sent him, suggesting that wearing it would help her have a safe pregnancy and delivery (History Extra, 2021). There are many accounts of other kinds of ceremonial practice. A learned text, compiled by the physician, Aldobrandino of Siena, in the 13th century, advised that two or three weeks before the birth, the mother should bathe in water steeped with herbs and lubricate her legs, thighs and vagina with camomile oil and chicken fat, no doubt to ease the delivery. Around that same period, birthing often involved practices which were more superstitious than medical, such as tying an eaglestone to the woman's thigh as it was believed to expedite the birth (History Extra, 2021).

The process of birthing is still a deeply moving, transformational process for society, as we welcome in the wonder of a new life. Births also bring members of communities together to give thanks for the new life, offer blessings, and provide support.

Workbook

Think about what the birth of a child means to you, and write down the adjectives that describe your feelings and thoughts. Draw/paint something that symbolises new life to you. Do not be afraid to includes fewer positive thoughts here - be open to your shadow side and include the more complex emotions or those that you may be in denial about.

Creating Ritual Purpose

Creating ritual purpose is about adequately preparing for the actual ritual. It is the time where we set our intention and thoughts about what we wish to achieve, and clarify our needs.

The practice of paganism offers much in the way of developing ritual purpose. If the pagan way is of interest, please read: Pagan Rites of Passage by Pauline and Daniel Campanelli. However, creating ritual purpose does not have to be linked to any specific spiritual or religious practice – you are welcome to create your own.

You could try to write to someone who did you bad. Write your feelings in full and honest detail, telling them about how you were impacted by them, then sit at your altar and burn the paper (carefully, with the obvious precautions). Make this as elaborate and/or as meaningful as you see fit. This is a good example of how to create a highly personalised ritual for your own therapeutic growth. There are an infinite number of reasons for a ritual though; here are some examples:

1. Letting go of experiences that still hurt through symbolism – writing a letter symbolically to someone who hurt you is a powerful way to let go of toxic experiences. Do consider carefully, though, which experiences you use in this exercise. You may not have thought about a particular experience for many years, so please take care and secure some support either side of completing this task if required.

To ensure some emotional depth, address the letter to the person who hurt you. As this letter is not going to be sent to anyone, you can write absolutely everything you feel. Use the tone of phrasing that feels right for you. Do not be afraid of using coarse or vile language – use the language that fits you. You may also want to protect yourself spiritually, which can be accomplished through meditating deeply and imagining yourself being encapsulated by a white sphere of protective light. Be explicit in your thinking about what it is protecting you from (e.g., contamination from old thoughts, spirits, whatever your belief system).

You could write an invocation – you may want to summon a god or goddess, or other being. Making sure you have a large pan with a lid or similar nearby and then light a candle; choose a colour candle that symbolises this ritual – maybe a red candle to symbolise your hurt. Some people tie items around the candle for symbolic protection. You could also light some incense and assemble other items that symbolise your recovery and growth – items such as jewellery or a crystal. Choose the time and day for the ritual – is there a special day to remember? When all is assembled, the house is quiet, you are alone and focused, begin the ritual. Be as focused and attuned as you can. If it does not work, stop. Try again another day. The ritualistic burning of the paper and watching the words burn away is symbolic and deeply cathartic.

2. Celebrating milestones such as abstinence from alcohol, drugs or over-eating is rewarding. It is important to mark the abstinence in some way, for example, saving the money you would have wasted on it, and spending the money once a year on something special. You could take a trip to the place you always associated with your addictive behaviour, but from a strengthened position. Some people in recovery use it as a time to invite their friends and loved ones to their home and prepare a celebratory meal. Rituals do not have to cost the earth. In fact, if you are trying to avoid addictive associations, you should avoid expensive components as they can trigger neurological reward systems. But you have done so well, so you deserve to mark the achievement with a ritual.

3. Rites of passage, such as starting something new – as we recover, we may start new jobs, new relationships, and adopt practices that are more nurturing and restorative to our well-being. It is so important that we acknowledge our new accomplishments and celebrate them with openness, excitement, and thanks. Practically, we may by a new car once we pass our driving test, and it is still common across the world to celebrate someone leaving a community with presents, food, and celebrations.

4. Providing honourable closure on something difficult, such as a relationship ending – sometimes, a ritual is required

to let go of those things which are sent to try us. We need to say goodbye to someone, or let go of something else, especially if they no longer serve us well. You may want to mark getting rid of a habit or a behaviour, or even saying goodbye to an old home or some of your belongings. Developing a ritual in this context will provide closure, however you set the ritual up.

5. Passage of time – there are a range of ways in which we celebrate, manage, and control how and when we interact with changes in time (or the seasons), all of which are complemented immensely by ritual practice. You might also want to honour other key dates, such as birthdays or anniversaries of important occasions in your life. Alternatively, the changing of the seasons could be marked by a change in your altar set up. In my house, we mark the changing of the seasons by putting up different wreaths, designed to illustrate the oncoming season.

Before planning how you will conduct a ritual, it is helpful to think about why you are doing it. It is important that your ritual practices become your own, and that you feel empowered to do this. Another vital part of rituals is to connect your ceremonial practice to your recovery. Do not just do a ritual for ritual's sake, make it specific to the issue at hand, which will ensure you get the utmost benefit from it.

Ritual Preparation

Once you have found the reason for your ritual, you need to prepare. A great deal of ritual preparation is spent envisioning your ritual, reflecting, and contemplating the actual activity. However, all the space leading up to the actual ritual is as important as the moment itself. The visualisation of the ritual is where we connect with our own heart and where we begin to look at what is behind the veil. We begin to understand what is really in our hearts. The more sacred the envisioning of the ritual, the more powerful yours will be.

Rituals do not need to be solitary affairs. They can be, and solo rituals often hold immense power, but try to involve other people wherever possible – even sitting with a friend, drinking hot chocolate under the full moon can be enriching.

Workbook

Consider a ritual you are planning and take a piece of paper with three vertical columns. In the left column, write the practical considerations, i.e., venue, time, purpose, people. In the middle column, write down the intentions, and in the final column, explore ideas as to how you will, through this ritual practice, benefit yourself and others.

Contemplating Space

Before any ritual, consider where you will enact it. Will you be incorporating a ritual at home? Will you go out into the wilderness to commune with nature or the gods? Will you meet with friends to share the experience? If we are attending a religious space for the ritual, we may dust off the cobwebs from our suit. You may wish to cleanse the body. As mentioned in other chapters, many people and religious practices consider water to be a very special element. Consequently, many people ensure that they shower before and after special rituals and thoroughly cleanse anything that is involved in their ceremonial practice. Cleaning does not just have to be with water, it can also be more ethereal, through burning sage or incense.

Many people have shrines in their home. I have an old, lacquered box on which I place candles, plants, incense, and a singing bowl. I sometimes cover it with silk scarves and always try to keep it clean and respectful. According to the season, I may add flowers; sometimes photographs of particular people

– for example, a spiritual guru for certain practices or loved ones for other rituals. I sit in front of the shrine to meditate and perform yoga there too. I would encourage you to set up a shrine somewhere, even if the only space you can find is a small shelf in your home. Your shrine is where you come to focus your mind, release toxicity, and engage in meaningful spiritual practice, which does not need to cost anything.

Perhaps you are creating a ritual from home to celebrate, for example, a new moon. I would again thoroughly clean and prepare the space in which you will conduct your ritual. Be clean, be thoughtful, and be thorough. Sandra Ingerman, in her book on ceremony, talks about 'powering up', spending time engaging in drumming practice or meditation without distractions, letting go of control, and allowing spiritual energies to work their magic, whatever they may be. Try not to rush, be deliberate in your actions and thoughts and be free of distractions. Be Mindful. You may want to think about the role of intoxicants or foodstuffs. Do you want to have a period of fasting prior to the ritual, or do you want to be free of intoxicants for periods of time? There are also options to include either food or drink within the ritual itself.

I always shower prior to a ritual and thoroughly clean the ceremonial area (which is usually an area of my house). I will update my shrine area with objects that help me to think about and connect with my ritual. For example, if I am celebrating Beltane, I may want to include some seeds to symbolise the onset of spring, flowers to represent growth, and even some herbs such as mint and rosemary to symbolise healing and recovery and survival of the winter period. I write down what I want to say and contemplate during the ritual. I might use particular poems from the poets I admire, or write it all out myself. If I want to think about a particular god or spirit, I do some research into that spirit and incorporate my understanding of them into the ceremonial practice. If I am conducting a ritual with other people, such as in a druid circle, I will circulate a script for us all to participate in, including lines for everyone.

These ideas are specific to me, so I want you to develop your own narrative for yourself. There is no template passed down from the ancients, so we have to rely upon our own intuition and personal sense of spirituality.

Ritual Clothing

Michael Solomon and Punam Anand at New York University studied the wearing of ritual clothing in depth and point out the importance of symbolic dress. When we dress for the occasion, we connect on a deeper level with our intention and purpose. Ask yourself the question, "What clothing will help me reinforce the purpose of my ritual? "

Whilst many people choose to wear special clothing to complement the ritual, other people may perform rituals naked or 'skyclad'. The 'skyclad' term originated within the neopagan movement and referred to practitioners working spiritually without clothing – this is where the clichéd idea of people in circles worshipping the devil may have originated. You may have heard of Gerald Gardner, who wrote Witchcraft Today in 1958. He advocated conducting rituals skyclad. Obviously, I cannot recommend that you be skyclad outside the safety and security of your own home, but I would certainly suggest that you at least practice one ritual skyclad for experimentation purposes.

Will the clothing have special significance? Pagans often get out their cloaks, and heathens get out their Norse regalia, including swords. I know other people who take great pains to make their own ritual clothing, decorating it uniquely. My suggestion is, as your ritual practice develops, you will begin to associate particular clothing with the rituals you conduct. You do not necessarily need to get out the sewing machine and knock up some intricate finery – sometimes just sitting with a special blanket can be meaningful enough for your practice.

I know people who have wardrobes of ceremonial and ritual gear that they get out throughout the year. If I am honest, I have various items that are meaningful to me; a gorgeous Green Man waistcoat that attracts much envy, and a cloak I can use if so inclined. I rarely go out parading myself in Anglo-Saxon garb - but it has been known. Being dressed for the occasion, especially for community rituals, can add a particular je ne sais quoi!

Workbook

Before starting any ritual, spend some time sitting, reflecting on the purpose of the ritual.

- **What do you want to accomplish?**
- **What do you want to let go of?**
- **What do you want to attract?**
- **What do you want to celebrate?**
- **Who would you like to benefit from this ritual?**
- **When your thoughts are clear, give thanks for the opportunity for you to sit and conduct the ritual.**

Then spend some time letting go of any surface feelings that are around for you. Imagine yourself letting go of these distracting thoughts as black smoke leaving through your nose and try to focus on the task at hand. Imagine a white light illuminating and protecting you from above, circling and covering you in light and nourishment. You do not have to believe there is actually something there, this is a way of connecting to intention through visualisation.

Ultimately, do you desperately need something to happen? It is worth being alert to a sense of desperation in your need for an outcome for your ritual. Marta Brzosko, in her blog (https://medium.com/mind-cafe/how-to-set-an-intention-for-a-spiritual-journey-19fa78dfdcfb), suggests that setting goals can lead to self-aggression. Brzosko suggests goals that are more reflexive and gentler, which you could find helpful. This extract sets out the goals, in her view, in full:

1. Phrase the goal as something you can be in charge of. To avoid turning intentions into goals, aim for a response to your circumstances — rather than particular circumstances themselves. Usually, this will involve an aspect of your mindset. How do you intend to relate to your thoughts, feelings, and behaviours?
2. Phrase it in the present tense. Setting the intention in the present drives you away from wishful thinking (I'd like to..., I will...) and towards the present moment (I do..., I recognise..., I honour...). This makes an intention valid from the moment you set it — rather than planning for it to come to life in a distant future.

3. Focus on the "vibe" the intention will give you. Your intention is something that should inspire you — or "resonate with you", as some people like to put it. Make it personal and relevant to what you know serves you in day-to-day life. Make it sound like you — authentic, beautiful, and moving in your own eyes.

4. Write it down in a place where you often look. Writing down an intention doubles its power, and putting thoughts into the written word is a signal to your subconscious that they are important. Additionally, if you write the intention where you see it — e.g., on your whiteboard or the cover of your journal — you will strengthen it every time you look at it.

5. Keep it to yourself. This is my big discovery from the past few years: keeping some things to myself can be extremely powerful. By consciously choosing not to share your intention with anyone, you turn it into something sacred — it remains yours and yours only. This can elevate your relationship with yourself to a whole new level because it shows that you can

trust yourself.

Many spiritual practitioners talk about the notion of the spiritual heart; our intention is a representation of what is in our hearts. Please make sure your intention comes from your heart. If you plan to undertake a ritual for negativity, if you want to hurt someone or to bring bad luck to somebody, then this does not come from a heart-felt, mindful, compassionate place. I am aware of some forms of witchcraft that practice spells with hostile intentions, but contemporary thinking is that this negatively affects one's karma. Rather than encouraging you to act on these feelings, I encourage you to reflect on why you want to complete that kind of ritual. I recommend that you then take those negative thoughts to either your therapist or healer – taking the negativity to the shaman, perhaps for ritual cleansing, may be more helpful.

Ritual Sound

Ritual sound is everything associated with our sensory attunement to the ritual process. We complement this with the use of instruments, voices, or even listening carefully to the sounds outside our heads. Music is known to improve respiration, lower blood pressure, improve cardiac output, reduce heart rate, and relax muscle tension. Dr. Santhanam Suresh stated, "Audio therapy is an exciting opportunity and should be considered by hospitals as an important strategy to minimize pain in children undergoing major surgery. This is inexpensive and doesn't have any side effects."

As a harpist, I bring the sounds of the harp into my ritual life – and any other area I can squeeze it into – as much as humanly possible. An 11th century music theorist, Guido of Arezzo, described a system, which appeals to me, called the 'solfeggio frequencies': six frequencies that are thought to support healing. The six syllables are:

- 396 Hz – liberating guilt and fear

- 417 Hz – undoing situations and facilitating change
- 528 Hz – transformation and miracles (DNA repair)
- 639 Hz – Connecting/relationships
- 741 Hz – Expression/solutions
- 852 Hz – Returning to spiritual order

Some people outrightly question these beliefs and the application of sound to therapeutic healing, but there is research on specific frequencies of binaural beats, such as 6 Hz and 40 Hz, which are shown to have a positive effect on stress reduction and memory.

When viewed on an oscilloscope, the harp wave forms come closest of all natural instruments to a pure figure 8 pattern. Irish harpists were required to be masters of three distinct types of music: Suantraighe (music to calm people); Goltraighe (music to bring about tears) and Geantraighe (music to awaken lightness and joy). The god, Dagda, used the harp to control men's emotions and change the seasons, and there is no doubt that the music can deeply affect people. But there are other instruments of joy to incorporate into ritual practice, especially as harps are not always within budget.

The gong is another useful ritual instrument, first mentioned in 6th century Chinese manuscripts, and have endured over time. Most recently, gongs are being recognised for their therapeutic benefits via gong 'baths', a complete immersion in a room where many gongs are being played simultaneously – truly a powerful practice. The therapeutic benefits of gongs are said to be profound, or are said to affect our brain waves. There is a lack of empirical data to prove this, but maybe we just need to find the evidence in the fact that gong baths have endured. Maybe you could purchase a small gong, or a Tibetan singing bowl, which also produces relaxing vibrations, and experiment.

I also recommend incorporating an element of drumming into your ritual. There is much evidence to support the idea that drumming is helpful to recovery. The Royal College of

Music conducted research in 2016, following two decades of evidence, and they found that a ten-week programme of group drumming reduced depression by as much as 38% and anxiety by 20%. A preliminary study published in *Psychotherapy and Psychosomatics* also revealed that a ten-week programme of group drumming can improve social resilience by 23% and mental well-being by 16%. These numbers do seem very precise for something so abstract. However, what is even more surprising is that when the subjects' saliva was tested for their inflammatory immune profile, drumming was positively associated with a move away from it. There is a raft of other research out there supporting this finding. So, I encourage you to get yourself a drum. It does not need to cost the earth, and even without training, simply banging on some drums is a beneficial start.

You could also simply use your voice. We have always sung in rituals, and continue to do so – work out a song, phrase or sound that complements your practice. Find some time on your own or with friends, and practise.

Practice

Take your instrument, sit comfortably, and take a moment to breathe. Bring your attention to your body and notice what is happening. Do not rush. Imagine a past hurt; re-remember what happened, the situation, the people involved, and your experience. Tap into the feelings again, as we are going to clear them out. Begin to drum the sound of the hurt, or pluck the strings, or use your voice) to beat the sound of the pain. Go for as long as you can, trying not to lose sight of your physical sensations. If it helps, just imagine the person's head on the face of the drum, and bang them into oblivion. Release the pain, it is time. This will help reverse the original stress response, and recalibrate your emotional experience.

The Ritual

We finally come to the actual ritual. You will have spent lots of time exploring different components, your preparation, your intention, and will have arrived here with an idea about your ritual (or at least the possibilities for yourself). You may also have got out a musical instrument to complement the health benefits of ritual practice. All you need now is to settle in and enjoy your ritual. Make sure you are undisturbed, and let go. We cannot talk about the ritual you have created for yourself, but we do not need to – ritual practice is sacred practice, sacred to you. Please respect that.

Finally, I encourage you to write up your experiences in your workbook. Write up actual rituals, use drawings and creativity to make your workbook a visually arresting account of what you did and how. Write up how it felt – journaling is another helpful way to support your recovery. And finally, where appropriate and safe for you, talk to others about their ritual practice.

9. Finding Your Tribe

The Caregiver

I have used the caregiver archetype to help us associate the idea of a clan. There may not be an obvious connection at first, however, I want us to begin by reflecting on the idea of what we associate with a caregiver. Caregivers are part of our community system, they come into our lives to help and support us and then move out of our lives. Caregivers are often supportive characters that can also make sacrifices for others. It is these qualities that are particularly beneficial and vital for our recovery in terms of having associations with a clan. I think of caregivers in literature as the nurse in Romeo and Juliet, or Mary Poppins, but they do not have to be powerful, such as Marge Simpson from The Simpsons.

The caregiver as an archetype is someone or a character who continuously and selflessly supports us and make sacrifices on their behalf. There are, therefore, issues such as lacking ambition or leadership. However, caregivers also have clear strengths, such as being honourable, selfless, and loyal. Within our interactions with clans in real life, it is important that we find the right clans, those people who can selflessly offer us the things we need, and to avoid those plans where there are issues with leadership or ambition.

Workbook

Take your workbook, and begin to reflect on the idea of the

caregiver.

- **What does the caregiver suggest to you?**
- **What does it feel like to reflect on those instances where you were a caregiver?**
- **How could you use the qualities of caregiver to help you move forwards?**

Our healing process often starts with ourselves. We spend time, perhaps in therapy, exploring our inner world, and also how we connect and interact with other people. But only ever in the third person; we do not bring the actual people into therapy with us. We may formulate ideas that we can use in life, and we may begin to feel differently about ourselves, but this is not inevitable, and often slow. Certainly, I found my own work transformational, but over years rather than months. My healing process was also consolidated with spirituality, but over time, the spirituality became more life-affirming, more restorative, and more healing. However, I realised that regardless of the work I did on myself, if I did not learn to interact with others differently, my growth would always be impaired.

And there are lots of reasons that we need, wherever possible, to incorporate the way we relate to others within our healing process. When we are hurt, in childhood especially, we adjust to the pain, often creatively, and it ensures our survival. We call this a 'creative adjustment'. Now, let's be clear, becoming controlling or avoidant as a child served us well, but in adulthood, you can probably understand how our creative adjustments no longer serve us well. Avoiding all conflict means people never truly know us or our boundaries, because we avoid the contact, and being controlling means that people are often going to struggle to be with us. Who wants to be around someone who controls everything?

Realising the issue of how we relate is incredibly difficult to accept. When we even begin to think about relating to other people and take responsibility for our own actions, we immediately trigger defence mechanisms. It is hard to recognise and then accept our limitations in the way we relate to others, it is far easier emotionally to simply leave the blame at someone else's door. Even myself, I would love to claim that my partner is responsible for every problem in our life, but this would not be true or accurate, it would just reinforce my own perception. Consequently, in this chapter, I want to help you begin your journey towards self realisation, and help you achieve everything you want to achieve in your life through adjusting your role in it. It may be challenging, and we may trigger complex intra-psychic processes, but you will be the ultimate beneficiary.

I believe that, especially now with social media, we read endless memes about 'knowing your own truth', 'dumping those that disagree', ad infinitum. Such memes reinforce the sense that the world is wrong and you are right, but that is not the case. You are the world, you are the connection with others, and everything that happens between you and someone else is co-created. You need to understand your role in this, and by doing so, we will be able to develop the way you relate to others in deeper ways, far more consciously and present. And the result will be a gift you will never want to let go.

As we will explore below, the importance of being part of a tribe is vital – not only for physical and emotional health, but to learn and process spiritual growth with others. Spirituality is not just a solitary activity – to gain maximum benefits, we should be with others.

Workbook

Open up Instagram or Facebook and tap the search option.

Search a few memes – type in 'happy', or 'sad', and see what comes up. You will be surprised, but the majority will be about you doing something for yourself rather than someone else.

Let's do another free association task. Pick up your journal and pen and write 'tribe' in the very centre. Now, free associate and write any idea that comes to you from your unconscious. Again, try not to judge or inhibit what you write, just let go with the pen. Once you are done with words, get another piece of paper and draw anything else that comes to mind. Do not focus on drawing a specific object at first, just let the pen flow wherever it wants to go. I would love you to share your drawings via Instagram when you can.

My History

My journey with tribes has been varied. There have been times when I felt part of a group, but in retrospect, I am not sure I was ever truly part of it. Even at university, as part of various societies, I was a member of the society, and would talk to some members, but not in any meaningful way. In hindsight, I was in the group, but not of it, or at least, not in the group for very long. At school, I was very much out of any group. I had a few friends I would hang out with when desperate, but rarely spent time with them out of school. I have always been naturally quick to fall out, fairly intolerant of anything, and often in conflict with people. Truly a microcosm of my own family unit.

However, joining my psychotherapy training forced me to sit in a group of people and stay with them over an extended period of time – four years, so I had to learn how to tolerate people coming to me to take me to a task. I could not run away as I needed to complete the training, so I had to learn how to be present with people, not dissociate or avoid. I also, most importantly, had to learn how to connect and remain connected with people, which was excruciating for me at times – my biology was frequently urging me to run for the hills, but my head made me stay put. This was an enormously beneficial gift to me as it offered me the chance to understand the joys and challenges of being around other people.

Over time, I gradually realised that relationships were not as scary as I had imagined. I began to like some people, not everyone (I am not perfect) but most importantly, I understood how valuable relationships were. The feelings of being connected with others, being part of a gang, was amazing, and I realised that anyone could learn how to do relationships differently, and even tolerate challenge, which, prior to that date, was impossible and threatening for me. In fact, if I could learn them, anyone could. The importance of this was consolidated further through the neuroscientific evidence that supported the importance and essential need of humans to be around others.

And now, nearly twenty years after my original training, I have kept my connections with those original people in my training group. They have seen me shout, cry, wail like a child, and I have witnessed and shared their sorrow. We have kept by each other, and they remain the most important people in my life. And even though we don't see each other frequently, I know that we will always remain connected in such a profound way. That kind of connection cannot be dismissed. It is time to understand how you can find your own tribe, or join mine, to get your own benefits.

Workbook

Take your mind back to your own life, beginning from childhood. Think about how you functioned at the different stages - pre-school, primary, secondary, and in work contexts. Write about how you felt, and how you experienced people. You may have been a typical extrovert and had large groups

of friends. You may have been introvert, with very few connections. However, the purpose is to explore not the amount of friends, just the quality of connection you were able to achieve.

History of Tribes

In anthropology, a tribe is a way that humans organise themselves socially. The organisation is often defined by traditions of common descent, language, race, or ideology. The term actually originated in ancient Rome; back then, the word 'tribus' denoted a division within the state. In Middle English, the word became 'Tribu', which is a borrowing from Old French. It may also be a reflection of how English uses a latinate word and drops the 'us'. Later on, as Europeans explored other cultures, they referred to them as 'tribes'. By the mid-19th century, anthropologists were using the term, as well as terms such as 'band' or 'state', to denote different stages in unilinear cultural evolution.

The term is now more contested, although it is still used as a form of technical shorthand in courses, schools, documentaries, and reference works. The term went out of fashion because some anthropologists felt that groups of people could not be precisely defined in this way. There were also issues with the colonial connotations of the word. African scholars in particular felt that the term was pejorative and inaccurate. The term that is tended to be used now is 'ethnic group', usually a group of people defined by their common ancestry and language, history, and territory. However, I will use the word 'tribe' uncomfortably because I apply it to the entire world, need to situate it within the Roman context, in particular, our collective history.

In these contexts, we understand a tribe to be a group of people who share a name - i.e., the Zulu in South Africa, or the

Caledonii in ancient Scotland. Some tribes are more advanced than others, and now we have a far more international mix of differences. Tribes are said to share territory, and work involved in maintaining that, such as building houses, agriculture, warfare, and ceremonial activities. A nation would be a larger tribe, consisting of various bands or clusters.

A preliminary search on Facebook using 'tribe' as a term immediately connects the importance of group with history. Every group using 'tribe' as their name also present a connection with history. On Instagram, the search produces more of a familial connection – groups of families, pets, and history. We most definitely have a pull to the past when we are thinking about tribes. Overall, associations with tribes also show an affinity or loyalty with others about something, whatever that is.

Workbook

Time for some research. I would like you to now do a quick search on one of the key social media platforms and search your own tribal affinities. Type in those hobbies or interests you have, and see which groups or people come up. Add them as friends, and begin the connection!

I could spend some time exploring the differences in how tribes structure themselves - i.e., some are egalitarian, others stratified, and others with more complex social ranking. However, this would detract from our real work here. We are not here to study anthropology - we need to understand the importance of being part of a tribe, and then work out how to improve how we function in relationships in order to improve our spiritual practice.

Most tribes no longer have a legitimacy to conduct their own traditional functions outside of the nation they reside in - they can only tithe and tax within the rules of the nation they inhabit, and all of us need to operate and abide by the laws within the nation in which we reside. Let's remember polygamy for example, this only occurs in certain countries where the law allows. In the U.K. for example, as it is illegal, it 'does not happen'... as far as we are aware!

Humans connect with others more familiarly on the basis of things, such as marriage, race, or gender, a process referred to as Homophily, which is a sociological concept that describes the tendency of humans to associate and bond with others similar to them. I am reminded of the term, 'birds of a feather flock together', which is an accurate way of talking about this concept. Over 100 studies have been completed that have observed homophily in some form or another. Similarity breeds connection. The homophily principles are that we will network on the basis of every type, including marriage, race, religion, work, support, information transfer, and friendship. We may connect on the basis of our interest in spirituality, but homophily in race and ethnicity creates the strongest divides in our personal environment, followed by age, religion, education, occupation, and gender following in roughly that order. I know we are in the age whereby we are supposed to embrace difference, but in doing so, we deny a significant part of our nature. We are tribal creatures; whilst we may tolerate and enjoy difference, we will always feel closer to that which feels similar.

When we think about tribes in history, Caucasians may initially be drawn to the ancient tribes of the U.K., i.e., the Caledonii. They may then think about wider Europe and remember the ancient Viking tribes. They may then move towards Rome and remember the Roman tribes, and their role in history. African folk may feel a pull more towards Africa, and the various tribes there, and so on. Tribal characteristics are such an integral part of our history that we have no problem in understanding, reading about, and processing their role in our lives. What we struggle more with now is the natural tendency to connect with sameness, within the umbrella of the nation, and the expectation to interact from a more logical place in our heads rather than our hearts. But what is the connection with tribalism and spirituality?

Virtually, every tribe in the world has a form of spiritual practice. Let's have a look at a few, however, to understand a few of the ways in which we connect and have connected with spirituality. In anthropological studies of tribes in India, indigenous tribal groups celebrate a nature worship, including prayers and rituals. Nature is revered as God, and elements of nature, i.e., trees, are worshipped. There is a distinct inter-relationship between the provision of nature and human thanks (Rowkith and Bhagwan, 2020).

The rich spirituality of Africa is also well documented. Traditional belief systems, based on openness and adaptation, endure. Jacob Olupona researched African spiritual systems, and he was keen to be clear that these are defined as pre-Christian or pre-Islamic colonisation of Africa. He goes as far to say that African spirituality cannot be separated from the everyday or mundane, and that it is holistic. Another key factor is that the system is not closed, that ancestry can be equal to deities, and ancestors hold such power that, if they felt a shrine was not being properly maintained, misfortune may befall the caretaker. It is only in the past 100 years that religious colonisation has occurred, prior to that, Africans wholly practiced indigenous African spirituality.

In pre-Christian Europe not so much is known, as mentioned in other chapters. This was due to the excision of everything that went before Christianity; in short, the Christianisation of Europe. However, we know that spirituality was polytheistic, meaning that there were multiple deities, and we know lots about who they are, although much has been lost. Different tribes would have worshipped different deities, depending on their particular beliefs. It seems that the belief systems would have probably correlated to those in Africa and India with a focus upon the seasons, nature, and fertility.

Workbook

Take a candle and sit in your meditation space. Spend some time in placement meditation (i.e., relaxing), using whichever technique fits for you. Then begin to take your mind to the tribes of the world, floating in and out of those you have knowledge of, and also those you do not. See what they wear, what they eat, and what it feels like for the members to be together. This is not an anthropological study, just a way for you to emotionally occupy the space within a tribe.

Finding Your Tribe

Now, we are no longer in 1,500 BCE, so you will probably find yourself somewhere in the world, probably not living in the Indian jungle. I am also not advocating that you pack up and move to the Outer Hebrides on an uninhabited island. You may actually live in a house or an apartment, and probably live somewhere near to a city or a large town. Even if you live rurally, you probably have neighbours nearby. I imagine you work, or have worked, and most will have some element of a family, even if estranged. You may have some friends, and you may also have some connections in your world. You may know some of your neighbours, and have different relationships. This is, for you, your primary tribe; likely a non-spiritual tribe – people whom you just share life with.

In terms of your recovery and healing, we now need to think about where to find your tribe, how to get it together, and what you bring to the table in terms of improving your current capacity. I am not going to spend too long on this point as the basic reality is a need to find groups of people who share common interests. You do not need me to describe how to identify your interests and how to connect with those groups. Let's do an exercise to make this clear.

Workbook

Identify the kinds of spirituality you are interested in.

- **Do you need to get back to church?**
- **Do you want to convert to a different kind of religion or spiritual practice?**
- **Is there a part of the world that you are drawn to?**
- **Are you interested in developing a kind of practice, i.e., insight meditation?**
- **Where are these practitioners based?**
- **What kinds of people do you want to be involved with?**

Once you have written some ideas down, jump aboard a search engine and begin the search. Obviously, be wary of the cults out there – I do not want you to sell yourself out to something you cannot get back from. So, please do your homework thoroughly.

In reality, given what we know about our inherent drive towards tribalism, you are more likely to enjoy the group that fits your own demographic – white adult women will enjoy connecting with others, and black adolescent men will get more from groups with that demographic. It is no coincidence that those kinds of groups are more popular than the more diverse ones. Now, to be clear, I appear to be supporting separatism here, but please do not get that impression, I am just generally encouraging people to get out of their comfort zone. In my fantasy, we can create wondrous groups full of diverse peoples who are able to put difference aside to connect in the most amazing ways. And I recognise the human's propensity to move towards sameness rather than difference. I encourage you to be realistic about the kinds of groups you will be more drawn to, but also open to getting yourself out of your comfort zone wherever possible – change and difference can lead to amazing things. Let's move back to our friends and family now for thinking about how well we make connections with others.

Exploring Your Relationships

Inevitably, you will have different levels of connection with different people at different times. You may be quite intimate with some people, and others you may not talk to at all. You may find that all your friends share your own demographic, but you may even have friends who share none of your demographic. I would be highly surprised if any of you who are over 30 regularly interact with groups of 18-year-olds, and vice versa. However your friendship circles work for you, you will inevitably find yourself going deeper emotionally with some people, and less with others. I want to share a diagram here to illustrate something.

The diagram below is the 'circles of intimacy'. I originally found this in a book by Herbert Fensterheim thirty years ago. Herbert is a master psychologist, therapist, and author. The diagram refers to levels of intimacy with others. The innermost circle is your most private parts that you may or may not share with others at all. The B circle is that which you may share with your closest friends and family, and the C circle is about the close friendships we have, and also some work colleagues we may have known for a while; maybe even our spiritual guides or companions. Circles D and E refer to the more superficial relationships with people we may not see often, the E circle probably being for those shopkeepers we may buy papers from once a week.

Circles of relational intimacy

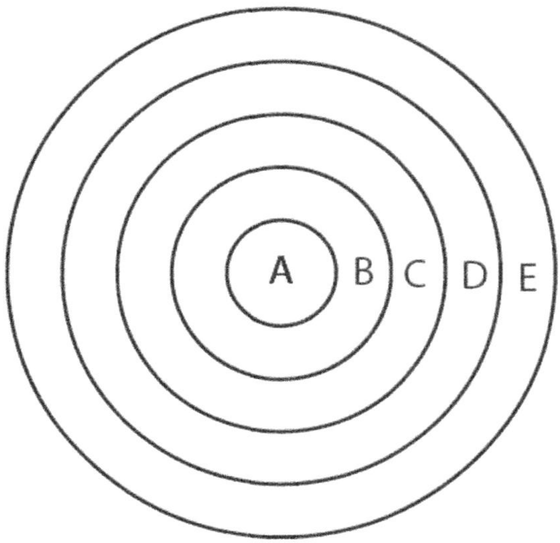

It should be said that this model is for real contact. This was developed before the internet and was a technique to support change in real time. Social media will not offer you anything in terms of developing connection with others in life. You can talk about your connections there, but this is not and never will be real connection. Even connection with real people on video conferencing feels very different to real life. Please bear that in mind when beginning to use this model in life.

Workbook

Re-read the information on the circles of intimacy and apply the model to your own circle of friends and acquaintances.

- **Who do you let into which circle?**
- **What patterns of relating do you notice?**
- **How do you feel you relate to others in terms of intimacy?**

Now, in the previous exercise, you should have been able to explore a little about how you do in terms of intimacy. I encourage you to not only think about when and what you share with people, but also reflect on why this is the case. What happened to you that got in the way of being healthily intimate with people? Do you over-share? Do you under-share? How could you work out a way of gradually and carefully getting yourself out of your comfort zone? Do you avoid real contact in favour of social media? As a clinician, I am extremely concerned by the number of young people who connect with others only on social media, and who just block someone when there is difference, which creates an unrealistic sense of how relationships with others work. You cannot just block your boss because she said something you disliked. You cannot block your dad because he makes you clean up after yourself. Therefore, when joining your tribe, I encourage you to find real tribes wherever possible. And in saying that, there are obvious cultural shifts taking place – we no longer have a job for life, meaning that those skills we had to deal with the people we worked with for years, not just a six-month contract, are being lost. Our capacity to tolerate and enjoy difference is diminishing.

Also, which time zone do you share from – do you share solely from the past, i.e., tell people everything that happened to you in the past, or do you share solely from the future? How do you deal with people you do not connect with, but need to? Do you use your phone as a way of reinforcing unhelpful ways of relating to other people? Do you only talk about what you want to happen? Are you actually present at all? Do you ever share anything from the here and now? I doubt it – it can sound weird, even though it is by far the most beneficial place to be in terms of recovery and healing. Our hurt does not occur in the here and now, and is a myth from our ego.

I also believe that there are important cultural differences with how we relate. In the U.K., we are typically more 'stiff upper lip'. We queue in orderly ways and engage in social chit chat much less. When we arrive in the U.S., it can be a huge culture shock for us finding a waitress expressing interest in our accents. I personally love the American vivacity, understanding it as a means of adapting to living in such vast, uninhabited areas, needing to connect with strangers competently.

Anxiety and Value

Many people who have survived complex abuse and trauma can end up struggling in relationships. Survivors of childhood bullying can, in particular, develop a real aversion and anxiety to connecting with people socially, which may be the case for you. I just want to say that how you survived what happened is ok. Many of us carry our wounds in this manner. In a way, what happened creates a template for further difficulties in the future. The research is unequivocally clear – childhood abuse and trauma often predict problems in adulthood. There is a notoriously challenging problem around survivors getting themselves into re-traumatising relationships as an adult. We victimise ourselves subconsciously, and inhibit our recovery.

This seems to be about our ego clinging with horror and disbelief at what happened and urging our mind in the present to continue to process and relive the experience. This is not about blame, but many of you may recognise how you always end up with the wrong kind of person – always end up being re-traumatised, or hanging out with people who act out difficult behaviours. I have news for you – today is the end of that. Today is the time for you to put all of that in the annals of history. Today is the time for you to step into the new you, the new way of relating where you get your needs met, and where you allow yourself to be loved.

And so, connecting with strangers can just seem too over-whelming, particularly when we are young and developing. I used to find connecting with strangers nigh on impossible, which is one of the reasons for coming across Herbert Fensterheim in the first instance! I still tend to be invisible in larger group gatherings. We may never properly disconnect from our childhood creative adjustments, but we most definitely need to be vigilant to them, so they do not contaminate our capacity to be present. As mentioned previously, creative adjustments were the ways we adjusted to difficult situations in childhood, which served us well, but less so now we are in adulthood. This is why we need to understand them and modify them. This is, after all, about heightening your capacity for connection with others and about making ourselves ready for contact with other people. But why is this so important?

Impact of Loneliness

As mentioned above, the importance of human connection is unequivocally clear – we need it for survival. Here are a few pointers to remember when talking about this. There is an increasing evidence base that points to the impact of loneliness on health. The mental health charity, Mind, reports that loneliness leads to various mental health problems, including depression, anxiety, low self-esteem, sleep problems, and increased stress. But the issues are not only psychological in nature. For older people in particular, loneliness and social isolation have been linked to a variety of higher risks for various health conditions – high blood pressure, heart disease, obesity, a weakened immune system, cognitive decline, and even death. Social isolation is associated with a 50% increased risk of dementia, and poor social relationships are associated with a 29% increased risk of heart disease, and similarly for increased risk of stroke. It has been variously cited across the world that loneliness can be a bigger killer than smoking. Take a minute or two for that to sink in.

Now, I would immediately jump on this and make the connection with what we know about tribes, and the impact on health. It is as though our bodies and minds are wired for connection. However, we can only truly relate to others in the present moment – we often, through anxiety, try to connect in some perceived future. This happens so many times on dating apps. I personally know someone who met another person on a dating app and agreed to meet the woman in person to run away together. He left a note for his wife and went to the train station. The woman did not arrive, and his wife did not want him back (curiously). Important lessons learned here, which I suggest you remain vigilant to. Engaging someone out of real time, via messaging, is not real life. Do not find out the reality of this when it is too late. It is very easy to take your anxiety from the here and now daydream about the future where it does not feel as threatening, and commit to contact in that time zone. But you could well pay the price somewhere along the line.

There is a difference between being alone and feeling loneliness. The former generally brings some benefits and calmness, whereas the latter leads to ill health. And what may feel a tolerable level of aloneness for one person may be intolerable for another. We all have our limits. During the Covid lockdown, I felt extremely lonely. Endless sessions and lectures on the computer with significantly less meaningful human connection than usual left me feeling quite lost a lot of the time. My mental health deteriorated, and as soon I noticed it going downhill, I made some important changes to transform my internal sense of self. The notion of contact, or being part of a tribe, is fundamentally important to our well-being, which is why the lockdown was so difficult for so many people. We are wired for contact, and engaging in spiritual practices is a way to consolidate relationships, sharing insight, and growing in relationship.

Let's look at attachment for a moment, an increasingly common term that has become part of the lexicon, particularly for therapists. The key principle underpinning it is that, essentially, mammals need to bond with other mammals to thrive. Mammals bear live children. Think about whales even, their off-spring are born live, and remain close to their mother throughout their 'youth'. Humans are no different. Our babies are, throughout the entire animal kingdom, more dependent on our primary care-givers for longer. Babies cannot even feed themselves for many months, and it takes years rather than days to stand. How many animals do you know that can stand immediately after birth? This is a requirement for survival.

During the time that all our needs are being met by our primary care-giver (this does not necessarily need to be a woman, although we are biologically predisposed to this), we are attaching to them. Our brain development happens as a direct result of this connection, or attachment. Our carer's availability impacts our growth and development. If they are unavailable or in another way, such as addiction, we realise that our needs may not be met. We become more self-reliant that is healthy, and in adulthood, we sometimes develop a chronic inability to take support from others. If a carer is scary and aggressive, this can lead children to develop fear responses, hyper-vigilance, and constantly wary of our needs being met. This distress can lead to what we call a 'disorganised attachment'. There are numerous ways in which we can be impacted by our primary care-givers, but the key is that we need to work out how we have been impacted. There are rough guidelines, and any reading of the attachment literature can be helpful, but you have to work it out yourself. Do not let anyone tell you or interpret it for you. I recommend that you read the book by Sue Gerhardt entitled, *Why Love Matters*? This will give you a distinct and comprehensive understanding about why this relationship is so fundamental. Attachment difficulties will most definitely impact you for life, although recovery is possible. This is why people like myself write books like this!

Workbook

Cast your mind back to your childhood and explore your relationship with your primary care-giver.

- **What stories are you aware of about you as a baby?**
- **Were you 'naughty' or 'unsettled'?**
- **What do you know about your primary care-giver?**
- **Were they 'available'?**
- **Did anything happen to you?**
- **Did you spend long periods of time in hospital?**
- **Were you ill?**
- **Is there anything else that might have interrupted your attachment?**
- **Most importantly, what do you feel is the impact on you now?**

Contact

Ok, so we have explored the importance of tribes, and looked at ways you can identify possible tribes to become involved with. We have also looked at how you feel you function in relationships. I hope that you have begun to develop an idea about your strengths and limitations. We now need to focus on what amazing connections are like – hopefully you can then begin to develop your own. Most importantly, know what you are aiming for – when our histories are so tarnished with problematic relationships, we need to sometimes learn from external processes to incorporate them in our own. And as importantly, improving our capacity to relate takes time. We cannot and should not expect to immediately be perfect at this. Certainly, being less encumbered by our histories or fears of the future will help connect now, but it can take years to fully develop our capacity to connect.

I am going to introduce the concept of Gestalt Contact here.

Although this is a psychotherapeutic term, it originates from Eastern philosophies and is also heavily influenced by the work of Martin Buber. And in itself, we could probably trace the concept back to previous times, when it was called something else. Contact happens at what is referred to as the contact boundary, the space between you and I in the consulting room. It is also the space between you and your lover on, say, a date. You are both there, attempting to contact, but with both having various skills and limitations; you may struggle with congruence (needing to be the same as someone else), they may struggle with honesty. Both negatively impact presence. You may struggle with congruence because you imagine that if you are fully authentic you will be rejected. Thus, you become concerned with the future, and possibly disconnect from the present. Your lover may have a similar process. Contact is not a space you can see, but it is there. We meet at the contact boundary, you bring yourself there, and I bring myself. What happens between us at the contact boundary emerges during the session. The key is remaining present, but the reality is often very different.

The contact boundary is also the space between your mind and Self. The Self is the formulation of your being. The mind is that which is referred to in the previous chapter. The Self contact boundary is vital for our self-awareness, our growth, and our healing. If we never situate our consciousness there, how can we ever truly heal? It is our mind that we access at the contact boundary. The boundary is where we explore the Self, raise our self-awareness, and learn about our Self as perceived by the mind. We access the subconscious through the conscious, and we need to open ourselves to whatever the universe shows us through this mechanism.

At the contact boundary with others is where we also learn about ourselves. We learn how we are perceived and how we support other organisms to grow and heal. We may also discover how we sometimes negatively impact others. Part of our task is to work out how to relate to others with love and care. In doing this, we have to differentiate between relating to people in an I-Thou way or in an I-It way. The former means that we attune to the other completely with care and respect – we immerse ourselves in their experience of us and modify what we do to help them be in the here and now. The latter is when we objectify people, dismiss them, and hurt them. Relating to someone in the I-Thou way requires skills around patience and understanding; most importantly, it requires empathy. Empathy often takes a hit when we are traumatised as we necessarily move from the capacity to care and be open to others to care for ourselves. Spiritual healing requires a courageous move away from meeting self needs to meeting and being with others. Contact is nigh on impossible to write about because most people read it retrospectively – contact is far better to learn about in person, observed.

Interestingly, our brains have developed as a direct result of contact with others. Originally, our brains were wired just for survival – to hunt, kill, and procreate. Over thousands of years, subsequent layers developed in our brain, leading to the idea of the triune brain. The outermost cortex is that which was developed in relation to others. As our tribes widened, and we needed to socialise with others in a more organised way, our brains needed to adapt. We developed skills of compassion, understanding, and to talk more coherently and fluently. We have, therefore, developed our brain to adapt to the need to be with others – let's not let it go to waste. Whilst our minds may continue into eternity, we are present here, now. And this is where our work is required. Anything we develop positively here will, regardless of which belief system you adopt, positively impact our futures.

Maybe this is an opportunity to talk briefly about karma, which refers to actions – the art of doing, and the impact of actions, which tends to mean that good actions result in better karma. Traditionally, many people have believed that karma is something we need to do to prevent problems in future lives, but that our lives here were impacted by the past lives. This may or may not be the truth. The reality, though, is that we are here now. I am sure you will all realise that if we do a bad deed now, this impacts us here and now. Let me give you an example. If you stole something from work and were found out, what would happen? You may be invited for an interview with the police. You may lose your job. Your colleagues may lose confidence in you, and your family members may also be impacted by what happened. This is karma in the here and now. We reap what we sow.

Let me give you another example. Whilst I worked as a social worker, I got extremely stressed, and became quite irritable and defensive. I would snap at people and thought nothing of being direct towards others to get what I wanted. This led to changes in my 'field'. I imagine that people grew more wary of me, and colleagues and bosses allocated me less responsibility. People inevitably lost faith in me. As my presence faded, my role at the contact boundary contaminated those I came into contact with.

In retrospect, I understand that my whole capacity to relate was absorbed in concern for the future and hung up in processing the past. Eventually, I realised what was happening for me, and I left social work. I have never regretted it, not just for the impact on my own life, but because the system is unfit for purpose.

I subsequently spent many years working on myself, trying to let go of the layers of hurt and harm I had experienced; vicarious trauma that I had subsequently been acting out towards others. It took many years of dedicated spiritual practice to recover from. My karma had also been impacted. As I developed a particular kind of reputation (I guess), people were less likely to want to work with me, and they formed an opinion about me. This shows how the here and now actions impact our future. I have worked hard over many years to make vital changes in the way I connect with others, and I share this not to scare, but to help you honestly reflect on how you relate to other people, and to think about how to do something different if you need to. Right now.

Back to contact. So, contact is, at its best, the superlative relationship. It is the most incredible connection we have ever had with someone. It is akin to being with the person who we love more than anything, and leaves us alive with warmth, connection, and a vibrancy. But contact is a constant process, rather than a specific state of being. It is therefore difficult to define as it also differs to each of us. What might feel like contact to one, won't feel sufficient for another. I think of contact as the way in which a mother looks at her newborn child. The child stares at the mother, and the mother stares at the child. The child is held with love, the most amazing love we can imagine. In that moment of the process, neither can get anything wrong, and both souls merge into a sense of oneness; contact. Both are utterly available for the other, both present, and both infinitely connected in the microcosm of the universe.

To experience contact, we need to surrender ourselves to it as well as the possibility, and the mechanism of what we can create. The essence of human existence is contact with both the Self and others. Contact is where one person meets the outside world, or the universe. It is also where we survive and grow to maturity. We cannot just do this alone. Some of you may feel that you are not capable of achieving such a high level of contact or relational awareness with another being. Most of us cannot, but that should not mean we should not try. Every organism is capable of effective and fulfilling contact with others in their own existence. The key is to be in the process of contact with others and the Self. There is no ideal or constant.

All contact is creative and dynamic. How I create contact in my world is different to you, but this is linked to the uniqueness of our role in the universe. Each experience between us unfolds as a creative adjustment between us, the organism, and the universe. Also, we only experience contact in the here and now. We do not experience contact in something that happened last week, and nor do we experience it in the future. We can all 'interrupt' contact in various ways, for example, through deflecting. A lover may want to connect on a deep way, but you feel nervous and crack a joke; deflection. You may be the kind of person who always keeps their feelings inside and keep a lid on things, which is called retroflection. Contact is also, however, not merging with the other. This is called confluence, and when we lose our Self in the other, this actually interrupts contact as we lose our sense of separateness.

Workbook

I would like you to calm the body, and just spend some time letting go of whatever is figural for you right now. Try not to attach to any thought. Then open yourself to the process of contact with the Self. Think about how you view yourself. Do you treat your Self with kindness and care? Are you intolerant? Do you fill yourself with shame? As you become aware of the mechanisms of connection with the Self, let them go. These do not serve you well and have no right contaminating your growth. Practice this frequently, and remain vigilant to how this part of your capacity for contact can creep in.

Ancestry

As we consider our tribal connections in the here and now, and as we relate to the universe in new, and more respectful ways, we most certainly improve our karmic tendencies. We attract more of what we need, rather than more of what we do not need. But the final component of this is the greater awareness of our ancestry.

As we grow, we may experience the loss of a grandparent, but as we get older, more and more people tend to drop off. We lose loved ones, partners, friends, and become increasingly isolated. We then eventually also pass, often having never fully lived. What I am describing here is the inter-connectedness of life; we are our ancestors. We are those subtle rhythms in this domain. We may well move away from consciously being like, say, our parents, but most of us will find their voices coming out of us at different times. We will find ourselves repeating certain concepts or jokes, and still probably eat similar foodstuffs to them. Even though our ancestors are not around us in the flesh, they still inhabit our existence. Take some very recent research which explores the exposure of pregnant mothers to stress; the female children in particular are indelibly marked with this stress for their life and their children. We pick up our grandparents' distress in the womb! Our ancestors are our genetic tribe.

Workbook

Find some images of people from your history. Go as far back as you can. Put the images on your altar, or your desk (if there is a difference!). During ceremonies, include their names. Pray for them to be around you during ritual practice. They will be there. They will hear your voice.

Each of our current benefits can and should be attributed to those who went before us. I thank my grandparents for instilling in me a love of language; my openness and love of language is directly from them. I thank my father for supporting me practically through my education; I learned because of him. I thank my mother for feeding me and teaching me how to relate. The way I relate is most definitely attributable to my parents and wider family. I still say 'cheese on toast' in a Yorkshire accent as my family hinted at me changing once I had moved away My family descended from their parents. And we learn generationally.

When I look at my DNA, I also realise that I am 99% from the UK. My ancestors were all from this land, and my DNA is that of my ancestors. I urge you to connect with your own DNA testing – find out where your ancestors come from to deepen your connection and awareness of your own history. I share the ancestry part, as it is with spiritual application and learning that we can understand the impact of our ancestry on us in the here and now. We can also connect and relate to them in the present through various spiritual techniques and processes. Whilst I could not teach you the art of spiritual journeying here in a book, and would not want to, I urge you to learn and attend those tribes where such practices are commonplace. Talk to your ancestors, connect with them, and love them. Fill in the gaps, say the things you always wanted to say but never could. Continue the here and now connection of your mind with theirs.

Conclusion

I hope you now have a greater awareness of the importance of attuning yourself to the need of contact with others. We need to find our clan. If you struggle to fit or to find someone, come and join mine. This is truly an integral part of our process, and we can use concepts such as the circles of intimacy and contact to really develop what we do, in the cold light of day, in the here and now. Our minds can and will only benefit.

10. A Natural Spirituality

The Everyman

The everyman isn't always something that we immediately relate to as an idea. However, I've used this archetype due to its meaning of being average and relatable. Plus, the everyone is found in everyday life. Indeed, the everyman is nature because nature is around us all. We breathe nature, we interact with nature, and we take nature into our bodies each day. Our lives are also controlled by the seasons of nature, so even though there is strange and curious, powerful magic in nature, it is everywhere, and we need to relate to this far more centrally and normally as an everyman archetype.

I consider characters in popular culture such as Homer Simpson, and any character played by Ben Affleck, as the everyman personality or archetype. And as we know, every movie we see Mr Affleck in, magic and growth always occurs. There are elements of heroism and change within the everyman, meaning that when we connect with nature as a transformative, normal process, we can also affect miracles.

In respect of the strengths and difficulties for the everyman, the first strength is that this archetype is grounded and the salt of the Earth. However, there are also weaknesses, such as a lack of preparedness for issues. Obviously, we cannot expect nature to be prepared for what the human population is going to wreak on it, but it is important to think about the how the land lies in terms of responsibilities.

Workbook

Take your workbook out, and write about the everyman as you understand it right now.

- **How does the archetype of the everyman resonate with you?**
- **How does the everyman resonate with your past?**
- **Is there a way that the qualities of the everyman could serve you well in your transformation?**

Nature is, for myself, the most important part of our spiritual journey; nature is what we are, and is what our existence is about. We are nature. And it is my view that the celebration and reverence of nature needs to be fundamental to our spiritual recovery and growth. We are the pulsing rhythm of nature. We may wish to objectify and separate ourselves from it, but this is foolish. By denying nature or minimising this, we deny our own existence. Within this cleaving unto nature, we obviously need to remain attuned to our own process, but not to forget or shut out the power of the universe in which we live.

As mentioned in previous chapters, we are innately attuned to the vibration of the earth (earthing), and dependent upon its functioning entirely to survive. Let alone thrive. We therefore need to situate nature at the forefront of everything we do. Going out and hugging the nearest tree may not seem to trigger the most powerful and immediate changes in our psyche, but the capacity to respect nature, to consider how dependent we are upon its successful operation, will affect change.

Subsequently, in this chapter, we will explore and work with the importance of nature as the obvious manifestation of the cycle of life. I will introduce you to a range of nature-based practices to re-attune your connection with nature, and as importantly, yourself. In order to do this, we will begin – perhaps predictably - by revisiting our historical drive towards nature, and then try to understand why nature was so important to our ancestors. And this is true wherever you are in the world, this isn't just a euro-centric phenomena.

In addition, we will also fill our workbook with ideas and plans to help develop our thinking and sense of nature as we see it in our minds. If I am honest, most people underestimate the importance of nature. We stroll along, mostly entitled, and oblivious to the wonders around us. We take the food on our table for granted, without the slightest interest in where it came from. We shovel huge amounts of food down our gullets without a care in the world for the depleting stocks. The fact that so many animals are becoming extinct or being farmed mercilessly seems to be out of our interest as long as our needs are being met.

Even more lamentably, we are also developing a desensitisation with the message that we need to do something drastically different. Many people are just tired of it all. Humans have become so self-focused that they have lost almost complete sense of the other; we probably won't realise this until it is too late, when the environmental changes cause such irreversible and catastrophic change, that there isn't a chance to do anything.

So many of us do nothing but read about the damage to nature complacently and then go on with our lives, doing nothing consequentially. Would we be as disinterested if someone hurt us directly? We would probably have lots to say as this would be in our direct field. Yet so many of us intentionally and consciously do nothing – how many times have you seen rubbish dumped, or fast-food wrappers thrown from cars? How many of us solely buy organic and move away from mass consumerism? Who litters in my street? What do big celebrations look like in your home – are they filled with black sacks full of presents that the children may open and discard after a couple of plays? Are there bins full of wasted food after every meal? How many of us intentionally try to reduce their footprint? Do you know people who do not have a clue about what an environmental footprint is? In the cold light of day, can you honestly say that you are doing enough, or at least as much as you can?

Workbook

Let us do an inventory of your home and lifestyle. Think about the last big seasonal celebration you had – Christmas, Hannukah, Ramadan – list the things you threw away in as much detail as possible. How much wrapping paper, how many feasts did you make, and how much food was thrown away? What kinds of things do you throw away more than anything else? Now think about what you could have done differently, and explore what it would have meant to either you or the family.

Wider Problems with Living Naturally

I often hear about how expensive it is to live ethically, and there is truth in this – organic foods are more expensive, and ethical goods have the ethical price tag. I also know that people in poverty especially often have other, more immediate things to focus upon, like surviving, or dealing with the impact of poverty. But this is not an excuse for doing nothing. And I say that as someone who has lived in poverty. None of us have an excuse. Having an excuse is the problem, and it is a way of describing a defence mechanism, which is way of avoiding feeling shame. Defence mechanisms also keep us in fixed patterns of relating, and as long as we are defending our position, we will remain stuck. This reality applies to everything.

I hear lots about how some people are anxious about what is happening to our wondrous planet, but how many of us are truly trying to do something significant? This is not a one-man job, it requires us all to pull our weight. However, we continue to watch Mukbangs on YouTube, comfy in our sheltered existences, happy to celebrate over-eating and over-consumerisation, completely unfamiliar with the toil required in producing the food and products we take for granted. We all want the latest gadgets, the latest clothes, the flashiest cars; immediate gratification. When did you last mend some socks? The most popular people on the planet are those who have lots of stuff, the biggest houses, the largest wardrobes – how much do we admire those with three hundred pairs of shoes? We watch the movie stars in their glamorous lives and want to be like the Kardashians (not me though, just to be clear). We are influenced by the influencers. We follow suit. But we are ultimately just too comfortable, and the universe feels it. The more immersed in consuming we get, the less spiritual we are.

Even with the climate crisis, there are some shocking trends. There is unequivocal evidence of the danger we are in. The primary achievement we could get is the removal of our dependence on fossil fuels. Instead, Governments are focused on recycling, in effect, putting the responsibility back on to individuals, when in fact, it is the Governments around the world that need to act decisively. Recycling is helpful, but more radical action is needed.

We walk around local parks and woodland, oblivious to the effort and skill that goes into making the space amazing. Many of us just have someone else do our dirty work at home because our properties are too large for us. We pay others to do what we could easily do because we are too busy, the task is too large, we have other concerns. How many of you have paid for cleaners or gardeners? How many of you would change your entire outfit every day, sometimes more frequently? How many take baths every day, and showers twice a day, lubricating our dried skin with endless creams and ointments? If we lived within our means, took less of the resources, this would not even figure. However, this is probably the tip of the iceberg.

We also have little interest in what goes on around us unless it is likely to directly impact us. We do not care about landfill unless we have to see it or live near it. We do not care about nuclear experimentation until the explosions could personally impact us. We waste resources without a thought in the world, as long as our needs are being met. We still justify a holiday abroad, four times a year, because we work hard. We will use the car five times a day just for convenience, and we tell ourselves it is because we do not have time. Good old time gets the blame for lots of things. It is no wonder we are becoming more indolent, more isolated. Human beings are consummately selfish, adept at meeting our own needs. And in that statement, I also deflected from reality – by talking about humans in the third person, I do not talk about myself, which is exactly how subtle the problem is.

Whilst this is happening, the universe is a ticking time-bomb. And all of this is an obvious, inconvenient truth that we are now desensitised to. I cannot tar everyone with the same brush, however. I know lots of people who have given their jobs and livelihoods up for the cause. In fact, as I write this chapter I am reminded of Wynn Bruce's self-immolation. This is a man who set fire to himself in front of the supreme court in America in order to demonstrate the danger we are in. The sacrifice was barely reported upon. In all, there are many, many people out there who fully realise the dire potential of where we are. And this is not just the Greta Thunbergs. I know many normal people making huge sacrifices, diligently recycling, walking more, trying to make some changes. And we all know there is probably too much to do in too little time, which is a separate matter altogether to begin to process.

But remembering nature as the embodiment of the universe in this dimension is vital to making changes. If we have a chance of avoiding extinction, it is an Earth-based practice such as this that will lead us back into awareness, back into respect, and back into a life that is based on nature. We have to create a symbiotic relationship with that which is vital to existence. We have to take ownership of what we do, why we are doing it, with full awareness of the impact on the universe. It is only through developing a love and reverence for nature that we can truly complete the purpose of our life. It is time to change. It is time to re-sensitise ourselves to nature. By reducing our exploitation of resources, even in practical ways, and offering love and toil to nature, we become more aligned to the natural rhythms of the universe in this dimension and create a new harmony, a new way of being, a new hope for life. By re-aligning ourselves to the rhythm and flow of nature, we step nearer to survival. And through our nature practice and the care and support we offer externally we can help develop our capacity to care for ourselves.

Workbook

Let's look at your defence mechanisms a little more. We need to go into ourselves to recognise the kinds of excuses we give ourselves for not doing enough to help nature. In the cold light of day, sit down and identify ten excuses that you have given yourself over the past six months.

*** How do you reconcile getting another takeaway coffee when you have tea in your staff room?**
*** What do you say to yourself when you throw litter on the ground?**
*** What do you say when you nip out to the supermarket in your car for a bottle of milk, when it could take ten minutes on foot?**
*** What are the factors that make you more likely to do something practical?**
*** What would lead you to make a larger commitment, now, to the climate emergency?**

Be brave, be honest, and work out the kinds of defences you have going on in your internal world.

___

___

My Story

Let me tell you a little about why this is important to me, and also what I have learnt. During my own distress in previous years, I lost sense of who I was. I had no awareness of anything other than my own hurt. I was consumed by my internal hurt, although I was clearly trying to stay alive and recover from the upset. In that hurt, I would eat anything, resist recycling, and have little insight into the effort it took to bring whatever I wanted to my table. I did not care, I had better things to do, and left the recycling to the 'hippies'. The more distressed I became, the less able I was to be present and open to the world. At the peak of my distress, I acted the worst towards others, which is common to us all. It is so easy to say we just need to do something, when in fact, we need to make sure we are emotionally able to do what we need to do. We often spout off so many simplistic statements without any understanding. How many times have you heard those ethical yet rhetorical statements such as 'Save the Planet' and just let them drift out of our mind? I was exactly the same.

But I was also stuck by this peripheral concern from the world leaders and spiritual gurus. Many were also delivering rhetoric, but nature was never the centrepiece of their existence. It was one of their many tasks, and although I imagine there is some genuine concern somewhere, the lack of responsiveness to where we are reflects the lack of deep awareness and capacity to empathise with our plight. My personal position is that if someone truly understood something empathically, if they honestly and fully recognised something completely, they would be unable to do anything different but change. If you honestly understood how you had hurt someone, and how their lives had been damaged irreparably, you could not help but be impacted. Part of the world leaders' defensiveness is about the reality that they won't fully experience the real impact – it will be our descendants - and this is also why they drag their heels; it is not real for them.

My change did not happen overnight, though, but over some years. There was no revelatory situation. I just noticed more going on in the outside world. I began to react to people fly-tipping, and noticing the impact on the environment. I engaged in dialogue with others and developed my opinions on the topics. Most importantly, it was the people I came into contact with who impacted me most.

I had someone who came to me in obvious distress about the impact of the environment on his children. Watching and hearing his genuine concern deeply impacted me – I remember thinking about how my own family could be impacted by this. He left his job and livelihood, devoting all his resources to a vital climate activism position. How could I not be impacted by this?

And with this in my mind, I would watch the 'leaders' with horror, especially the spiritual leaders, who had nothing in their manuals or books that suggested a need to incorporate nature centrally within everything we do. I would meditate faithfully, hear the rhetoric from spiritual leaders, and see no meaningful action. I also probably gave my own autonomy to them – I expected them to do something; giving the responsibility to someone else is another example of a defence mechanism. I can then, in some future time, blame them. Religious organisations also focused on filling their pews with practitioners, or ensuring that people came to the mosque five times a day. This also contributed to my disillusion, and me stepping back from the larger organisations.

There are many spiritual organisations out there (who will remain nameless), who, on the surface, have great environmental credentials, but also have limitations. They still need to earn money from people to support the ones who live in the sanctuaries, and they do this by encouraging people to travel for massive journeys, often to remote areas of the world. I have been one of those people. Whilst I have also travelled there, and whilst they are probably one of the most ethically aware organisations out there, there are still limitations. Prior to lockdown, one particular organisation's members would earn millions each year from charitable income and from visitors, most of which went to salaries. They recycle food waste and do some gardening, and they are involved in various green projects outside the centre to be fair, but they also build new, large houses frequently on the site, eating up more resources. We cannot get more land, is my point in this.

The Buddhists also have problematic practices, take one large Buddhist centre on the border of Scotland, for example. It started as just a farmhouse on the land, but gradually and systematically, they have built more houses and more buildings, and the land now looks like a Tibetan theme park with towering, gold statues of Tara, and a huge temple over several floors, much of which is not even used, just saved for important visitors. Nature seems to have been forgotten in the quest to convert. None of us are above nature. I know these comments are probably controversial, but it is time to own the inconvenient truths; none of us are exempt. And more importantly, we need to do something about it. When I have shared that feedback with the relevant organisations, the denial is astonishing. I have no doubt that things will continue as is, but will continue to work on an optimistic outlook wherever possible.

Do not worry though, this book is not going to expose climate deniers – I want to just highlight the kinds of problems that are getting in the way of the climate crisis – greed, lack of awareness, defensiveness, and insecurity. And more importantly, I want us to consider how we can make the changes we can make, for no other reason than that we can. I also hope we can begin to feel inspired by other people – it is through this inter-connectedness that we may have a chance. And it is important for me to be absolutely explicit in my position. That over with, let us move onto the history.

Workbook

It is time to get outside. I want you to spend the next free day outside, rain or shine, and put your feet in water, on grass, and touch the bark of trees. Meditate on the side of a hill and breathe in the air. Feel the ground beneath you, feel the rocks, swim, and do so in both light and dark – go out in the morning to see the sun rise, and be there when the sun sets. Write everything you experience in your workbook, your emotional responses, but also your observations. What do you know about what you see? What are the types of trees?

History and Definitions

Let us now explore the history of our relationship with nature. I want to begin by defining the term. Nature refers to the natural, physical, material world and/or the universe. We study nature and the natural resources as a part of science. We often, as mentioned above, consider human activity separate to natural phenomena. However, we are intrinsically dependent on nature. We survive through nature's bounty, and the Earth fuels nature's capacity to provide this, with human intervention. Nature is also often taken to mean the natural environment, or the wilderness. Again, separately, like it exists apart from us. Nature is also considered that which is untainted by humanity – the natural rocks and streams and woodlands. A building is not nature, albeit consisting of natural products manipulated by humans. We also consider 'nature' to be the human, primordial natural state, i.e., it is our nature to be greedy, it is natural to want to eat.

Science also sees nature as 'matter in motion', meaning that nature obeys no laws, that science attempts to understand through measurement, observation, and testing. This is why 'physics' is the study of nature. Matter is that which physical objects are composed of, and is observable - we can see it, and often we can touch it. The universe is everything, but the visible components of the universe are now only thought to be 4.9 percent of the total mass. The remaining amount is believed to consist of 26.8 percent cold dark matter, and 68.3 percent dark energy. Physicists continue to investigate these components. It is the physical laws that describe the way in which matter and energy move in the observable universe. There is so much we do not understand yet observe, which is a key point for everything spiritual. Alain de Botton stated that our position has changed, from originally being in awe of the power and stature of nature to now being in awe of the way we have negatively impacted nature. I have to agree with him.

Humans were once an average, discrete part of the earth's wildlife. We were hunter-gatherers, eating to live, and living to eat. We had little effect on the planet, but as the last ice age abruptly ended about 11,700 years ago, and the advent of human civilisation emerged, our relationship with the world dramatically changed. Let's have a look at some of the key points in terms of harm (Bear in mind that it is only over the past fifty years or so that we have been taking an avid interest in the fate of the planet). It was in 1859 that Tyndall first noticed that the concentration of greenhouse gases could cause climate change. We often believe climate change is new, but humans have unsuccessfully tried to tackle this for decades now. It was also our need to control oil fields that drove World War 2. This is probably the major sticking point – whilst there is money and gain to be had, this need will keep people stuck. We need to work out how to make the prevention of climate change sexy and profitable.

Also, some of us really tried to accelerate thinking about climate change in 1970 when we celebrated the first Earth Day, which always leads me to think about how much concern people need to hear before acting on it. Alongside this, we have the environmental disasters – such as Chernobyl in 1986 and Fukishima in 2011 – that create scarring on the Earth's surface, all man made. Combined with the U.S. blocking calls for serious action on climate change in the UN framework convention in Rio de Janeiro in 1992, there is no wonder we are where we are. We are now in the position where the West Antarctic ice sheet collapse may be irreversible, but my belief is that we probably won't do anything until we need to – sadly, only when we are in dire straits will action be taken. This may, unfortunately, be too late. And sooner than we imagine.

Workbook

Now, the previous information was probably triggering at some level. In a way, I hope it was if it leads to action. However, I am sure my readers are more attuned to the crisis than most others. Let's spend a moment reconfiguring. Spend some time noticing what is happening to yourself on a cellular level.

- **What twinges and aches are you becoming aware of?**
- **What is happening to your jaw?**
- **How about your breath?**
- **Once regulated, use your workbook to write a stream of consciousness regarding your position in respect of nature.**

Comment also on the impact of yourself. If you wish, pick up a brush and paint.

Seasons

As humans became 'enlightened' and 'civilised', we turned our back on nature. It was up until this point (around the 1800s) that nature was central to everything we did. We were, and still are, totally reliant upon nature. I will include some examples that we know about, purely because they were written down. (In terms of writing though, bear in mind that writing only began in ancient Sumer between 3400 and 3100 BCE (but does not constitute 'literature' at that point). But in recorded history, writing began during the start of the pottery phase of the Neolithic period when we used clay tokens to record commodities. This spread throughout the rest of the world through cultural diffusion).

So, when we review what we have written about the past, we know the importance of nature. In terms of the seasons, four seasons are recognised in both temperate and sub-polar regions, they are the result of the Earth's orbit, and changes are due to the intensity of the sunlight. Animals hibernate or migrate, and plants can become dormant, depending on the time of the year. Meteorological seasons are reckoned by temperature, and as we all probably know, summer is the hottest, and winter the coldest in the Northern Hemisphere. All the seasons have specific names. In the English language, the season's names naturally derive from Old English, French, and Latin, with some Germanic names.

In literature, the seasons have always been represented, and it is through winter that we understand how important the seasons are and always have been. Winter has always been associated with despair and hope. Take The Lion, the Witch, and the Wardrobe, for instance – this book uses winter as a time of despair and hopelessness. Spring has always been associated with a time of joy and love. Themes of renewal, and birth abound. Robert Burns used lilac blossoms as a seasonal symbol. Chaucer's Canterbury Tales revolves around the beginning of spring and people readying themselves for pilgrimage after surviving winter. Summer is associated with reflection and searches, and is also the season when people travel, explore, and are filled with joy. Think about 'Summer Nights' in Grease as an example. Autumn is associated with bounty and changes; things become ripe, and John Keats wrote a poem, To Autumn, referring to the season as a labourer that brings harvests in conjunction with the maturing sun. In history, surviving winter was less certain, and spring was always more of a relief.

In terms of how we celebrate the seasons, there are infinite variations, depending on where you are in the world. I tend to use the pagan calendar as a way of navigating the seasons, but I will use the standard names here as opposed to the pagan ones. Spring is the time of rejuvenation and survival, a time to celebrate surviving another winter; the chances of doing so obviously diminish over time. Cover your altar with spring flowers, light candles, and items that represent eggs and birth. I walk in areas where there are lambs and celebrate the new births in the animal kingdom. I make willow wreaths and cover them in dried flowers. It is also the best time for planting, and even if you just have one small plant pot, try to get into the habit of sowing something.

I have to say that summer is my least favourite season. People are everywhere, and life seems crowded and hot. I try to remain out of the world and commune with myself more. I find myself waking earlier and earlier, and my altar becomes full of symbols of fertility and the seasons. I encourage you to meditate on the values of generosity and giving, and also preparedness in the summer. We are waiting for summer to end so we can begin to harvest but need the heat from the sun to accomplish this. Collect wonderful (secondhand) scarves and altar fabrics in bright oranges and yellows to represent the warmth and vital essence of summer. If you can, get to a henge for the longest day. Incorporate all of this book into your life.

For the darker part of the year, I feel more connected to the earth and the weather. I encourage you to notice more of what is happening around you. Look at the plants and shrubs and identify sources of harvest. What are the fields doing? Do you notice anything about the animals? In autumn, I find the apprehension for winter coming, but a joy and wonderment at what bounty nature can still offer us. My wreaths change in colour and tone, mainly vibrant reds and browns, and my altar gets a clean and tidy for winter. I attend monuments and stone circles every sabbat, but especially Mabon. In winter, my preparations are, like many, centred around Yule and preparing for the solstice, cleaning the house, and ridding my space from clutter in the process.

A lot of my energies are preparing for the journey, and I seem to connect more with others as we hunker down for winter. I also seem more energetic and partake in more sports and physical activities. Much of the winter is also spent in meditation, and daily yoga practice. I eat well, and a lot of time is spent in self-care, preparing for the energy-sapping rejuvenation of spring. Modern life now demands far more from us in terms of forbidding our natural response to the seasonal changes - we no longer work less during winter, we work the same. And we are paying the price.

Humans tend to only the consider the weather as either good or bad with no grey area. We are either in the darkness of winter and its hatefulness, or summer and the joy of being outside and warm. This polarising is part of the problem. Weather is all kinds of things, and we flow gradually through them all. The issue is also about humans liking weather because it suits their needs, or hating it because it prevents them from doing something. I am intentionally separating myself from humans here with language – as long as I talk about them wretched humans, I can distance myself a little! But even more widely, different parts of nature have a different draw for us. Waterfalls may draw us in with their power, their allure, and their romantic nature, and the stars may trigger us to be more introspective.

Workbook

It is time to work out how you can incorporate the seasons into your life. Write down each of the seasons in your book and free associate. Identify colours with specific seasons that work for you. Think about your ritual practice and also how you can weave your spiritual activities in with the ones of nature. It is time to become the embodiment of nature.

In terms of spirituality, the seasons are as important as anything else, often because what we practice has endured for centuries. For some examples, Baha'is believe that spring is vital for spiritual renewal and rejuvenation. The Americans celebrate summer with barbecues, whereas the Swedes celebrate Swedish Midsummer, or Midsommarstång, eating herring and potatoes, and procreating. The calendar is a way of many religions, such as Christianity organising their spiritual practices, with certain events happening at similar times throughout the year. Islam is a divinely ordained way of life. Celebrations happen at specific times of the year, impacted by the moon. Interestingly, as Muslims have migrated to the U.K., their religious practices have needed to adapt to a different day length for Fajr and Maghreb. The pagans in particular revolve their practices around the four primary seasons, although celebrate eight events throughout the year to include the equinox and solstices (Yule, Candelmas, Ostara, Beltane, Litha, Lughnasadh, Mabon, and Halowe-en). The pagans seem more aligned with the movement of the seasons throughout the year, and it is always known which part of the year they are in according to the relevant sabbat. This is also important because the pagan practices are more aligned to pre-Christian practices, evidencing the importance in previous times, despite the shortage of evidence of nature within spiritual practice.

Workbook

Take your journal and scribble down your current associations with seasons. How important are they? Do you celebrate them? What comes up for you when I talk about reconnecting with the natural rhythm of the universe?

Nature as Deity

It is perhaps also no coincidence that elements of nature have figured significantly within our deity practice across the world. This is also, perhaps presumably, a vast field; humans love their deities. Thus, I won't endeavour to explain every deity in the world, just a few to perhaps stimulate your own research and your own journey towards that which fits for you. Let's start with Africa.

Africa has a rich relationship with nature. There are goddesses of the moon (Zulu), patron of new harvest (Oko), and gods of the sky and thunder (Unsondo). Aztec mythology had Xochipilli as the god of art and flowers, and Xochiquetzal as the goddess of fertility. And also, obviously, amazing names. The Incas had Pachamama as their fertility goddess. Vodou have Baron Samedi as the loa of the dead, with Grand Bois associated with trees and plants. In China, they have Gonggong as the god of Water, and Zhurong as the god of Fire. Agni is the god of fire in Hinduism, and Indra is their god of rain. In Armenia, there is Vishap, a dragon associated with water. Celtic mythology has the likes of Cernunnos (the horned god of fertility), and Sucellus, the god of forests and alcohol. You may be well aware of a number of the Ancient Greek gods and goddesses, such as Zeus and Apollo (gods of thunder and sun respectively).

The names may not mean much to you as an individual, but

just a quick glance over the kinds of names and energies that the gods and goddesses preside over indicate the concern of our ancestors. We were bothered by fertility – we needed high reproduction due to low survival rates in childhood. We wondered about thunder as we did not understand how it happened. We were amazed with fire because although valuable, we did not comprehend the magic of how and why it happened. Deities were ways of articulating that which we feared, and as Christianity replaced this belief system in most of the world, we became focused upon one god, which science has gradually removed for us, and the god of science became that which we worship. Deities explained what we could not understand, and due to the enormity of what could happen to us, and usually what was happening to us, we revered and tried to influence the deity power through ritual, ceremony, and commitment.

Our concern with nature also took us, and takes us, out of the here and now. It is because we were so concerned with bad things happening in the future that we lost sight of the present. We were so intent on avoiding a future point where death occurred through the failure of nature that we would do anything possible, including the less tangible prayers and magick to avoid the inevitable. We used the past to fuel our current actions to manage the future.

Nature was fundamental because we were more intimately affected by the reality. If there was a bad season, we would starve. If the winter was too harsh, we or our children may freeze. If someone close to us died, we would not understand the complex reasons behind it, so would find a reason to explain it. Finding reasons gave us certainty and made coherent that which was not. And if we found a reason that others bought into, this would also give us power. Science offers the same assurance, albeit with more clarity, but not as much as we should believe. This process of creation is also a way of keeping us safe, but also explains not only the importance of nature for life, but how spirituality itself emerged.

This is not to say that spiritual practice is about providing explanations for what we do not understand. I am also definitely not saying that in reverting to historical relationships with nature, we should also deny science or ignore reality. My method of spirituality is incorporating it all – using the benefits from both in the most fulfilling and rewarding way possible. We can complete rituals, for example, on things we understand perfectly. We should not imagine that we can pray to the god of thunder for a storm in the morning – we can (fairly well) trust what the meterorologists are saying. What we can do, is identify and accept that the role of spirituality has changed.

I also wanted to talk a little about astrology, the practice of identifying characteristics in people as a result of planetary positions. Some of us will be apportioned signs as a result of when we were born. Those of us born in the darkest of wintertime are Capricorns, and those in the midst of summer are Virgos. Good old science has reported that scientific testing has found no evidence to support the premises or purported effects outlined in astrological traditions. However, science also reported that smoking stopped Alzheimer's, when in reality, smokers did not get Alzheimer's because they tended to pass away from lung cancer before that could take hold. So, do not worry so much about this as science is not always right, and is often led by politics rather than ethics!

The reality is that astrology has not demonstrated its effectiveness in controlled studies and has no scientific validity. But do not deduct that there is no validity. Although astrology is considered pseudoscience amongst the high and mighty scientific community, this does not mean there is nothing to take away from the practice. I definitely do not dispute either the practice or science. It may be that the methods of scientific enquiry do not fit the practice, or it could be that astrology is a way exploiting vulnerable people for money. I do believe that those of us born in midwinter carry a certain heaviness, and those born in midsummer are often more gregarious. I include this practice because it may well fit for you, and if it fits for you, definitely use it.

I believe there is actually some middle ground with astrology. We should not ever throw the baby out with the bathwater, but we, from our subconscious, make associations with different times of the year and apply that helpfully to people born at those times. Our subconscious may also be a conduit to or representation of guidance from the universe, so do not discount it, just trust your instinct. Also, read the astrological conjunctions that other people are writing – take what you will, and discard the rest. This is what most astrologers do.

My own experience with astrology is an interesting one. Growing up as part of the traveller community, there were lots of beliefs that people may refer to as archaic. Many people portend things, and the community is highly attuned to interpersonal dynamics. Astrology was, for us, embedded within everything we did and do. We know Peter is fiery because he is Aries. We know Izzy is good with people because she is Gemini. We know the relationship between Larry and Janet was strong but intense because they are both Scorpios. Now, if science can, through ten questions, give a diagnosis of a personality disorder to someone, I can describe someone as a Libra. There is no difference. The only apparent difference is that I do this in real life with friends and family, and the psychiatrist does it under the respectable auspices of the N.H.S. A diagnosis of any mental health condition is as helpful as that of a star sign in a fundamental way.

Let's now move towards some direct nature practice. I have split this up in to three parts again. The first will help us think about and remind us about the power and importance of being present; the second will be about empathy, and empathic attunement with nature, and the final practice will be about helping you develop and revitalise the way you approach nature moving forwards.

The Power of Presence

We experience nature in the present. Although we understand the role of nature in the past, and we have a sense of the possibilities in our collective future, we only experience both in the here and now. We are here now. You are here now. We can only exist now, and we can only act now. The future has not happened yet, and the past is already done. The first point to consider is accepting that we are here now. The importance of presence is also that universal consciousness is manifested within the present. We are conscious in the present. If we are not conscious, we are not present. Your primary purpose is to re-connect with conscious awareness of nature.

Many, many spiritual practices help practitioners to focus on the here and now. Being present is no radical proposition. Part of being present is moving away from regrets, which is important for us now in terms of what we have done to nature. There is no going back, but can move forwards. We need to remember this trajectory to free ourselves from what has gone before. Being stuck in the past also leads to blame and guilt. These are also strong and painful emotions. I may also be guilty about not doing enough sooner, but if I held onto those feelings, I would retard my growth. I have to let go of my previous actions completely and honestly.

Workbook

Cast your mind back to what has gone before. Look at your life and your relationship with nature. What do you identify as a regret? What did you do that was not helpful. List everything on a piece of paper, or a few pieces! Be honest, confront your reality, and then stand over a candle with a bowl of water next to it, or a safe way of extinguishing the paper. Speak your truth. Open up to what happened, but more importantly, confirm what you want to do to change.

Then light the paper and let go of this.

Empathy

If you are going to eat meat, it would be helpful for you to situate yourself in the conscious mind of the animal. What is it like for the animal to be taken away from its own tribe and placed in a stainless-steel cell? What would that be like for you? What do you imagine the animal's experience will be when they smell the fear of the others? What will it feel like when they realise there is no escape, and they are about to have their lives taken? What would it be like for you as a sentient being? If you rationalise it being ok for animals, how would it be to consider the actions towards our Jewish brethren during the second world war? The reality is there is no difference. I ask people to do this exercise simply to get into the minds and souls of others, and to take ourselves out of our own heads. This is how we begin to develop our capacity for empathy.

My position is, in terms of the crisis we find ourselves in, that there is no need or reason to eat meat. We are in the era of trying to save and maintain our planet. There is some important housekeeping to do, and this is not the place for defending our previous actions. Part of our planetary recovery requires us to repair the planet, and we cannot do this when there are huge amounts of CO_2 being emitted through factory farming. Your burger may well taste good, but it did not feel good when it was a sentient being.

We also need to appreciate more of the toil that goes into bringing our foodstuffs to our table. If you were the only one responsible for all your foodstuffs, would you waste as much? I would guesstimate that you would not. I would imagine you would be far more careful and considered about how the foodstuffs were being eaten and used by your family.

Workbook

We can improve our relationship with nature by, firstly, going vegetarian. I do not recommend veganism, but can make that decision if you so wish. I also recommend that you set up your own allotment and try to live off as much as you can grow. Also, perform the experiment with two plants. Just talk to one, and water/feed both the same. Identify the benefits of engaging with plant life in the here and now. Again, the plants do not benefit from future good wishes, they benefit from someone being there now.

Next Steps

This chapter introduced you to a general reminder of the crisis we are in. We need to act now, in the here and now, not tomorrow. Tomorrow is too late, and we can't regain yesterday. Revitalise everything you do. There are huge amounts of information out there on how you can make important and lasting changes to the environment. However, being spiritual is not just about making practical changes, it is also about developing your capacity for real and powerful connection with the natural world. Increasing your capacity for empathy will improve your capacity to be present. And in the presence, you will have the experience. Hug those trees. And revitalise your relationship with nature.

11. Final Words - Turbulent Times; The Role of Spirituality

Since I began this book, we became engulfed by the Covid pandemic, and soon after I had written the final chapter, the war in Ukraine started. I no longer know how long any of us will survive, given the vile threats made by Vladimir Putin. We are currently in such difficult, distressing times; darker and more threatening, perhaps, than ever before.

I will presume that everyone is aware of what is happening in the Ukraine. Russia has invaded, and we are now inundated with images of suffering, unhappiness, and loss. We hear of pointless acts of aggression on the streets of Kyiv, with the civilians bearing the brunt of the force; the politicians started what the populace will need to finish. How the people of the Ukraine are managing the invasion, I do not know, but I am certain that there is distress, anxiety, and anger around for them. And now we have the explicit threat from Putin of nuclear apocalypse, it is hard to imagine what worse times could befall us.

As I write this, my heart is filled with sadness and distress for the Ukrainians. How does one process the invasion of an army? How do you make sense of the aggression from one group of humans to another? For we are talking about humans, even though their behaviour may seem inhuman. And I am lucky as my country is not being invaded (yet), but I can empathise with those whose countries are. I imagine what it would be like for us in my country to have soldiers lining the streets and buildings being bombed. Totally devastating at best. However, man's propensity to go into war is also a useful mechanism to think about before I end this book.

Most of us think that humanity has come a long way in many ways, but events such as this provide proof that we have not developed at all. Our intrinsic quest for power, destruction, and division is still abhorrently apparent as it always has been. And this most recent act of aggression is from one of the most advanced nations in the world. But it is the threat of nuclear disaster that appalls me the most. Not just the possibility, as we have known that for decades, but the fact that it is on the tip of someone's tongue. A man dared to utter the words as a threat to the world, which is evidence that he consciously thought about ways to hurt others. So consumed in his own rage, his own disordered sense of power and justice, that he has expressed a clear and wilful wish to destroy millions of people; perhaps the world. This, in itself, is a crime against humanity; the Ukraine does not need taking out, he does. Call that 'hard' spirituality.

I am reminded of how war has figured within our lives throughout history. War has been apparent in all stages of history and in all continents, and it is what all humans have in common, as common as spirituality. Whether it is Europe battling the Nazis, or the Japanese engaging in the Thirty Eight Year war in the first century, we have all engaged in both war and spirituality, and somehow, for whatever reason, we have felt it appropriate to take the call to arms and fight.

It is interesting that there is always a defence. The attack on the Nazis was justified because they were threatening everyone's safety. Both North and South Vietnam felt justified for different reasons. Some Muslims felt justified in terror attacks because of American hostility and interference (as one position). Wars emerge when one group of people move into someone else's space, usually when there is also power and greed on the table. This indicates the eternal truth of humanity, that in greed and power we lose empathy for the other. We are also fundamentally clans-folk.

For our primordial experience of groups is our family. We are protected in the family group, and we take support and nurture from the group, which is often why the notion of 'gang' is interspersed with family. We learn to function most effectively in groups, and it is when one group collides with another, or seeks to expand their group, that problems begin. Even in schools, how easy was it to feel territorial with our home groups and see other forms as the enemy? The same idea is also seen in gang warfare. Gangs form through fear of hostility from other gangs; their violence is, thus, immediately and irreconcilably justified. These are often individual acts, but consisting of and emerging from a collective identity. The Russian gang, in this instance, is behaving no differently. And I imagine many Russians will see the Ukrainians as antagonists.

And so, we can only sit and watch as the events pan out. We are all, I am sure, praying for peace. We are also at the will of the universe – howsoever Putin and the rest of the 'leaders' are minded to act, we will soon see. For myself, I just sit here horrified and alarmed that for people such as Putin, his concern is war rather than the real threat to humankind, environmental destruction. Are his actions actually about hastening the destruction? Is this something he wants? Will the rest of his cabinet sit by and allow this to happen? Is this the solution he yearns after? I do not know, I am not Putin, but I know that wars cause loss of lives, ruination of families and livelihoods, and never in the history of humankind have wars ever been seen to be a helpful commodity.

To prevent further fallout, now is the time to cleave unto our faith. We need to consider this as the ultimate calling to connect in spiritual love and harmony with a view to develop our own capacities for Awen. More importantly, to help others develop theirs. 'Awen,' as mentioned previously, means spiritual enlightenment, which happens when we use spirituality to raise self-awareness. We need to generate Awen to raise our collective self-awareness. It is only through Awen that we can begin to empathise with others, to act in humble and pragmatic ways, and to ameliorate the suffering of others, not the pain caused by our own ego.

And this is my call to arms for you. I urge you to connect with everyone you can and encourage them to find their own Awen. We can affect change, but it requires us to change ourselves first through the development of Awen. Use this book to affect your own and then encourage others to affect theirs. We can use the war as an opportunity to fall apart or come together in unity, love, and harmony. We can die from this or grow. Just one of us can be the shoot we need to see in the frosty ground of the end of winter. That tiny element of care that you offer to someone else could be the trigger for them to offer the same to another person.

Please do not underestimate the power of contact with others. I also urge you to attend our courses and begin to develop your capacity for nwyfre and awen. We can do this, but we need to do it in connection, not separation, which is incredibly hard, but we can do this. Incorporate that mantra into your way of being and believe in the possibilities of change; for in that belief will follow change as reality.

And before I leave you to continue with your own spiritual journey, I would like to say that change is a process, not a final event. You have the capacity to change for the rest of your life. None of us need to remain stuck in problematic ways of being and feeling. We all have the potential to relate differently to the self and others. This is not just a belief for me, but an actual way of being. We need to develop faith in that possibility. Many years ago, a distinguished professor taught me that faith is like salt. You know what salt looks feels, and tastes like; this is exactly what faith is – expecting something to be as you know it to be, or at least want it to be.

Sometimes, faith can be so strong that we discount those things that contradict it. We may believe so powerfully that someone loves us that we ignore, deflect, or minimise from information that contradicts this. We may have faith in our ability to complete a seemingly insurmountable task, but by perseverance and self-belief, we may complete that task. I am minded of the Mountaineer, Kenton Cool. If he did not possess any faith that he had the potential to climb Mount Everest 14 times, he may never have started in the first instance. It is the faith that starts our journey towards change, and I encourage you to nurture faith in the possibility of your own journey as your starting point. Your journey may also feel as arduous as such a mountain climb, but it is the faith in the possibility that will start that journey towards success.

And as I finish this book, I realise that I had faith in my ability to complete it. Even though I spent many times doubting and questioning, still am, I held an ounce of faith in the ability to get it completed. And I have held faith in many other elements of my life. I encourage you to do the same.

ABOUT THE AUTHOR

Andrew Smith, PhD is a registered psychotherapist, with twenty years' professional experience. He divides his time between working as a lecturer in London, and as a psychotherapist in private practice.

Andrew has been involved with spirituality organisations and practices for thirty years. He has lived for five years in a Buddhist centre, trained as a yoga teacher in Tamil Nadu, and has been trained in a wide range of techniques such as past life regression therapy, thai massage, and mindfulness.

When not in work, Andrew plays the harp, and is an exhibited portrait artist and collector. He lives in Yorkshire with his partner, son, and three dogs. He blogs weekly.

www.doctorandrewsmith.com

www.therapp.org

Printed in Great Britain
by Amazon

13999787R10153